AGAINST
LONG ODDS

AGAINST LONG ODDS

CITIZENS WHO CHALLENGE CONGRESSIONAL INCUMBENTS

JAMES L. MERRINER
AND
THOMAS P. SENTER

Foreword by
Honorable Richard D. Lamm

Westport, Connecticut
London

Library of Congress Cataloging-in-Publication Data

Merriner, James L., 1947–
    Against long odds : citizens who challenge congressional
  incumbents / James L. Merriner, Thomas P. Senter ; foreword by
  Richard D. Lamm.
        p.   cm.
    Includes bibliographical references and index.
    ISBN 0–275–96642–9 (alk. paper)
    1. Electioneering—United States—Case studies.   2. Elections—
  United States—Case studies.   3. Election funds—United States—
  Case studies.   4. Incumbency (Public officers)—United States—Case
  studies.   5. United States. Congress—Elections—Case studies.
  I. Senter, Thomas P.   II. Title.
  JK2281.M47   1999
  324.7′0973′09045—dc21   99–15394

British Library Cataloguing in Publication Data is available.

Library of Congress Catalog Card Number: 99–15394
ISBN: 0–275–96642–9

First published in 1999

Praeger Publishers, 88 Post Road West, Westport, CT 06881
An imprint of Greenwood Publishing Group, Inc.
www.praeger.com

Printed in the United States of America

Copyright Acknowledgments

The authors and publisher gratefully acknowledge permission for use of the following material:

Excerpts from *Mr. Chairman: Power in Dan Rostenkowski's America* by James L. Merriner, copyright © 1999 by the Board of Trustees, Southern Illinois University, reprinted by permission of the publisher.

Every reasonable effort has been made to trace the owners of copyright materials in this book, but in some instances this has proven impossible. The author and publisher will be glad to receive information leading to more complete acknowledgments in subsequent printings of the book and in the meantime extend their apologies for any omissions.

*To Charles T. Merriner
and all challengers, especially Lionel Kunst*

CONTENTS

FOREWORD

You would be surprised at the number of years it took me to see clearly what some of the problems were which had to be solved. . . . Looking back, I think it was more difficult to see *what* the problems were than to solve them.

—Charles Darwin

Against Long Odds can be read at many levels. It is first of all an exciting contemporary history of some immensely interesting political races; it is drama; it is political science. The book also tells very readable stories of courage, determination, and dedication; and treachery, cynicism, corruption, and idealism. *Against Long Odds* succeeds on all these levels—but it particularly fascinates me as a metaphor for the deep problems within our political system and our democracy. You cannot read this book without realizing that the survival of our democracy itself is ultimately at stake.

Significantly, voter participation fell below 50 percent in 1996 for the first time since 1924. Indeed, voter turnout has decreased twenty-five percentage points since 1961, with a significant decline (except for Republicans in the South) of both Democratic and GOP partisan registrations. So many local party organizations are just a shell of their former selves. What wins today is nothing like the reasoned debate that often took place previously. American politics has become a race to the bottom. Meanwhile, reforms enacted to "empower" the people actually have replaced our political parties with what has been called a "lobbocracy."

In his book *The Roar of the Crowd*, Michael O'Neill observes that "it is no longer statesmen who control the theater of politics but the theater which controls the statesmen." Michael Wines of the *New York Times* notes that the constant impact of television, mass fax transmissions, and daily polling has debased the legislative process from "a slow and contemplative thing into something more like a 500–channel democracy, with the clicker grasped in the hands of the electorate." He says elected officials now move "in sync with the opinion of the moment as gracefully as blackbirds rising in unison from a field. The blackbirds, of course, often go nowhere."

Historian Alan Brinkley said we live in "an age in which government, politicians and even politics itself have become objects of indifference and contempt," and that party conventions are "slick, shiny infomercials, almost indistinguishable from many other packaged artificial events that populate our culture."

How can democracy exist when the politicians look at the public as sheep to be manipulated, and the public considers politicians just a bunch of crooks? This is far from what our founding fathers envisioned. We have no honest broker of the national interests. This will come to haunt us, for as Robert Louis Stevenson observed: "Sooner or later we must all sit down to a banquet of consequences." We do not have institutions equal to the magnitude of the problems facing us. A democracy requires that people have faith in their collective decisions.

The progressive degrading of that faith is illuminated in gritty and fascinating detail in this book. These are not *issues* problems the authors are writing about here; they are *structural* problems—which we are not even seriously debating, let alone solving! These problems may be beyond the ability of the normal political system to fix. The individual chapters in this book show that neither political party has a monopoly on either virtue or vice; in fact, it is doubtful whether either the Republicans or the Democrats will be able to reform the system. To voluntarily change the way politicians campaign is like trying to housetrain chickens.

There have been times in American history when neither of the major parties was able to solve the nation's problems. At those points, great pressures emerged to form a third political party. In the vast ma-

jority of cases, these movements add to the dialogue but did not suc-
ceed in building a permanent organization. Political scientist Richard
Hofstadter has observed that the third party's role is "to sting like a bee
and then die." This truly has been the fate of third parties for the past
140 years. Many of them deeply impacted public policy, but they did
not become institutionalized. Their issues endured, but their party disappeared. Republicans in the 1850s were the last start-up party to become a major party.

There is no divine right of political parties any more than there is a divine right of kings. Political parties were not part of the vision of our
founding fathers, and are not mentioned in the Constitution. George
Washington actually opposed their formation. They were necessary,
however, as a way to focus political choice in the new republic. Because
they are a pragmatic people, Americans needed some way to organize
various philosophical and policy differences. As a result, Federalists and
Anti-Federalists soon emerged. Americans kept these two parties only
as long as they played a useful function, and then easily developed new
ones when the old ossified or failed to address the political needs of the
new country.

Reading this book has reinforced my fear that *neither* party today can
do what needs to be done economically for the United States to remain
a great country. Bringing America's expectations in balance with our
revenue will be a terribly painful and monumental task, currently pro-
jected budget "surpluses" notwithstanding. We shall have to substantially downsize some of our most popular programs. But in our
catch-22 situation, the best politics is the worst long-term policy. Neither Democrats nor the GOP can afford to take the steps in campaign
reform to solve these politically volatile problems. Short-term political
concerns eclipse long-term public interest considerations. I judge it to
be substantially beyond the ability of either party in the present political
climate to deal successfully with these structural problems. Politics, like
nature, abhors a vacuum.

In the past, the answer of the Progressives to the ills of democracy
was something the existing system could not or would not give the nation—more democracy: recall elections, referenda, direct election of
senators, primaries. Above all, primaries. Progressives said that by taking the nomination process out of the hands of the pros in their smoke-
filled rooms and giving that power to the people, suddenly there would
be clean politics. In many ways, this worked. But in the age of TV and
high-rolling special interests, primaries have extended the political
"season" to a nearly continuous process costing huge sums of money.

We have a structural problem that cannot be solved with "politics as usual." As political scientists Thomas Levergood and Todd Breyfogle point out: "We must realize that our current crisis of self-interested bickering and anarchy derive neither from our own selfishness, nor from the dishonesty and incompetence of politicians, but rather from political institutions that are no longer able to restrain the worst within us." In short, individuals are not to blame; the system is. How the system operates is explained in this book.

It is hard for me to imagine a scenario in which either of the parties meaningfully reforms the campaign laws. A Congress elected under one set of rules is unlikely to change them. Yet, campaign reform is imperative and overdue. A giant "For Sale" sign hangs over America's political system. The biggest correlation of victory in politics is not one's issues, character, or energy; it is how much special interest money one is able to collect. The reform group Citizens Action has found that 34 percent of the funds spent by federal candidates was directly contributed by no more than one-tenth of 1 percent of the voting-age population. Not the ideas in one's head, but the money in one's pocket is what matters. Voter cynicism and alienation are at all-time highs, and such scorn and estrangement strike right at the heart of a democracy. As Michael Lind puts it, the two "parties" today are really the party of the voters and the party of the donors. And, as *Washington Post* columnist E. J. Dionne wrote, "A democracy which hates politics cannot remain as a democracy." We must act to restore the public confidence and rescue our nation from factionalism and cynicism. I do not believe this can be done within the existing two-party system.

Power tends to corrupt all human institutions, but the Constitution with its balance of powers has worked well to deal with corruption or abuse of power. The two-party structure plays a real role in this process in debating issues and exposing self-interest. To a remarkable degree, we have enjoyed a self-correcting system. Now, however, the special interests have taken over *both* political parties. They advance their coercive agenda by electing all or most of those who make the rules. It does not matter whether someone is a Republican or a Democrat—do they support and defend your particular interests? The "lobbocracy" often can pass and, more readily, stop legislation at will. Their actions are becoming increasingly blatant. Lobbyists' campaign checks are being handed out on the floor of the Congress. What better symbol of how corrupt the process has become? It is not the validity of one's cause that prevails, but how one works the system. We use the resources of the uncomplaining many to satisfy the complaining and self-interested few. Eventually, this is a political Ponzi scheme that is bound to crash.

This dilemma seems to be beyond the reach of the normal political process. An end-run strategy has developed that controls public policy through election laws, party rules, and special-interest money. Still, the Constitution remains an effective document. Our problems are more with our funders than with our founders. It is not our Constitution that is flawed; it is this end-run strategy that now elects, funds, and lobbies all our elected officials. We cannot express the national will because we are unable to get around those with a special agenda. It is Thomas Jefferson's ultimate nightmare: Alexander Hamilton's "economic elite" has taken over *both* political parties.

The first step in solving a problem must be to correctly identify its nature. As Abraham Lincoln observed, "The hole and the patch must be coterminous." We have an institutional problem more than a political problem. Both parties are for sale; both are hopelessly compromised by special-interest money. Our political institutions, instead of becoming part of the solution, have become part of the problem.

Only a new political coalition, unencumbered by the past, can take the money out of politics or reduce its caustic influence. Real political reform will require a constitutional amendment allowing limits on campaign spending, or possibly publicly funded campaigns, and nothing short of a political revolution will garner the needed support. The Republican and Democratic foxes will *never* adequately protect the henhouse. The historic solutions themselves have become the problem.

There is an important distinction here. Special interests will always be with us; they are not inherently evil. James Madison, in *Federalist Number 10*, even saw them as integral to democracy. However, when they change their *modus operandi* from argument and logic to buying political influence, it is time to act. They must inevitably exist; they do not have to invariably control the process.

Still, American politics is not driven by ideas or idealism, but by organized special interests. Confidence in the existing political system is low and will likely diminish more as both parties use congressional hearings on campaign reform to expose the wrongdoings of the opposing party. Time is not their friend. When both parties have the same disease, it is unlikely that one of them will offer the cure.

But, there is a natural coalition in the nation for a new political movement. Take the pro-choice Republicans and the economically realistic Democrats and you have the core of a new party—the fiscally responsible Democrats and the socially progressive Republicans. Lop off those who despise government and those with a blind faith in it and organize the remainder. Most Americans neither want to dramatically extend the power of the federal government, nor dismantle it. The center of American political opinion is ripe for conversion. The need is great—and the time is now!

Honorable Richard D. Lamm
Governor of Colorado, 1975–1983

PREFACE

One of this book's strengths is that both authors are well grounded in research techniques, though in different disciplines. James L. Merriner, a political reporter for thirty years, has won journalism awards for feature writing, spot news coverage, and investigative reporting—a rare triple play. Dr. Thomas P. Senter, a practicing physician who has published many medical papers, was selected in 1978 as a VA Clinical Scholar in the combined University of California at San Francisco/ Stanford Robert Wood Johnson Program. He was the first and—until 1998—the only dermatologist to be so honored.

Merriner suspected that conventional journalism, no matter how thorough, detailed, and informed by "insider" information, somehow was not telling the real story of the modern incumbency preservation system. Senter, because of his extensive involvement in the Ross Perot presidential campaign of 1992 and a 1996 U.S. Senate race in Alaska, learned first-hand the operations of that system. Prior to those campaigns, as a board member (and the only noncandidate for public office) of the bipartisan Coalition to End the Permanent Congress, he was impressed by the grit and determination of his fellow coalition members in their unsuccessful efforts to unseat congressional incumbents.

In January 1998, Merriner and Senter met in Anchorage and decided to write this book. After further research, they discovered that political scientists, like journalists, also have not adequately examined the incumbency preservation system. Thus, the need for this book, aimed both at general readers and political specialists, seemed clear.

"We should like to thank"—at this point one usually stops reading, but the authors wish to stress that this book would not have been possible without the freely given help of many people. To be thanked first and foremost are the political challengers who agreed to relive their painful experiences of losing by graciously submitting to our questions. In many cases, top campaign staffers and friends of the candidates also were queried; in a couple of instances, the challengers declined to talk with us and so those chapters rely largely on interviews with staffers and friends.

Besides interviews with challengers and their advisers, sources for the chapters include media reports, public records, and the authors' own experiences. Featured incumbents also were invited to comment, but almost without exception, they declined. Details of sourcing may be found in the bibliographical essay.

Statements of fact in the book are based on on-the-record interviews, public records, or the authors' eyewitness accounts. No statement of fact rests on uncorroborated, "blind" off-the-record sourcing. Interpretations of the facts are, of course, the authors' alone.

The authors also wish to express gratitude to Heather Ruland Staines, editor at Praeger Publishers, who saw promise in this project from the start. Richard D. Lamm not only contributed the Foreword but offered useful suggestions along the way. Tom D'Armore Jr. also was helpful.

Both Tom Hood and Doyle Crane deserve thanks for carefully reviewing early drafts of this manuscript; their suggestions were invaluable and greatly improved the book. THRO (Throw the Hypocritical Rascals Out) founder Jack Gargan was supportive of this work from the beginning. Others who helped with information, insights, and suggestions include Howard Phillips, Paul Jacob, and Gary Ruskin. The late Lionel Kunst, who had the vision and courage of a true reformer, inspired the authors by his determination to open up the political process to challengers of all stripes.

James Merriner also would like to tip his hat to those who provided moral support through the writing of this book. They include Sharon

Davis and Joel Davis, Michael L. McCluggage, Charles M. Merriner, the late Charles T. Merriner, Stan Palder, and Betsy Chapin Palder.

INTRODUCTION

The American system of democracy is the most comprehensive and widespread the world has ever known. According to the Census Bureau's count of the federal government, those of the fifty states, and roughly 80,000 units of local government, the nation has more than 526,000 elective offices. One state, Illinois, even elects its members of Mosquito Abatement District boards. No other country has anything close to these immense and diverse ballots. It means, among other things, that at least 526,000 people must be willing to offer themselves for public office, inviting their fellow citizens to scrutinize their character and qualifications.

Rarely noted is that this astonishing breadth of elective office depends almost entirely on volunteers. There is, constitutionally, no inherited nobility. Nor, theoretically, is there an established political class. True enough, an array of family dynasties has provided generations of Adamses and Kennedys in Massachusetts, Byrds in Virginia, Longs in Louisiana, and Tafts in Ohio, among others. To be sure, big-city political machine bosses in decades past had the power to appoint, in effect, the holders of elective offices. But by and large, any citizen may offer himself or herself for public office, from the local school board and town council up to the U.S. House of Representatives and Senate, and even the presidency itself. The patrimony of this tradition dates to eighteenth-century colonial America, arising from the cradle of the New England town meeting or perhaps even further back to the Mayflower Compact of 1620. Self-government is a long-standing and largely unsung fixture that has long been taken for granted.

A parallel American tradition, of course, is scorn and mockery of politicians for their mediocrity, venality, and egotism. This custom is rich and largely justified, but it slights the courage and public-spiritedness of people who volunteer—nobody forces them—to serve in public office. A political system requires politicians. A ballot requires candidates. *Somebody* has to run for office. One of the authors' aims is to honor citizens who volunteer to serve, incumbents and challengers alike, but especially challengers.

This book examines the efforts of fifteen citizens who volunteered to run against U.S. House and Senate incumbents during the 1990s. Most challengers had been successful, sometimes spectacularly so, in the private sector. They assumed that they could transfer their skills and success to the political realm. But they quickly realized that the system is rigged against them. To a person, they were shocked to learn how ruthlessly congressional incumbents protect themselves *and* one another against challengers.

The current techniques of this congressional self-protection are a new phenomenon and a blight on the American system of government. Incumbents always have had natural, built-in advantages and consistently have exploited them. If nothing else, an incumbent already has passed the rigorous test of voter approval at least once. What is new is that incumbents' advantages have been *institutionalized*—by statute and by practice.

The statutes are the Watergate-era reforms of the 1970s, especially the Federal Election Campaign Act amendments of 1974 and their subsequent interpretations by the courts. The practice is the management of campaigns by a new class of political and media technicians paid for by special-interest contributions to incumbents, contributions that challengers cannot easily match unless they have personal riches that they are willing to use. Even then, incumbents normally have the upper hand.

Congressional incumbents now are virtually guaranteed re-election. This holds across the spectrum, for Democrats and Republicans, liberals and conservatives. As recently as the 1940s, a 75 percent re-election rate for incumbents was the norm. By the 1970s, government watchdog groups started noticing elevated re-election rates. Now the figure routinely exceeds 90 percent—even in the supposedly revolutionary year of 1994, when Republicans overturned forty years of Democratic rule in the House, shocking the respectable opinion mongers.

In fact, out of 387 members of the House who sought re-election in 1994, only four were defeated in primaries and thirty-four in the general election. With the public in its angriest anti-incumbent mood in recent memory, 90.2 percent of those who ran for re-election were returned to the House. Nor did many even face close calls. On average, incumbents won by a landslide with 64 percent of the vote.

Back in 1974, the aftershock of the Watergate scandal tossed forty House members out of office for an incumbency re-election rate of 89.6 percent. It has not dipped below 90 percent since. For example, in 1988 the number was a record high 98.5 percent. Ten years later, incumbents nearly matched that record at 98.3 percent.

The trend in the 100–member Senate is identical, although re-election rates tend to swing more widely in the smaller body. Twenty-six out of twenty-nine incumbents who sought re-election in 1998 won, for a typical success rate of 89.7 percent.

What the public thinks about this virtual lifetime tenure for incumbents might be inferred from voter participation figures. Ruy A. Teixeira, author of *The Disappearing American Voter,* said, "We know that people only vote if they feel a connection between the outcome and their individual vote." Thus, boycotting the polls could represent less of an abdication of the duties of citizenship than a realistic assessment of the odds of changing the status quo. Certainly, something is keeping potential voters at home. In 1998, just 36.1 percent of eligible adults turned out to vote. This was the lowest rate since 1942, when millions of Americans were overseas fighting a war.

Political analysts and commentators—a sizeable industry—in 1998 fixated on the fact that Republicans lost five seats from their House majority, violating the rule that the party in opposition to the White House always gains seats in midterm elections. Pundits remarked at length on the GOP setback, the surprising victory of former professional wrestler Jesse "The Body" (or "The Mind") Ventura as the Reform Party governor of Minnesota, the outlook for the 2000 presidential election, and so forth. Somehow, job security for incumbents and escalating voter alienation scarcely entered the mix—except for some occasional solemn-faced tut-tutting. Questions of how incumbents managed to create and sustain the present electoral system do not seem to trouble the pundits.

As the following chapters will demonstrate, incumbents win through intimidation of their challengers' supporters; an institutionalized near-monopoly on money, local media and other establishment resources, and outright dirty tricks. A political class indeed is in place, tantamount to an inherited nobility, or perhaps more like the privileged Praetorian Guards of the Roman Empire. This is something new under the American sun. The founding Federalist aristocracy lasted only twelve years—the George Washington and John Adams administrations—before Thomas Jefferson turned them out in 1800. Periodically thereafter, members of Congress were replaced wholesale with the ups and downs of various parties. The tradition was for parties to rotate House seats among their leading spokesmen every term or two. For instance, a young and ambitious Whig Party politician, Abraham Lincoln, stepped down after a single term in 1848.

But the new political class has ruled now for about a quarter-century. Whether in its Democratic or Republican branches, this elite clique comprises incumbents, the special interests that bankroll them, and the professionals who manipulate their campaign imagery.

One of America's highest values, upheld in the sacrosanct First Amendment, is the belief in vigorous and robust public debate. A contemporary congressional contest with the incumbent holding all the high cards and generally refusing to meet a challenger in a face-to-face forum, while both candidates try to trash each other's reputations in televised attack ads, is hardly a debate of ideas at all, let alone vigorous or robust. Thus, it is not just the electoral system for Congress that has been fractured. The marketplace of ideas has broken down.

The challengers featured herein, taken together, are a fascinating assembly of human beings. Taken one at a time, they ran because they believed in certain ideas—liberal, moderate, or conservative. Without exception, they found that ideas are overwhelmed by the professional and institutional system of incumbency preservation. This was true in cities, suburbs, and farmlands, from Massachusetts to Hawaii.

Commentators often warn that campaigning for high office has become so expensive, so nasty and bitter, so destructive of personal privacy and reputation that good people will refuse to run. This perennial warning apparently has not caught on because there never seems to be a shortage of politicians—a by-product of our 526,000 elective posts. But the alarm should be heeded. We asked challengers whether, in light of their experience, they would advise a close friend or family member to run for Congress against an incumbent. Almost always, the answer was no.

Our message is not that challengers deserve to win and incumbents should lose. Many incumbents prevail because they are, plainly and simply, better candidates with more appealing positions on the issues. The point is that the national political tradition of volunteerism is in peril. Even years after their campaigns, some challengers interviewed for this book winced in pain at memories of their forfeiture of privacy, exhaustion of personal finances, subjection to slander, and hurts to friends and family members. "Politics ain't beanbag," as the adage goes—it always has been a rough and tough game, not for the faint-hearted. But, again, the contemporary system of incumbency protection has added a dimension of intensity while subtracting a measure of fair play. What rational person would volunteer himself or herself for public office in such circumstances?

Ironically, the stacked electoral deck was dealt by professed champions of reform and fairness. Illustrating the social scientist Karl Popper's "law of unintended effects," the Federal Election Campaign Act amendments of 1974 were supposed to reduce the influence of money in politics but accomplished the opposite. The whole system of "soft money" and "issues ads" and multimillion-dollar Political Action Committees (PACs), which so scandalizes reformers, sprang up after Congress imposed supposed *limits* on money.

The law restricted individual contributions to $1,000 per candidate in each primary or general election. PACs formed by interest groups, as well as political party committees, were limited to $5,000 per candidate per primary or general election. In addition, ceilings were placed on the amount that candidates could spend—$70,000 for a House district and eight cents per eligible voter for a Senate seat.

In the private sector, this system would have been seen for what it was: a scheme to restrict competition by erecting barriers to entrants in the market. Later court rulings have left many hurdles in place while making a muddle of campaign regulation in general. The Supreme Court struck down the *spending* limits as unconstitutional. The $1,000 and $5,000 *contribution* limits were left standing—except that candidates could contribute as many of their own dollars to their own campaigns as they wished. In other words, one's personal money is an inviolable instrument of free speech, but other people's money is not. Such was the curious judicial reading of the First Amendment.

In 1979, Congress, disturbed by declining voter turnout rates, passed yet another "reform" law allowing political parties to raise unrestricted sums of money for voter registration drives and get-out-the-vote efforts. This provision has led to unlimited "issues advocacy" spending by interest groups. Unregulated contributions for issues advocacy or party sustenance became known as "soft money," while $1,000 and $5,000 donations to specific candidates were "hard money." The temptation to mingle hard and soft money has proven irresistible to many campaigns.

Advocates of the present system might argue that contribution limits apply fairly to incumbents and challengers alike. Unfortunately, not all campaign dollars are equal. Congressional incumbents already enjoy many "free" electoral benefits by virtue of holding office. Available are hundreds of thousands of dollars in taxpayer funds for free mailings, long-distance telephone service, access to congressional broadcast studios, staff assistance for constituent services ("casework"), district offices, mobile offices, round trips home from Washington, and more.

Just one of these benefits, free mailings—what is called the "franking privilege" (or "frank") for official business—allows each congressional office on average to send more than a million pieces of mail a year. At bulk-mail rates, the annual cost to taxpayers exceeds $52,600 per congressman. Much of the mail goes to constituents in the form of official "newsletters" that amount to free campaign publicity. Challengers obviously do not enjoy this privilege and must pay to get their message out.

Thus, an incumbent's first $1,000 contribution for re-election is, in a sense, gravy, whereas a challenger's first $1,000 is absolutely critical. He or she probably is unknown to most voters and must gain lots of publicity quickly.

Unless a challenger has personal wealth and is committed to spending it, he or she must somehow rustle up enough $1,000 and $5,000 donations to raise the several hundred thousand dollars needed to mount a credible race. As a result, nearly all challengers are underfunded. In 1996, fewer than one-fifth of House members faced challengers who could raise even one-half the amount of the incumbent's campaign fund.

Not only have contribution limits hobbled challengers' campaigns, they have served to stifle ideological debate. In 1968, a few wealthy patrons financed Senator Eugene McCarthy's antiwar challenge to President Lyndon B. Johnson. But no longer can like-minded rich people gather to underwrite a candidate with out-of-the-mainstream views. Instead, raising a large sum in $1,000 trickles mandates a broad, bland, mainstream appeal. A challenger with unorthodox opinions often finds that they are best silenced. It is not surprising that voters complain about campaigns dominated by personal attacks and quarrels over trivialities instead of serious debates on the issues.

But even if contribution limits were repealed tomorrow, congressional incumbents still would have enormous institutional advantages. Because they are in a position to influence policy while challengers merely have potential influence, interest-group dollars naturally flow to incumbents. A Federal Election Commission study showed that PACs give more than 90 percent of their funds to incumbents. Many PACs have discovered that incumbency matters more than party labels, explaining apparent anomalies such as Republican-oriented business groups giving money to Democratic congressional leaders. As pundit Mark Shields observed, PACs are the "mutual funds" of politics. Money in search of political influence trumps partisan and ideological differences.

Even if campaign funding is disregarded, the modern Congress has constructed immense institutional self-protections. Two in particular, which will be examined in the upcoming chapters, are ladling from the federal pork barrel and providing constituent services. Of course, pork and favors for the home folks go back to the earliest Congresses. What has changed is that the exponential expansion of the federal government since the New Deal has created not just a difference in degree but also in kind. Washington's myriad of regulating and subsidizing activities has handed voters a vested interest—quite apart from their partisan or philosophical concerns—in keeping their incumbent on the job. More seniority equals more pork. This self-interested voting explains the paradox of polls showing low public esteem for Congress coupled with high regard for the voters' own congressmen. Incumbents distribute favors and pork. Why throw them out?

The self-guarding Congress has proven impervious to real reform. For example, members of Congress, increasingly sophisticated about mass media, have taken to the Internet, using public funds to finance World Wide Web sites for their offices. These sites offer biographical data about the congressman along with position papers, speeches, lists of bills sponsored, and similar self-promoting information. In 1996, CompuServe, a private Internet service provider, offered free Web sites to congressmen *and* their challengers. In stepped the Federal Election Commission, nominally an independent regulatory agency but effectively controlled by Congress. The FEC disallowed CompuServe's offer as an illegal "in-kind contribution." In effect, the system sought to lock out challengers from free use of a new mass medium, the Internet. This was an entirely typical and yet all but unnoticed piece of fallout from the Watergate-era reforms.

The modern Congress is so entrenched that many academic political scientists, such as Susan Welch, no longer bother to analyze incumbents' races. She wrote that she now scrutinizes only "open" seats, with no incumbent on the ballot, because they offer the only opportunity for shake-ups in the composition of the body.

Meanwhile, the media naturally focus on winners without asking losers in-depth questions about what went wrong. Exactly what happens to credible citizen-challengers who go up against entrenched incumbents is an untold tale. This book tells the stories of fifteen citizens who volunteered to serve in Congress—against long odds.

1

MASSACHUSETTS

MITT ROMNEY (R) v. SENATOR TED KENNEDY (D)

Mitt Romney was far from politically naive. He grew up in politics. His father, George W. Romney, former head of American Motors Corporation, was governor of Michigan in the 1960s and made a brief run for the Republican presidential nomination in 1968. His mother had tried for a U.S. Senate seat in Michigan and, later, a former sister-in-law did the same.

Unlike some candidates featured in this book, Romney was not recruited by party elders to run. He decided on his own to challenge Senator Edward M. "Ted" Kennedy of Massachusetts. Romney was inspired in part by the "man in the arena" quotation from President Theodore Roosevelt, who said a fighter deserves our admiration even if he stumbles, however much critics might fault him. A script of this passage hangs on Romney's office wall. Richard M. Nixon quoted it in letters to friends after losing the 1960 presidential election to John F. Kennedy; it is something like holy writ for Republicans and closes as follows: "Far better it is to dare mighty things, to win glorious triumphs, even though checkered by failure, than to take rank with those poor spirits who neither enjoy much or suffer much, because they live in the grey twilight that knows neither victory nor defeat."

Romney figured he could fight for his beliefs as a "man in the arena." Nearly as important, he could help the Republican Party by forcing national Democrats to divert money and consultants to Kennedy's reelection. Kennedy had sat in the Senate for thirty-two years, elected six times over weak GOP opposition. Without a free ride in 1994, Kennedy would have to call on Democratic resources that otherwise would have been deployed in other states.

Modern media politics is driven by a new class of professional campaign consultants, pollsters, and media producers. How much these technicians actually determine the outcome of elections is debatable, but certainly they have taken over the operations of campaigns. Once shaken from his complacency, Kennedy was impelled to summon to Massaschusetts a top-drawer Washington, D.C., consultant, Robert Shrum. He had been the strategist for Kennedy's 1980 presidential nomination campaign against President Jimmy Carter.

The national GOP noted Shrum's decampment northeast and scarcely could believe its good fortune in acquiring Romney's candidacy. He seemed to be the perfect citizen-challenger in what was shaping up as an anti-incumbent year. As a wealthy venture capitalist, he could finance his own campaign. Always looking as though he had just stepped out of his tailor's shop after visiting his barber, Romney embodied that peculiar combination of telegenic coolness and personal warmth that media politics bless: He was young (forty-seven), handsome, well spoken, enthusiastic but without a hard ideological edge, and a stranger to scandal. A family man who had married his high school sweetheart and fathered five children, he neither smoked, drank alcohol, nor consumed even caffeinated beverages, taking milk and hot chocolate instead. Further, as a Massachusetts resident for twenty-three years, he was inoculated against a charge of carpetbagging. Texas Senator Phil Gramm, chair of the Republican National Senatorial Committee that year, must have been delighted by Romney's candidacy.

In contrast, Ted Kennedy in 1994 was sixty-two years old, portly, puffy-faced and wrinkled, seemingly weary and unfocused, and burdened by personal scandals. He was divorced and remarried in a heavily Catholic state. The 1969 Chappaquiddick incident in which a young woman in Kennedy's car had drowned was long behind him. But in 1991 he had roused his nephew, William Kennedy Smith, from bed late one night at the family's mansion in Palm Beach, Florida. The two went bar-hopping, and Smith took home a young woman who later charged him with rape. Although Smith was acquitted at trial, the senator's own reputation as a womanizer constrained him to sit mute while the Senate

Judiciary Committee considered the Supreme Court nomination of a judge accused of sexual harassment, Clarence Thomas. Later that year Kennedy went to his alma mater, Harvard University, to give a speech beseeching forgiveness for "the faults in the conduct of my personal life."

Mitt Romney was a rich, young, energetic, good-looking, articulate insurgent against the status quo, surrounded by a photogenic family—in sum, he was a reprise of the 1960s image of the brothers Kennedy—an ideal anti-Kennedy Kennedy. Still, he was going up against a Kennedy in Massachusetts, an endeavor rather like volunteering for a hanging. Indeed, registered Republicans were only 14 percent of the state's electorate. No fool, Romney figured from the outset that he had a 10 percent chance to win.

He said later, "You know that the field is slanted against you, the referees are working for the other side, and the scorekeeper is not helping you either. But it's still a great, enthusiastic experience . . . so long as it is not how you define yourself. I define myself as a human being on the basis of my relationship with my wife, my family, and my faith."

That last self-definition—faith—proved to be troublesome for the Romney campaign.

In Massachusetts, Mormonism is, strictly speaking, a cult, using the writer Tom Wolfe's sociological definition of a cult as a church that lacks political power. In Utah, Mormonism is something close to a state-established church. But in New England, the faith group is so small that its members are regarded as, at the least, curiosities outside the mainstream.

A youthful Romney had gone to France to fulfill his faith's prescribed two years as a missionary. In Boston, until he launched his campaign, Romney was the lay president of the metropolitan "stake" of fourteen churches, appointed by church elders in Salt Lake City to counsel members and handle administrative tasks.

In response to his political instincts, Romney in 1993 had assigned Richard Wirthlin, who had been Ronald Reagan's pollster, to test the Mormon question. "There was a very significant percent of voters in Massachusetts who were less likely to vote for a person who was Mormon," Romney said in an interview. Wirthlin also had queried voters' reactions to a businessman and a nonpolitician and "most things were very encouraging," Romney said, "but one that was not" was Mormonism. "I didn't worry about that too much, but Richard Wirthlin pointed out that that could be used against me by my opponent. So that was in the back of our minds."

The efficient ruthlessness of the Kennedy machine has been a staple of American political folklore since the 1960 presidential race of John F. Kennedy. It was confirmed once more in 1994, when Ted Kennedy's campaign simply was smarter and tougher than Romney's. In that sense, Kennedy deserved to win. Except that one critical Kennedy maneuver was a dirty trick.

Like many other incumbents faced with unexpected serious opposition, Kennedy seemed to sleepwalk through the election-year summer, disbelieving that his throne was endangered. But he agreed to run Shrum-devised television commercials lest he concede the air war to his foes. By the time it became clear that Romney would win the September 20 Republican primary, the competitive edge of Kennedy and his corps was rehoned. The thrill of the chase rejuvenated the senator, even though his handlers continued to fret about his rambling and dull public appearances.

In the primary, Romney easily defeated another millionaire businessman who outspent him, John Lakian. In a previous campaign for governor, Lakian had inflated his educational and military credentials. With such ethical baggage, he was no match for the squeaky-clean Romney.

However, shortly before the primary, Representative Joseph P. Kennedy of Massachusetts, who called himself the "pit bull" of his uncle's campaign, detonated the political equivalent of a neutron bomb. (Officially, his late brother Michael, another son of Robert F. Kennedy, was the campaign manager.) Joe Kennedy declared that Romney would have to answer for the institutional bias of his Mormon faith against blacks and women.

Joe Kennedy's questions about Mormonism naturally made headlines and topped the TV newscasts. The issue carried an ironic sting because John F. Kennedy in 1960 had made history by overcoming anti-Catholic bias to become the first Catholic president. JFK famously had confronted Baptist ministers in Houston and said he did not speak for his church on religious matters and the church did not speak for him on public policy. He also had appeared at Mormon headquarters in Salt Lake City and praised that faith's "successful battle to make religious liberty a living reality."

Joe Kennedy had blundered in that he did not know the Mormon church had rescinded its ban against blacks assuming the priesthood in 1978. On this particular point, he apologized to Romney. But regarding the general issue of Romney's faith, Senator Kennedy insisted it was a proper concern. On September 26, he challenged Romney to explain his feelings on Mormonism's history of racial prejudice and its ongoing sexual discrimination. With calculated timing earlier that month, Kennedy had announced his opposition to the Vatican's prohibition of the ordination of women, a tenet common to both his and Romney's faiths.

"The victory that John Kennedy won was not just for forty million Americans who were born Catholics, it was for all Americans of all faiths," Romney responded. "I'm sad to see that Ted Kennedy is trying to take away his brother's victory." He said the 1978 action allowing black priests was "one of the most emotional and happy days of my life." But he refused to discuss his religion further.

Kennedy was duly scolded by high-minded editorialists for raising the religious issue—the Constitution states there may be no religious test for public office. The senator quickly deployed his "spinners" to insist to reporters that the question concerned racial and sexual bias, not religion. Unimpressed, the *New York Times* suggested in a news report that the religion tactic had backfired against Kennedy (which meant that it had backfired with the eminences of the *New York Times*). Martin F. Nolan, who had covered politics for the *Boston Globe* for a year longer even than Kennedy had been a senator, understood more clearly what was going on. He said that the Kennedy objective was to make sure that every voter in Massachusetts knew that Romney was a Mormon.

In the spring of 1994, an independent academic poll had showed that 70 percent of Massachusetts independents—they are a plurality of the state's electorate—wanted a fresh face in the Senate. Even 45 percent of Democrats wanted someone new, a deadly figure for a Democratic incumbent. Later polls showed Romney running neck-and-neck with Kennedy. But a Gallup poll released on September 27, after the Mormonism issue flared, gave Kennedy 53 percent to Romney's 44 percent.

Certainly Mormonism was not the only thing that turned the race. Even Romney does not think it sank him. "There's no question that where the Kennedy campaign was most effective," he said, "was in the area of this striker individual."

The ground for "this striker individual" had been prepared from the start by the Kennedy campaign. The senator can be either a rip-roaring orator or a mumbling dullard, depending on his mood. On one particular September day he was neither. He went to Hanscom Air Force Base in Bedford, Massachusetts, and gloated, "You make the long speech when you haven't got good news. I'll tell you, we can make a short speech here today."

Then he grinningly thrust his hand into the inside pocket of his suit coat, ceremoniously retrieved and unfolded a letter from Deputy Defense Secretary John M. Deutch—a constituent and friend of Kennedy (and later director of the Central Intelligence Agency)—and read that at the senator's urging, the Phillips Laboratory Geophysics Directorate in Bedford would escape Pentagon cutbacks, thereby saving 550 jobs.

The Bedford scientists made high salaries and probably leaned Republican. But Kennedy "had the clout to make this happen," one scientist whose job was preserved noted with due gratitude. Kennedy, the heir of Camelot, was running as an insider wheeler-dealer who delivers pork.

At an "export conference" in Boston with 100 Republican CEOs—Romney types—Kennedy announced a $26 million federal grant to Raytheon Corporation, based in Massachusetts, to build aviation equipment in Hong Kong. Reporters who assumed that big business is anti-Kennedy and pro-Republican were surprised at the CEOs' praise of the senator. As one CEO put it, "I don't necessarily like him, but he brings a lot to the state."

Kennedy had a mythical name, the Kennedy political organization, thirty-two years of seniority, virtuosity in pork delivery, the tacit backing of many GOP businessmen, and the support of the state's dominant newspaper, the *Boston Globe*—the paper's political editor was Ben Bradlee Jr., son of the former editor of the *Washington Post*, who had written a book about his friendship with John F. Kennedy. Romney had a markedly less famous name, some money, and telegenic quality.

Kennedy was portrayed as a public benefactor while his opponent was drawn as a robber-baron tycoon. "This striker individual" perfectly fit the incumbent's message. Romney boasted that as a venture capitalist he had created 10,000 jobs at sixty companies. This invited Kennedy's opposition researchers ("oppo," in political-speak) to try to knock the claim down. They found a stationery factory in Marion, Indiana, where 265 workers had been laid off—followed by a strike—after Romney's firm acquired it.

Here was an irresistible opportunity to portray Romney as antilabor. At the time, organized labor had a major beef with Kennedy—he had voted for the North American Free Trade Agreement, which labor contended would eliminate domestic manufacturing jobs. But labor's attitude was "never mind, Teddy's our friend." The Kennedy campaign sent a film production crew to Marion to interview workers, then brought five of them to Massachusetts to harass Romney at campaign appearances.

Romney said, "There was a woman who came on TV and said, 'I worked for this company thirteen years, I am a single mom, and Mitt Romney fired me.' " The first such ad "went up," in political jargon, on September 19. "The [campaign] spending was over two million dollars over two weeks. I, at the beginning of that, was slightly ahead of Senator Kennedy in the polls. At the end of the two weeks I was down by twenty-two points. . . . My campaign and I really did not find a way to blunt the effectiveness of that ad, nor of the press, which got that issue, and we just failed to recapture the agenda."

Romney's side of the story was that he was on campaign leave from his firm when it bought that Indiana company. He had no seat on the company's management or board of directors, no personal financial interest in it, and no involvement in the layoffs or strike. This rebuttal dutifully was reported in the text of newspaper articles, but the charge itself naturally filled the headlines.

The TV spot was devastating because Massachusetts was one of the few states in the country in 1994 where "corporate raider" was a worse epithet than "tax-and-spend liberal." Romney said, "If you're in the newspaper business, part of your business is entertainment, and they like reading that people have feet of clay, and they like reading that big bad business people, you know, they're tough on workers."

Signifying the seriousness with which Kennedy took Romney's challenge is that he borrowed $2 million against his $6 million McLean, Virginia, estate, to underwrite Mitt-Romney-fired-me and other TV ads. It was the first time he had taken out a personal loan in a campaign and also the first time he "went negative" against a challenger.

The Romney campaign was destroyed in a span of ten days, from Joe Kennedy's explosion of the Mormon issue to the airing of the Marion worker ads. This happened despite the appearance of negative stories about Kennedy later in October. Romney questioned Kennedy's treatment of workers at the family-owned Merchandise Mart in Chicago and also turned up an old, sweetheart land deal in the District of Columbia that had benefited the senator. A Romney TV ad featured some unflattering television news footage showing Kennedy—fat and wrinkled—sitting down slowly, creakingly, painfully onto a park bench (he has worn a spinal brace since suffering a broken back in a 1964 plane crash).

Still, the challenger did not campaign on what Kennedy called "the faults in the conduct of my personal life." Not that he deserves special credit for this. He recognized that everyone knew about Kennedy's private life and he might appear churlish by emphasizing it. GOP activists and even a friendly reporter or two urged him to go personal, but he said it would be "neither savory nor effective." This was a wise decision—election-day exit polls showed that only 10 percent of the voters cast ballots based on Teddy's personal life, and they hardly needed Romney to remind them about it.

Meanwhile, the campaign rumbled on. Joan Bennett Kennedy, Ted's former wife of twenty-four years, went to court in late September to overturn parts of the couple's divorce settlement of 1982. She had gotten $5 million in cash, alimony, child support, and two residences. Her petition was sealed, and her lawyer would not disclose what more she wanted. A week later, three days before a scheduled court hearing, she agreed to postpone the action until after the November election.

On October 24, the Senate Ethics Committee confirmed to inquiring reporters that it had dismissed charges of sexual harassment and drug use by Kennedy. The committee had never publicly announced it was investigating such charges, brought in 1992 in a book by a former Kennedy staffer, or its decision in June 1994 to close the probe. Republicans and Democrats on the committee had rejected the charges unanimously. (The operations of congressional ethics committees will be examined in later chapters.) Kennedy's exoneration statement was cosigned by the ranking Republican Senator Mitch McConnell of Kentucky (who also will be revisited).

One day Romney campaigned in Dorchester, a once-tony Boston suburb that had housed "lace-curtain Irish" but now was a slum of urban desolation and the drug culture. One of the Kennedy camp's designated harassers shook a placard in Romney's face and said, "Don't you ever forget, you're in Kennedy country." Romney looked around at the boarded-up buildings and forlorn streets and retorted, "It sure looks like it."

Romney thought he had hit on a winning slogan—Dorchester as an emblem of the failures of 1960s liberalism. In his closing statement at the candidates' second and last televised debate, October 27, he expounded on the bleakness of "Kennedy country."

The Kennedy camp responded instantly and professionally. The senator hastened to Dorchester for a rally to denounce Romney for insulting a proud community and to demand an apology. Promptly, reporters went to Romney's downtown Boston office to ask for a response. By Romney's account, he was more bemused than alarmed. He thought, "An experienced campaign team [against] a novice team like mine . . . I chuckled to myself, of course, that's just doing a better job."

Actually, the Kennedy forces already had done a better job the night of the second debate. At the first debate, two days earlier, Kennedy's camp demonstrated its mastery of imagery by demanding that his podium be extra-wide so that Kennedy would not appear fat behind it. This debate had been rated a draw by the *New York Times*, a Kennedy win by the pro-Kennedy *Boston Globe*, and a Romney win by the pro-Romney *Boston Herald*. In the second debate, Romney clearly scored some points against the sometimes fumbling Kennedy. The challenger's camp was elated.

After a debate, reporters leave the arena to trudge down a hall to a temporary press room to file their stories on portable computers. In this hallway—"spin alley," as it is called—they are accosted by campaign aides who spin their candidate's performance. The Kennedy supporters said the debate was boring, nobody watched, who cares. Kennedy people clearly dominated spin alley, far outnumbering Romney backers. In fact, viewership was down only 20 percent from the first debate. But Romney once again was plainly outgunned and outmanuevered.

The next day's brief press reports treated the debate as ho-hum, the equivalent of a summer sit-com rerun. This is not to say that reporters merely were manipulated by spinners. The second debate lacked the media virtue of novelty—just as Nixon perhaps had out-pointed JFK in the second 1960 presidential debate, but John Kennedy's smashing performance in the first debate defines that campaign to this day.

Although the race was already decided, both sides sprinted through the endgame. Romney undertook a Trumanesque "whistlestop" train tour with his father, George, his mother, Lenore, and no fewer than sixty-eight Romney family members aboard—let the Kennedy royalty try to match that! They wore "TKO" sweatshirts for Take Kennedy Out. For his part, Kennedy campaigned with Hillary Rodham Clinton and also bestowed more pork—a $330-million federal grant for Boston mass transit.

On November 8, Kennedy won 58 percent of the vote, his smallest percentage since 1962, to Romney's 41 percent. Kennedy spent $10.5 million, with no money from special-interest PACs, which he sanctimoniously spurned, and ended up with $1.6 million in personal debt. Romney spent $7.6 million, with a negligible $2,000 from PACs, and $3.1 million in personal debt, which he knew was mostly gone forever if he lost.

"I got into it, as most people do, because I thought I could make a difference," Romney reflected. "Obviously, that isn't what the race is all about."

"It's about mechanics and money?" he was asked.

"Yeah. That's one of the great frustrations a lot of people that I have spoken with have. They got into it out of lofty ideals and found the race had little to do with that."

The aftermath is a tale of two treadmills.

In July 1995, George Romney was running on his treadmill in Lansing, Michigan, collapsed, and died at age eighty-eight.

For Christmas 1994 a relative gave Kennedy a treadmill. He worked out for thirty-five minutes at 6:00 A.M. each morning, had only soup and salad for lunch, got in shape, and seemed re-energized to thrust his lance against the newly Republican Senate. "It's sort of a new time in my life," he said. Even Republican senators such as Kennedy's close friend Orrin Hatch, a Mormon from Utah, took note of his reconstituted "vig-uh." It could be said that running against Romney was one of the best things that ever happened to Kennedy.

In October 1997, Kennedy, looking ahead to his re-election campaign in 2000, said that, on second thought, he would accept PAC contributions after all.

2

NEW YORK

JOSEPH J. DIOGUARDI (R) v. REPRESENTATIVE SUE KELLY (R)

"Joe, don't do it." The words were those of House Speaker Newt Gingrich of Georgia, recognized as the father of the conservative Republican capture of Congress in 1994. "Joe" was Joseph J. DioGuardi, a long-time friend who had served with Gingrich in the House in the 1980s during their bomb-throwing days against the Democratic majority. DioGuardi had even been the national finance chairman of GOPAC, the political action committee headed by Gingrich to promote Republican candidates, in 1987–88. But now the two men confronted each other via opposing press conferences. The place was Westchester County, New York. The time was March 1996.

What was Gingrich warning DioGuardi not to do? Run for Congress against a liberal incumbent Republican.

DioGuardi replied, "Newt, you're a good friend, but you are not a voter in the Nineteenth Congressional District of New York."

After DioGuardi refused to drop out of the race, Gingrich turned nasty. On June 17, he sent DioGuardi a letter signed by himself and his four fellow members of the House GOP leadership, telling him to withdraw. Sternly, it was headed, "Mr. DioGuardi:" (no formal courtesy of "Dear" in the salutation) "Should it become necessary, the House Republican Leadership is prepared to commit time and extensive resources to [Representative] Sue Kelly's re-election efforts," the leaders declared.

This was no idle threat. Shrugging it aside, a political science professor at Vassar College, located in the district, opined, "Congressional races, particularly those for the House, are local affairs. What people in far-off Washington prefer by way of a candidate, the local voters tend not to pay a hell of a lot of attention." Doubtless true, but beside the point. Gingrich and his cohorts could cut off DioGuardi's sources of campaign funds and punish his supporters, which they proceeded to do.

At first glance, Gingrich's stance seems curious, even inexplicable. Why would the conservative champion stab a conservative friend, not in the back, but practically face-to-face? DioGuardi could be stiff-necked and sharp-tongued, whereas Kelly was pleasant, but personalities had nothing to do with it. The explanation concerns American regionalism and power politics.

In ancient times—that is, during the Roosevelt, Truman, and Eisenhower presidencies—the Republican Party was a subsidiary of the Northeastern establishment, the WASP enclaves of New York, Boston, and Philadelphia. The Yankee "Rockefeller Republicans" were then eclipsed by the presidential nomination of Senator Barry Goldwater of Arizona in 1964. Although Goldwater was annihilated by President Lyndon B. Johnson, conservative dominance of the GOP endured until it climaxed with the election of President Ronald Reagan of California in 1980, followed fourteen years later by the Republican seizure of Congress. The Republicans had become the party of the South and West. Crudely put, the rebels and cowboys had beaten the Yankees. Yet, here was cowboy rebel Gingrich backing the Yankee Kelly over his old friend DioGuardi.

Gingrich and his House leadership fellows lived in constant fear that Democrats would retake the House in 1996, given the reanimation of President Bill Clinton's popularity after the federal government shutdown of December 1995 during a budget standoff, an event that Clinton ingeniously managed to blame on the Republican Congress. Gingrich and his cadre, supposedly so astute, had lost the public relations battle to Clinton just a year after their electoral triumph. Thus, they determined to support every Republican incumbent, even Yankee liberals such as Kelly, in hopes of preserving their precarious House majority.

Kelly said she had not known of the letter in advance, but she was "delighted. . . . It puts people on notice that the leadership is not going to put up with people within their own party turning against their own members."

Presidential politics were also behind the Kelly endorsement. Senate Majority Leader Bob Dole of Kansas, the party's presidential nominee-to-be, wished to demonstrate that the GOP was not inflexibly dogmatic on the abortion issue. Why, the party was "a big tent."

At the Republican National Convention in San Diego in August 1996, pro-choice candidate Kelly was among the threatened incumbents given a televised turn at the podium. This video parade was orchestrated by Representative Bill Paxon of Buffalo, New York, head of the National Republican Congressional Campaign Committee (NRCCC), and the husband of Representative Susan Molinari of New York City, the convention's keynote speaker. For what it is worth, both members left Congress in 1998, Molinari resigning to take a TV commentator's position, Paxon retiring at the end of the term to "spend more time with my family." Paxon had drafted the June 17 go-away-Joe-DioGuardi letter signed by Gingrich.

Blatant interference by outside party elders in a local primary is considered bad form. Only in extreme circumstances is this protocol violated. This has been the rule at least since President Franklin D. Roosevelt campaigned against his Democratic U.S. Senate foes in the 1938 primaries and was embarrassed by their re-elections. The Gingrich gang's assault on DioGuardi was no routine political tactic but a declaration of civil war in their own party.

DioGuardi had seen it coming and tried to prevent it with a May 24 "Dear Bill" letter to Paxon. Amid the presentation of his partisan *bona fides,* DioGuardi declared, "No Democrat can win in this overwhelmingly conservative Republican district"—meaning that either he or Kelly could keep it safely in GOP hands, so why not let us fight it out alone?

This was an exaggeration. True, the Appalachian foothills of the lower Hudson River valley north of New York City had been the bedroom domain of wealthy suburbanites since the nineteenth century. In the twentieth century, the region attracted big-business headquarters for such firms as Reader's Digest, IBM, Pepsico, and Texaco. The area's congressman for decades was the staunchly conservative Hamilton Fish, one of the Republican trio famously derided by FDR—himself a member of the Hudson Valley squirearchy—as "Martin, Barton, and Fish."

Like hundreds of others, the district was transformed by the social tidal waves that followed World War II. African Americans moved into

the southern part of the district closest to the city. The district also en-
compassed rich Jewish and Catholic, as well as middle-class, ethnic
communities. It was less Republican than most suburban areas. Still,
politicians tended to pigeonhole it as liberal Republican; after all, the
Rockefeller estate was located at nearby Pocantico Hills. But, in fact,
before Kelly won in 1994, the area had not been represented by a liberal
Republican since 1972.

DioGuardi was first elected in 1984, beating an aide to the retiring
Democratic congressman by just two percentage points. Controversial
feminist celebrity and former Representative Bella Abzug of Manhattan
moved into the district to challenge DioGuardi in 1986. He defeated
her by nine percentage points, becoming, in Republican eyes, a liberal
dragon slayer. No political pushover, DioGuardi ran TV spots featuring
news footage of liberal Democratic Governor Mario Cuomo sputter-
ing, "Bella, you're a liar." Then, in 1988, despite the national landslide
for George Bush, DioGuardi narrowly lost to another female Democrat, Nita M. Lowey. He later fell victim to a reapportioned district in a
comeback attempt in 1992.

In the 1994 Republican primary, Sue Kelly, in a field of seven candidates, won 23 percent of the vote, defeating runner-up DioGuardi by
three points. Because New York does not require a run-off election
when no candidate wins a majority, a margin of only a few hundred
votes and a plurality of 23 percent gave Kelly the GOP nomination. In
the general election her Democratic—yes, Democratic—opponent was
yet another Hamilton Fish (known as "Hammy"), grandson of FDR's
Republican nemesis and son of the newly retired GOP congressman.
Kelly won 52 percent of the vote to 37 percent for Fish and 11 percent
for DioGuardi, who was on the ballot as the nominee of the Conservative and Right to Life parties.

DioGuardi never held anything like a safe seat, so he cannot be considered as enjoying an incumbent's systemic advantages, but he might
be viewed as a chronic candidate. He never closed his 1994 campaign
office or stopped running.

After he refused to genuflect to Gingrich in 1996 and slink away into
oblivion, Gingrich moved swiftly to humiliate DioGuardi's leading
congressional supporters. Representatives Bob Dornan of California
and Chris Smith of New Jersey, probably the two hardest-edged conservatives then in the House, backed DioGuardi and even helped out
with fund raising in his district. In July, Gingrich removed them from a
conference committee of House and Senate members who would work
out a final bill on defense spending, even though both men had solid

claims to the seats. Dornan was a former fighter pilot with twelve years seniority who chaired defense and intelligence subcommittees. Smith had fourteen years seniority and chaired international relations and veterans subcommittees.

These moves by Gingrich were not mere internal House processes of no concern outside the Beltway. Rather, they were illustrations of how seriously incumbents take the electoral security of fellow incumbents. The Speaker of the House traditionally defers to his members' seniority and rarely upsets their claims to committee seats lest he violate congressional protocol and decorum, even after the congressional antiseniority reforms of the 1970s. Gingrich's actions were tantamount to King Arthur's expelling dissident knights from his Round Table.

With characteristic defiance, Dornan declared, "I'm an Air Force officer. I will not be punished by the likes of Newt Gingrich." Sure enough, he was restored to the conference committee after more than thirty Republican congressmen signed a letter to Gingrich demanding it. Smith, more accommodating, said only that Gingrich's actions were "bad form." The Speaker's mouthpieces said Smith's deletion from the conference committee roster was just a mistake. For his part, Gingrich blandly said, "I have no comment on internal affairs of the House as it relates to our members"—a statement indistinguishable in its smug arrogance from those of his Democratic predecessors as Speaker. To make sure he got the point across, Gingrich later booted Dornan and Smith from airplane manifests for congressional overseas trips, something wholly in the Speaker's power. Although Smith then headed the Helsinki Commission—a product of the Ford administration to monitor human rights in what was then the Soviet bloc—he even was barred from a flight to Bosnia to supervise elections there.

The party hierarchy dutifully supported Kelly, although the rift of cowboys versus Yankees caused concern. Dick Armey of Texas, Gingrich's House majority leader, traveled to Westchester County, New York, for a Kelly fund raiser. He "worked the crowd," shaking hands and chatting with folks who spoke with what must have been to him strange New York accents. (This event might be taken by social scientists as an episode of enduring American regionalism.) But Armey signed the June 17 go-away-Joe letter. He also called potential DioGuardi contributors in New York to ask them not to give money to him.

Kelly was no daughter of the Hudson Valley upper class but an upper-middle-class Ohioan, born in 1936. She married a man she had met at Harvard, where she was a botany researcher. They moved to Katonah, New York, and raised a family while she owned and operated a florist shop with a sideline building-renovation business. Her husband, Ed, prospered in construction and real estate.

She has been labeled as a liberal Republican, but the term is relative. Kelly supported Gingrich's Contract with America down the line and in 1996 compiled a respectable American Conservative Union voting record of 70 percent. But she also voted for some social welfare spending provisions and gay rights, which angered the party's obdurate conservatives. However, the issue that really inflamed them was abortion. She favored legalizing late-term abortions, which pro-lifers call partial-birth abortions.

Neither was DioGuardi—raised in New York City—a native of the district, nor was he neatly clothed by a political label—conservative, in his case. He supported human rights at home and abroad, by actions and not just words. DioGuardi and an African American congressman from Houston initiated legislation to confer Medals of Honor on overlooked black heroes who had served in the segregated military of World Wars I and II. With a California congressman, DioGuardi went to Albania for the first official U.S. visit in fifty years. He still works for human rights for ethnic Albanians in Macedonia and for their self-determination in the neighboring Balkan province of Kosovo. Indeed, DioGaurdi has made about twenty trips to Eastern Europe in pursuit of human rights. He further labors for self-determination in what he decorously calls not Northern Ireland or Ulster but "the north of Ireland."

The DioGuardi family is a classic immigrant American success story. DioGuardi's father arrived in New York from Naples, Italy, at age sixteen in 1929, just before the Depression. With no work available, he shined shoes, did odd jobs, and saved his nickels so that within three years he opened his own vegetable stand in Harlem. By the late 1930s he had a neighborhood grocery in the Little Italy section of the East Bronx, where DioGuardi was born in 1940. DioGuardi had believed that his father spoke a rare Neapolitan dialect of Italian, until he learned much later that the senior DioGuardi actually was speaking Albanian. He was descended from Albanians who fled from the Ottoman Turks across the Adriatic Sea more than 500 years ago.

When DioGuardi was sixteen, the family moved up, geographically and socially, to Westchester County. After years of loading crates of vegetables part time before and after school, DioGuardi graduated from Fordham University and spent twenty-two years, twelve as a partner, with the top-drawer accounting firm of Arthur Andersen & Co. In

1985 he became the first practicing certified public accountant to serve in Congress.

The first CPA in Congress was dismayed to find that Washington keeps the national books with unsophisticated accounting that would get any big-business board of directors in trouble with the Securities and Exchange Commission and probably ousted by angry shareholders. Technically, the federal government is "out of trust" in entitlement trust funds such as Social Security and Medicare and does not follow Generally Accepted Accounting Principles. DioGuardi's pet issue in Congress was "truth in federal budgeting, accounting, and reporting," and today he still lectures and writes about it. (His book, *Unaccountable Congress: It Doesn't Add Up*, was published in 1992.) But, in 1996, the issue that motivated DioGuardi to run in the Nineteenth District was not finance but abortion.

The Kelly-DioGuardi race was personal and ugly on both sides. The Catholic Coalition of Westchester issued a "Hey! Do You Know Sue Kelly[?]" brochure with a gruesome line drawing and textual description of "the abortion procedure where a late term baby is partially delivered and has its brains suctioned [out] to kill it." The mailing also featured a "Sue and Gerry" section noting her cosponsorship with Representative Gerry Studds of Massachusetts of homosexual-rights legislation. As the flier pointed out, Studds had been censured by Congress in 1983 for having sex with an underage male congressional page. Further, the brochure said Kelly had voted against reducing spending for the National Endowment for the Arts. The endowment had subsidized art works such as "Piss Christ" and "Junkie Christ." Pictured was a representation of "Junkie Christ," with most of it blanked out under a banner reading, "CENSORED!!! This 'art' is too blasphemous for us to show in full, but not too blasphemous for Sue to cut federal funding with our taxes for 'art' like this!"

After all of that, the mailer appended a disclaimer including the sentence "We do not advocate, whether express or implied, the defeat of any candidates for federal office." This grotesquerie was required for the group to maintain its tax-exempt status under campaign-spending "reform" laws.

The Kelly campaign did not shrink from responding with personal attacks of its own. Kelly accused DioGuardi of violating campaign-finance laws in "a money laundering scandal." Actually, although a major DioGuardi campaign contributor in 1988 had been convicted, the former congressman and his campaign committee were cleared by a Federal Election Commission letter, which had arrived with customary

FEC tardiness in 1993. Though exonerated, DioGuardi had been forced to pay large legal fees for his defense—another typical FEC circumstance. In the meantime, Kelly allegedly used DioGuardi's FEC reports to obtain the addresses of his contributors, then sent them negative mailings. The challenger's camp filed charges against this improper practice with the FEC; they were dropped after the election.

Kelly continued negative campaign tactics by suggesting her opponent's tax-exempt Truth in Government foundation was illegally involved in his 1996 campaign. Representative John Boehner of Ohio, one of Gingrich's congressional leaders, wrote the Internal Revenue Service a letter requesting an investigation of Truth in Government and sent a copy to DioGuardi. If this was a tactic to intimidate the challenger, it failed.

DioGuardi, in a stretch, wrote the Presbyterian Kelly that "your choice of words [money laundering] is a clever code for communicating ethnic prejudice by reinforcing stereotypes." He accused her of the same for her refusal to condemn the alleged "anti-Irish-Catholic shenanigans" of interests opposed to a planned Irish American cultural center on a certain piece of Nineteenth District real estate.

DioGuardi's campaign also highlighted Kelly's pro-abortion picketing of Representative Hamilton Fish's local office in 1992. She had worn a full-length black chador (an East Indian shawl) and carried a sign saying, "Fish Equals Women in the Dark Ages." In a later newspaper interview, Kelly recalled that after every spring break at her upper-crust Sarah Lawrence College, a few young women did not return because of botched illegal abortions.

Further, DioGuardi proclaimed that "multimillionaire Kelly paid no federal income taxes" for four years. This was true but perfectly legal under the haywire tax code. Kelly wrote off her congressional salary against her husband's losses in real estate on their joint returns. DioGuardi compared her to convicted tax cheat Leona Helmsley, with a brochure picturing both women under the headline "Guess Who Didn't Pay *Any* Federal Taxes Last Year." Also, Kelly had "voted to cut Medicare," an odd charge from a conservative committed to reining in ruinsome entitlement spending—Kelly's vote had supported Gingrich's position.

Kelly said of the tactics of DioGuardi and his supporters, "That's scary! That's like Hitler!" Later, her Democratic opponent in the general election called her "Machine Gun Kelly" because she took large contributions from the National Rifle Association.

All of this overheated name-calling and charge-countercharge was standard fare in the debasement of the marketplace of ideas under modern media politics. But the real action was in structural partisan politics, supposedly withered away under media politics.

Kelly won most of the Republican county, city, and town organization endorsements, as an incumbent normally would. In August, the state Board of Elections surprisingly decided to place Kelly on the ballot in both the Republican and New York Conservative party primaries, even though state law required her, as a registered Republican, to obtain the Conservative Party's permission first. Under this ploy, Kelly would have a chance to keep DioGuardi off the Conservative ballot line in November. State election laws and commissioners normally tilt toward incumbents; New York's election board members presumably were pressured by the machine of then-Senator Al D'Amato to rule as they did for Kelly. An enraged Conservative Party went to court and, three court rulings later, managed to knock Kelly off its ballot on the eve of the primary.

At the national level, Gingrich's warfare against DioGuardi and others, such as hard-right challenger Ron Paul in Texas, continued to bedevil the conservative establishment. Conservative honcho Paul M. Weyrich, head of the Free Congress PAC, whipped out faxes and letters to right-wing mailing lists damning Gingrich for the go-away-Joe letter in June. House Majority Whip Tom DeLay of Texas, apparently untroubled by the cowboys-versus-Yankees divide, encountered Weyrich at the GOP convention in San Diego in August. The two had been close friends for years. But DeLay followed Weyrich out of a meeting room and loudly berated him for his apostasy.

Meanwhile, Kelly refused all invitations to debate her challenger, following the common wisdom, do not publicize your opponent (although DioGuardi as an incumbent had debated Bella Abzug eleven times). Once, while campaigning on sidewalks along storefronts in Mahopac, Kelly called to a passer-by, "We still have a stupid primary, so come out [to vote]!" This was an unwitting expression of incumbents' belief in a birthright to their office—"stupid" primaries, indeed.

In the September 11 Republican primary, Kelly won 53 percent of the vote to DioGuardi's 42 percent and 5 percent for a minor candidate. DioGuardi spent $492,000, with just $31,000 from PACs and $77,000 of his own money as a contribution and $48,000 as a loan. Through the primary, Kelly reported spending $353,000, although her total spending for the 1995–1996 election cycle was $907,000. Of this amount, $418,000 came from PACs and none from her own pocket-book.

In November, Kelly won with 46 percent of the vote to 39 percent for the Democratic-Labor candidate and 12 percent for DioGuardi as the nominee of the Conservative and Right to Life parties.

In 1997, Kelly—looking ahead to the 1998, election—came out against partial-birth abortions. In 1998 she lobbied hard and secured the Conservative Party nomination without a primary by giving in on another issue, parental consent for minors' abortions.

Meanwhile, DioGuardi had become intensely involved in the cause for Albanian rights, especially in Kosovo. Back in 1985, somebody overheard DioGuardi's father speaking Albanian during a birthday party for his son while he was in Congress. The next morning, twenty Albanians appeared at the congressman's front door in Scarsdale with a case to plead. In 1998, as volunteer president of the Albanian American Civic League, DioGuardi testified four times to congressional committees. Also, he conducted demonstrations at the United Nations and the U.S. Capitol against American foreign policy in the Balkans.

DioGuardi had no intention of running again for Congress in the Nineteenth District but consented when the Right to Life party asked to place his name on the 1998 ballot. DioGuardi spent less than $11,000 in an inactive campaign and won 4 percent of the vote. Kelly was re-elected with 63 percent of the vote to 33 percent for the Democratic candidate.

3

PENNSYLVANIA

CHARLES GEROW (R) v.
REPRESENTATIVE BILL GOODLING (R)

In 1996, Charles Gerow took on a twenty-two-year incumbent, ran a surprisingly close race, maintained his optimism and good humor, spent the next two years gathering more money and support, and challenged the same incumbent in 1998. Then he got clobbered. What happened? He threw a scare into the incumbency protection racket, which rallied in its hour of danger.

The story dates back to 1960, when George Goodling was elected to the U.S. House from the southeast Pennsylvania district that includes the historically important towns of Gettysburg and York on the north side of the Mason-Dixon Line. Solidly Republican since the Civil War, this area of rich rolling farmland kept George Goodling in office until 1975, except for a two-year interruption following the Lyndon Johnson landslide of 1964. Upon Goodling's retirement, he was succeeded by his son, Bill.

Incumbents tend to view their office as a birthright—in Bill Goodling's case, literally so, a bequest from his father. After winning in 1974 at age forty-six, he was re-elected eleven times. A former high school teacher, administrator, and coach, he is one of those bland, obscure, moderate congressmen who usually do not make news but who do the actual, gritty work of legislating in the House. He flew the Republican flag in the Democratic-controlled Education and Labor Committee. When his party won a majority in 1994, Newt Gingrich awarded him the chairmanship of that committee, renamed the Economic and Educational Opportunities Committee. Goodling had no reason to fear his re-election in 1996 was in jeopardy.

Charles R. Gerow fits the profile of the typical challenger—a young lawyer, politically active, and convinced that the incumbent was out of touch with his district and a mere tool of the party leadership in Congress. Under Speaker Gingrich, Goodling had drifted steadily to the right, but not far enough to suit Gerow. Early in 1996 he called together about a dozen friends and local party leaders to announce his intention to run in the April 23 primary. His plan was not taken very seriously, even though he was not some malcontent off the street but a person of some stature in the district. He taught government at Dickinson College in Carlisle, one of the original thirteen colonial colleges, and was the state chairman of Citizens Against Government Waste.

"One gentleman who has been involved in the Republican Party for many years, a community leader, very well thought of, laughed at me," Gerow recalled. "He said, 'Charlie, I think Bill Goodling is worthless, but unless you've got $700,000, you can forget it. Do you have $700,000 on you right now?' I said I was a little light. And he laughed. He said you just can't beat these incumbents unless you're prepared to spend that kind of money." Undeterred, Gerow declared his candidacy on January 24. "I have the courage of my convictions, so I stepped up to the plate."

He made it almost too easy for the oppo people. All they had to do was drive to the Cumberland County courthouse and pull some files. As early as March 12 the *Harrisburg Patriot*—the state capital's newspaper, influential in Goodling's district although Harrisburg lies just outside of it—reported that Gerow had tax problems.

The IRS had filed a lien against Gerow for $11,700 in federal taxes allegedly owed for 1991–92. He also had been delinquent for two years on property tax payments and faced a mortgage foreclosure in 1995.

Gerow had answers for these allegations, but the critical point is that he was forced on the defensive when he was struggling to put his campaign in place. He said the IRS lien had been satisfied, although he still was disputing the amount actually owed. Likewise, his property taxes now were up to date. As for the foreclosure, a bank had filed one against Gerow and his ex-wife for $123,456 in principal, interest, and attorney's fees, but the bank later withdrew it after acknowledging an improper filing and paying all costs of the action.

Drawing attention to personal finances was pretty cheeky on Goodling's part because the congressman's re-election had been threatened in 1992 after he bounced 430 checks totalling $188,000 on the notorious House bank. At that time, Gingrich and Vice President Dan Quayle roared into the district to campaign on his behalf and the incumbent was re-elected in a three-candidate general election with a plurality of 45 percent of the vote. Two years later, Goodling won with no primary or general election opposition; Democrats did not take the trouble even to field an opponent. "One of the reasons incumbents win," Gerow concluded, "is because they are never challenged."

From Goodling's point of view, he had reason to feel surprised and irritated by the upstart challenger. Gerow's supporters wrote letters to editors of newspapers—a common campaign device for incumbents and challengers both—reviving the bounced-checks scandal and demanding a candidates' debate. But in the era of twenty-four-hour televised news, the House bank was ancient history. Meanwhile, Goodling naturally spurned debates. "He said, 'Oh, I'm willing to debate, but of course my schedule won't allow it, blah blah blah,' " Gerow said.

Another problem for Goodling was his promise that the term he had won in 1994 would be his last. But when his party took the House and he was given a chairmanship, he decided to stick around. Although the promotion was an important matter to insiders, it was not to voters. "I never heard one person on the street say, 'Oh, Mr. Goodling, he's a committee chairman.' The only people that I heard say that were political insiders and media types," Gerow said. However, those are the people who define campaigns.

Republican hard-liners of the conservative House "class of 1994" spoke bravely of eliminating the Departments of Education, Commerce, and Energy as needless bureaucracies. The rebels soon butted heads against the permanent Washington establishment, and those three departments today are healthy, growing, and ensured of eternal life. As chair of the committee overseeing education, Goodling helped to renew the Elementary and Secondary Education Act and create other programs. While he questioned the all-but-sacrosanct Head Start program, he shunned the idea of terminating the Department of Education. Gerow, by advocating abolition of that cabinet office, invited attacks that he was an out-of-the-mainstream radical.

Gerow hit back with criticisms of Goodling's votes for tax increases. Studies have shown that the longer members serve in Congress, the more they tend to support additional taxes and spending. Thus, Gerow's case against Goodling could be—and is— framed by many challengers against many long-time incumbents: They have forgotten the home folks, grown too cozy with insiders, and raised our taxes.

Goodling responded that he had voted for the Bush administration's 1990 tax package (the one that rescinded the president's "read my lips" pledge) in order to support Pentagon spending that kept military bases in Pennsylvania open. This was disingenuous. An independent commission decided which installations would close and Congress could overturn its work only by a straight up-or-down vote without any local base-saving amendments. Still, as the incumbent, Goodling had the resources and money to drive his message, while his opponent did not. So Gingrich and the National Republican Congressional Campaign Committee did not consider that Goodling was in peril.

"The Republican leadership was in most cases downright rude," Gerow said, "but the rank and file responded very well." His stands on school choice, term limits, and downsizing government probably fit more snugly than did Goodling's with those of the conservative voters in the district, which was middle-class, white, and still 50 percent rural.

Even though Gerow was making headway with these issues, he felt that media coverage continued to favor the incumbent—a universal belief of challengers. Tilting toward incumbents seems to be a media characteristic, no matter how sincerely individual journalists might try to uphold standards of impartiality and fairness. Gerow perceived one reason for this: Incumbents "feed them stories" from their inside information. There are other factors. Because they hold high office, congressmen have built-in access to media attention, while challengers often are little known and uneducated in media processes. Another reason might be that, like all human beings, newspeople like to go with winners.

"My guess is, they said, 'Who's this untested, untried guy who is coming in here to run against someone who we've known for two decades?' You had to earn your spurs with them," Gerow said. Once, when a reporter wrote a negative article about him, Gerow tried to call to give his side of the story. "They said, 'Oh, he's out playing golf.' We later found out that his golf partner that day was Bill Goodling."

Gerow spent only $73,714—about one-tenth of the $700,000 he had been told was needed—including a personal loan of $21,000 and $3,500 in donations to his campaign. During that election cycle, Goodling spent $305,541. Although he took no special-interest PAC money, personal contributions poured in from other states from people who had business before his committee.

In spite of everything, Gerow won 45 percent of the vote, a performance that amazed the GOP. The man who had teased him about having
$700,000 said, "You showed us, kid." Encouraged, the forty-year-old
Gerow resolved to try again in 1998.

One thing he had noticed about the 1996 race was that "every time
we saw Mr. Goodling, we saw a paid member of his staff." A few days
before Goodling won the November 1996 election with 63 percent of
the vote against a Democratic nobody, the *York Dispatch* published a
story about the incumbent's apparent misuse of staff for campaign
purposes.

Large staffs are a feature of the modern Congress. Fifty years ago,
House members were allowed up to five assistants; senators were allowed six—not counting separate staffs for committees. Now, representatives may hire twenty-two personal aides. Senators are not limited,
but most employ thirty to forty people, depending on the size of their
state. These public employees are prohibited by law from doing campaign work on the job. Anyone who has ever made a personal phone call
on company time can understand how easily this line is crossed.

About one-third of the staff of a typical member of Congress now
works outside Washington in the home district, primarily to handle
constituent problems and requests, a task known as "casework." As the
size of the federal government has exploded, congressmen have em-
placed staff troubleshooters to navigate through the galaxies of its
regulating and subsidizing universe. Many members of Congress will
say privately that the quality of their casework is more important than
their voting record in getting re-elected. A challenger by definition can
do no casework or stake its claims on voter loyalty. In short, big government reinforces incumbency.

Attentive voters might recognize that the number of a congressman's staffers laboring in the district increases dramatically at election
time. Indeed, one common ruse is to grant congressional aides unpaid
leaves of absence to work on the campaign and then, after the election,
bestow salary increases or bonuses to make up for the time off. This
post-election largesse is handed out regardless of whether the incumbent wins, loses, or even retires and merely wishes to give his or her
aides parting rewards. For example, Goodling placed his district office
chief on leave to manage his 1996 campaign, then paid him a bonus after the primary and general elections were won. One watchdog
group, the National Taxpayers Union, computed that 1996 post-election
staff raises in some congressional offices ranged from $180,000 to

$428,000—compared to an average office payroll of $570,000 per year.

Besides staffers, members of congress go home to campaign. As recently as 1962, taxpayers paid for congressmen to take only three round trips home from Washington a year. Early in his career, Democrat Dan Rostenkowski and two Republican House colleagues would drive to Chicago all night every Thursday and back to Washington all night every Monday at their own expense. But this was unusual; most members of Congress stayed in Washington on weekends except for those eastern seaboard members who caught quick, cheap train rides to New York, Philadelphia, or Boston. With the political ascendancy of the South and West and their congressmen's more demanding travel costs, the number of paid trips home steadily was liberalized through the years until it now is, in effect, unrestricted. Members of Congress just charge their trips to their overall office budget (technically, the Member's Representational Allowance, or MRA).

J. P. Kurish was the *York Dispatch* reporter who pursued the story of Goodling's apparent assignment of staffers to campaign work. Kurish recalls an internal editorial debate over the propriety of running a story damaging to one candidate so close to election day. In the end, neither the timing nor the substance of the story mattered. Goodling maintained he had sent his aides home on official business, but then they attended political events on their off-hours. He skated to re-election and his use of staff never was officially examined.

After this review of congressional staff and travel perquisites, it is important to note that Goodling was not an egregious abuser of them. Rather, he was their ordinary beneficiary. The National Taxpayers Union ranked his MRA spending in 1996 as 377th out of 435 representatives—he spent $674,662. Similarly, he ranked only 329th, spending $15,406, on postage under the "franking privilege" of free official mail.

One new aspect of the "frank" deserves notice, although Goodling is not involved. Congress continually enacts "reform" laws, taking care to insert loopholes to outwit the reformers. A recent statute forbade mailings of "constituent newsletters"—thinly disguised campaign brochures—within ninety days of an election, a change from the previous sixty-day rule, enacted with self-congratulations for congressional probity. However, members still may use public funds to advertise the time and place of so-called town meetings with constituents, which are actually campaign appearances. Disclosure forms reveal that a member of Congress might spend tens of thousands of dollars for such print and radio ads.

Despite his loss, Charlie Gerow figured the case against incumbency was even stronger in 1998 than it had been in 1996. His 1996 race was a slapdash, ninety-day lunge, poorly funded and organized. The 1998 race would be different, both in field work and in soft-money support from the national term limits movement.

In 1990, Colorado became the first state to impose by referendum a limit on the number of consecutive terms allowed its members of Congress. During the early and mid-1990s, Goodling's re-elections were faced with expanding sentiment for term limits as a tool to break apart the "permanent Congress," even though—or perhaps partly because— the opinion-mongering elite abhorred it. In Massachusetts, one of Mitt Romney's most popular bumper stickers read "Term Limits for Teddy." States around the country enacted congressional term limits only to have the Supreme Court in 1995 declare them unconstitutional.

As for Goodling, he compounded his problem by pledging in 1998, as he had in 1994 and 1996, that his next term would be his last. Yet by 1998, the term limits drive had fizzled, defeated not just by the Supreme Court ruling but by disagreements among conservative groups.

In 1996, the group spearheading the issue U.S. Term Limits, "didn't weigh in at all" on his race, Gerow said, because the organization focused on state ballot initiatives. (Nor, to bring up Rostenkowski again, did the group target his district in 1994, although he was under criminal indictment and served as a literal poster boy for the national term limits movement that year.) The conservatives' dilemma was that they had to rethink their cause after Republicans won the Congress. "The problem for the movement is that Republicans got in [office] favoring term limits, but pray every day that it will go away," said the executive director of U.S. Term Limits.

For example, Goodling signed a U.S. Term Limits promise in 1996 to support a constitutional amendment restricting House members to three two-year terms and senators to two six-year terms. Then he voted against the amendment six times and abstained once.

Even so, U.S. Term Limits, based in Washington, did not back Gerow in 1998, although the group's executive director made campaign appearances with him. Another group, Americans for Term Limits, based in Madison, Wisconsin, dropped $300,000 of soft money into his race.

Goodling responded quickly and professionally. He ran a TV spot denouncing Wisconsinites for presuming to tell Pennsylvanians how they should vote. "I hope you're as incensed as I am," Goodling intoned. The commercial did not mention just what policy the Wisconsin folks were pushing. As at Ted Kennedy's Dorchester rally, incumbents are skilled in communicating that local pride requires their continuation in office.

However, Goodling was not adept at modern communications techniques and could spin that ad only with outside instruction. It arrived after Newt Gingrich went to Lemoyne, Pennsylvania, on February 21, 1998, to speak on Goodling's behalf. Gingrich was used to addressing crowds of hundreds, but only a few dozen folks showed up at Lemoyne. The disgruntled Speaker flew back to Washington. At a House GOP leadership meeting a few days later, he said, "We need to do whatever it takes to get [Goodling] renominated. . . . We need to take care of him."

He was taken care of. A top National Republican Congressional Campaign Committee official was assigned full time to the Goodling campaign. A pollster who had worked for Bob Dole's presidential campaign likewise was dispatched. So was the media consultant who had produced the notorious "Willie Horton" ad for George Bush in 1988. Majority leaders Trent Lott of the Senate and Dick Armey of the House flew to Pennsylvania to speak at Goodling fund raisers. NRCCC chairman John Linder of Georgia gave Goodling the maximum $5,000 allowed by law, plus the maximum $55,000 in "coordinated expenditures" of national and state party organizations—another incumbency-protection ruse. Republican members of Congress called reporters to attest to Goodling's conservative *bona fides*; he's our guy, not that far-right-winger Gerow.

Thus, the GOP congressional primary in Pennsylvania's Nineteenth District became a proxy fight among national advocacy groups, quite apart from a test of which policies the district's voters might prefer. "I kind of felt like a rowboat out in the Atlantic Ocean, just kind of rolling around in all this money coming in from all over the place," Gerow said.

Goodling was favored by the Christian Coalition (technically, not an endorsement) and backed outright by the U.S. Chamber of Commerce (big business), the National Federation of Independent Business (small business), and Gingrich's GOPAC. The head of Americans for Tax Reform was lobbied hard to support Goodling, but he defiantly backed Gerow instead. So did the Family Research Council and President Reagan's former attorney general, Edwin Meese. Americans for Term Limits ran soft-money "issues advocacy" ads calling Goodling a "careerist politician" and reprising the House bank overdrafts: "Now he defends himself by saying [check bouncing] was not a crime. Bill, if it is not a crime, what is it?"

Amid this welter of dueling conservative organizations and celebrities, there was never a question of a Democrat's winning that seat in prime Republican territory. Incumbent or challenger? That was the only real issue.

Aside from national soft-money aid, Gerow strived to fight an old-fashioned "ground war" of door-knocking and handshaking. He estimated his troops knocked on 35,000 doors. In fact, between January and April, Gerow raised more money than Goodling did, shocking the Gingrich forces. Before Gingrich and Linder's NRCCC came riding over the hills like the cavalry, Goodling's campaign was "straight out of 1958," one Republican said in wonder and disbelief. In the final weeks, Goodling waged an "air war" of media and refused to debate, seeing "little overall value to debates in the contemporary political system." As self-serving as it is, this statement may well be valid under the system of attack ads and soft money that trivializes issues to slogans.

On May 19, Gerow won 17,245 votes—fewer even than in 1996— for 32 percent of the total. He spent $151,044, more than double his 1996 outlay, not counting the soft money from Americans for Term Limits. This time, Gerow gave only $2,000 and no personal loans to his effort.

Goodling backed down on accepting PACs contributions—a change of heart common to threatened incumbents, such as Ted Kennedy—taking $90,659 of their money. For instance, USA Loans, a firm that provides government subsidized college student loans, contributed a "bundled" amount of $63,000 from its members, curiously arriving in one day. "It seems like all these executives woke up one morning and said, 'I've got to help out Bill Goodling,' " Gerow said dryly. Goodling's total spending exceeded $425,000, again without considering soft money. He followed his practice of chipping in none of his personal funds.

The morning-after-the-morning-after-election-day, the *New York Times* report, datelined Camp Hill, Pennsylvania, opened, "Here lie the tatters of the term-limits movement: disconnected phones, empty doughnut boxes, blank computer screens and an exhausted, unshaven Congressional candidate, slumped in a chair in shorts."

Goodling had said he really, truly would not seek re-election in 2000. Gerow told the *Times* reporter, "He was emphatic this time. He said, 'I'm chairman, and I can deliver things for this district, and this is my swan song.' It's a sentimental appeal and, in some people's eyes, a practical appeal. And it worked."

But that does not explain the passion with which Gingrich and his band propped up the chairman (of the renamed once again Education and the Workforce Committee). True, Goodling opposed some of President Clinton's education initiatives, but he was hardly a full-battle-stations conservative. As in their scuttling of New York's Joe DioGuardi in 1996, the House leadership feared losing its majority in 1998 and valued incumbency over ideology. In this they differed not at all from the previous Democratic majority—or the current Democratic minority.

This is conjecture, but dread of the national media reaction to a Gerow victory might have motivated Gingrich and his lieutenants as well. The media are prone to painting Republican primary and convention fights as "struggles for the soul of the party" and warning that the GOP is about to be captured by right-wing extremists. These characterizations did not seem to bother Gingrich when he was a House rebel, but they apparently did after he became Speaker. In 1998, the Republican Congress did not pass a tax cut under a budget surplus, an omission as perplexing as though Democrats had failed to support increasing the minimum wage. If the Republican party has a soul, it is hard to locate.

Representative William F. Goodling indulged in no such speculation but merely called the conservative opposition to him "baffling." On November 3, 1998, he crushed his Democratic opponent with 68 percent of the vote.

4

VIRGINIA

Oliver L. North (R) v.
Senator Charles S. Robb (D)

December 9, 1968: Lyndon B. Johnson wore formal tails, an indignity
he had refused to suffer for his own presidential inauguration in 1965,
to give away his daughter Lynda Bird in marriage to Marine Captain
Charles S. Robb. Five hundred guests attended the ceremony in the
white and gold East Room of the White House, followed by a reception
in the Yellow Oval Room. Robb had been a member of the ceremonial
Marine guard at the White House, but he knew he was headed to Vietnam in four months.

February 22, 1969: Marine Second Lieutenant Oliver L. North
was atop the tank in Vietnam, directing his troops into a defensive
arc amid an ambush. The tank turret swiveled around and slammed
North to the ground. With ribs broken and a lung punctured, he
spurned medical attention, grabbed a grenade launcher, crawled
back up the tank, and led a successful counterattack. Seven enemy
soldiers were killed. North was either a hero or a maniac, depending
on your point of view—President Ronald Reagan later called him a
hero. North was awarded a Bronze Star with a combat "V" for valor.
Three months later he earned a Silver Star in another action. On November 23, 1969, North flew home to greet a baby girl he had never
seen.

A quarter-century later, North and Robb ran the nation's meanest
and oddest U.S. Senate race, featuring two clean-cut former Marines
both soiled by scandal, two politically ambitious All-American boys,
who—no matter who might win—had their reputations trashed by
modern media politics.

Also, the incumbent won.

Somewhat stiff and bland but displaying an attractive, boyish earnestness, Robb wanted a political career and earned a law degree at
the University of Virginia after leaving the Marine Corps. He was
elected lieutenant governor of Virginia in 1977, governor in 1981, and
U.S. senator in 1988. Although a Democratic rising star, he was given
to missteps—literally and figuratively.

During the night of the March "Super Tuesday" primary in the 1988
Democratic presidential race, he went to the ABC-TV bureau in Washington, where many newspaper reporters assembled to cadge early
exit-poll results, catch the first vote returns, and gather comments ("re-
act," in the trade) from high-profile Democrats hanging around the
place. Robb chatted with a friend, shook hands goodbye, turned to
walk down a hallway, and immediately smashed his forehead into a clear
glass door. He was knocked cold. Regaining consciousness, Robb
waved off the alarmed network staffers, rose from the floor, and wob-
bled on down to the newsroom. There he met with reporters, shaking
his head against the cobwebs. After the newspersons determined that
Robb would be okay, they laughed heartily.

Much worse media attention came in August 1988 when newspaper
stories said that Robb, while governor, attended parties in the resort
town of Virginia Beach where cocaine was used. He denied having
taken the drug himself. In 1991, the media reported that he had a nude
massage from a former Miss Virginia. Governor L. Douglas Wilder, the
nation's first black elected governor in the twentieth century and a
Robb rival, called a friend from a car phone in glee over the Robb scandals. Robb's staffers electronically intercepted the call and played a tape
of it to reporters. The fallout was ugly all around; three Robb aides had
to resign and later pleaded guilty to conspiracy charges. In 1993, a
grand jury decided not to indict Robb. He soon declared his candidacy
for re-election in 1994.

Back in 1987, Oliver North, by then a lieutenant colonel, had been
summoned to testify before the congressional committee investigating
the Iran-contra scandal. The Reagan administration had assigned
North, a National Security Council aide working in the White House
basement, to handle secret and apparently illegal arms sales to Iran.

Some of the cash then was covertly sent to rebel contras fighting the Marxist government of Nicaragua, possibly violating an on-again, off-again congressional resolution banning aid to the contras.

Appearing before the congressional committee for six days in a starched green Marine uniform, bemedalled, ramrod-straight, and projecting a Boy-Scout earnestness exceeding even Robb's, North buffaloed the members of Congress. As Hollywood says about certain actors, the camera loved North. Marines call this quality "command presence." Although North's spoken testimony was unconvincing, his televised persona as a stand-up Marine with sincere, bassett-hound eyes wowed the public, or at least many conservatives. That the Reagan administration apparently had driven holes through the Constitution did not seem to bother these true-blue right-wingers.

North was indicted for lying to Congress; shredding, hiding, and falsifying documents needed for evidence; and accepting an illegal gratuity to pay for security at his home. His credibility was fiercely attacked in court by yet another boyish-looking but highly skilled political amateur, Chicago attorney Dan K. Webb, who was working for the Iran-contra special prosecutor. (Incidentally, Webb later became the defense counsel for Chicago Congressman Dan Rostenkowski, indicted for misusing public and PAC funds.) Although a jury convicted North in 1989, the conviction was overturned on appeal a year later because the case was tainted by publicity from the televised hearings. Full of righteous indignation, retired from the Marines, North decided he wanted to be a U.S. senator. It would mean defeating Charles Robb in 1994.

In January 1994, the Iran-contra special prosecutor released his final report, which stated that North was "guilty beyond a reasonable doubt" of felonies. North's opponent for the Republican nomination, James C. Miller III, who had been Reagan's budget chief, said, "The Iran-contra controversy is going to stay in the news and will continue to be an issue."

Again, the special prosecutor's findings did not seem to bother North or his supporters. Probably neither man would appreciate the comparison, but both North and the Reverend Jesse L. Jackson have a tremendous gift for expressing the vivid image that can electrify their crowds. North said, "This is our government, you stole it, and we are going to take it back," and—in particular—recapture it from a Clinton administration teeming with "twenty-something kids with an earring."

Such rhetoric should have delighted the national Republican Party. Not so. The party elders fretted that North was so controversial that he would jeopardize a good chance to defeat so damaged an incumbent as

Robb. In turn, former president Reagan issued a statement in March 1994 that he was "getting pretty steamed about the statements coming from Oliver North," specifically that North had lied to Congress on orders from Reagan. North blamed the schism with his former president on media misreporting. Shortly afterward, North's private pilot dropped him off in Washington, flew back to Frederick County in Virginia, crashed, and died. It was not a happy time for the North campaign.

Both party establishments were glum about their prospective but flawed nominees. Governor Wilder, stepping down under Virginia's one-term gubernatorial limit, wanted to challenge Robb, but then withdrew. The Virginia Democratic chairman, Mark Warner, also balked. He declared his candidacy, only to back down for the sake of party unity.

Another Warner, Republican Senator John W. Warner (no kin, as they say in the South), declared North unfit to serve in the Senate.

The Virginia Republican Convention packed the Richmond Coliseum on June 4, 1994, with nearly 15,000 delegates—the state party claimed it was the largest political gathering in U.S. history. The party, in a shrewd fund-raising ploy, said anyone could become a delegate by paying a $45 registration fee. A predictable scramble by the Ollie North and Jim Miller forces to enlist delegates followed. North's advantage was his support by the Christian right. Indeed, the Christian Coalition rented a mailing list of 36,000 of its supporters to North but refused to rent one to Miller—a questionable action for a tax-exempt group that is not supposed to take sides in elections. (This maneuver by the Christian Coalition was unknown until the Associated Press broke the story in 1997.)

Balding and rotund, Miller fell far below North's level of charisma, but he nimbly threw conservatives some red meat without angering North's supporters. "If we Virginia Republicans nominate a candidate who loses to Chuck Robb, Democrats from Hollywood to Manhattan [Sodom and Gomorrah, in right-wing code] would insist that Americans don't mind if politicians break promises, raise taxes, and promote bigger government," he said.

Anticipating Miller's defeat, GOP Senator Warner already had promoted former state Attorney General J. Marshall Coleman to run as an independent in the general election. Coleman's candidacy was Warner's own project—there was no collusion with Robb about it. The convention nominated North over Miller, 55 percent to 45 percent. Then Wilder, after dropping out of the Democratic primary, started making noises that he might run as an independent, too. A nasty, four-way Senate race was shaping up— North, Robb, Coleman, Wilder.

Robb easily won renomination in the Democratic primary of June 14. Four days later, Wilder declared his candidacy as an independent.

The national GOP was beside itself trying to decide what to do about Oliver North. Initially, Senate Republican leader Bob Dole publicly refused to endorse him. Still, the Christian right had been President Bush's only solid core of support in his 1992 race against Bill Clinton. The party could not afford to antagonize this group. So, staffers on the National Republican Senatorial Committee—which funds candidates—were told they would be fired if they backed Marshall Coleman. Freelance campaign consultants likewise were advised they would never work for national Republicans again if they helped Coleman. Even Dole was induced to spend a day campaigning with North, and James Baker, who had been Reagan's chief of staff and Bush's secretary of state, pitched in with fund raising. But other top Reaganites continued to balk.

The state that had cradled George Washington, Thomas Jefferson, James Madison, and Robert E. Lee now witnessed a campaign of bumper stickers proclaiming, "I Don't Vote for Felons" (a slam at North) or "We Believe in Marriage" (a hit on Robb). The National Education Association (NEA), the largest union in the state, poured in soft money for Robb. On the other side, North's direct mail campaign drew in more than 270,000 contributors from across the country.

Robb needed NEA dollars because he could not rely on the old southern Democratic courthouse crowd. This bunch—the sheriff and the tax assessor and the local banker, straw-hatted and palavering and spitting tobacco juice while seated on a magnolia-shaded, wrought-iron bench placed behind the Confederate monument gracing the lawn before the courthouse—forms a stock tableau from southern mythology. But with a few rural-county exceptions across the South, the courthouse machines were long broken up by the 1960s civil rights laws and the later, underappreciated phenomenon of the expansion of public-sector unions for teachers and government workers. Robb was no creature of those courthouses but rather had become famous for the woman he married (just like Senator Warner, the sixth husband, if Richard Burton is not counted twice, of Elizabeth Taylor). For Robb to beat North he would need to sweep the Washington, D.C., Virginia suburbs—populated with government workers—and the Third Congressional District.

The voting-age population of Virginia was about 15 percent black, with most of it gerrymandered into the Third District, the historical seat of U.S. slavery. In 1619, the first slave ship eased up the James

River to offload its human cargo. In 1991, the area, known as the Tide-water, was redistricted to ensure blacks of at least one African American member of Congress in Virginia. In 1992, the district elected Bobby Scott, a Robb supporter and a Harvard classmate of Vice President Al Gore.

So North concentrated on the largely white, rural counties of south-ern and western Virginia—with their Wal-Marts, Dairy Queens, court-house squares, and church pulpits—putting 279,000 miles on his motor home. He christened it "Rolling Thunder," the code name of an LBJ bombing campaign against North Vietnam. He left small blue stickers saying "Ollie North was here" seemingly placed on the win-dows of every gas station in the state. Beyond this grass-roots cam-paign, North ran a high-tech operation. "Rolling Thunder" had a satellite uplink installed in the back.

North likes to say that he overrode his consultants to publish a cam-paign platform with fifty-three policy points. "It said, 'Here's where I stand on each one of these issues.' I handed it out in both a long version and a short version, a full booklet and then kind of a profile, so that peo-ple would not have any doubt as to where I stood on an issue."

By doing so, North broke two unwritten laws of electioneering. First, the common wisdom is that if you take a specific stand, voters on the other side of that issue definitely will vote against you, but the pro-ponents will not necessarily vote for you because they might be swayed by other issues or trivial considerations such as they do not like the way you squint your eyes against the TV floodlights. The second rule is never to hand your opponent a "laundry list" of issues so that he or she might pick the best ones to turn against you. Thus speak the consultants.

Nonetheless, "I can assure you that after I was done campaigning, nobody had any doubt" that the fifty-three-point platform was the right thing to do, North said. Although he won this argument with his consultants, at least in the immediate tactical sense, in the later stages of the campaign his handlers controlled him. They choreographed his ap-pearances as rigidly as a symphony conductor and kept him away from reporters.

If cornered for an interview, North would snap, "Fire!" and take questions like a Marine in a combat training drill. "The media was hos-tile throughout, but I'm a big boy and I expect the media to be hos-tile," he said later. On October 22, 1994, the *Washington Post* ran a story that probably confirmed North's suspicions. It said the Nicara-guan contras secretly funded by North had been involved in illegal drug trafficking. The news value of this report was hard to detect, for nearly all its information had been disclosed in the 1980s (nobody was prose-cuted on drug-related charges in the scandal, but the special prosecutor said after the *Post* report that he had lacked time to delve into that area, although his investigation lasted seven years). One day after the contra drugs story, the *Post* endorsed Robb.

For his part, Robb talked to reporters as though he were the inno-cent novice and North the polished media pro. Like other incumbents, such as Senator Larry Craig in Idaho, he played the role of a wounded fawn when the campaign turned negative. Robb marveled at how swiftly North's handlers had put him in a pressed plaid shirt after a for-mal debate so that the candidate would appear folksy in a subsequent parade. "I mean, he's as good as Reagan at delivering the line," Robb said in wondering admiration. Then, before the cameras, his wife Lynda Bird kissed him and his mother-in-law, former first lady Lady Bird Johnson, hugged him.

Despite North's detailed policy platform, the campaign was personal from the start. September saw a dreadful exchange between the two former Marines regarding their war records. North sneered at Robb as an "Eighth and I" Marine, a reference to the street address of the Wash-ington barracks that housed the White House detail. Robb blasted back that he had been decorated for combat in Vietnam. For those who keep score, North received the Bronze and Silver Stars, two Purple Hearts, and a Navy commendation medal; Robb was awarded a Bronze Star, a Vietnam Service Medal, and the Vietnamese Cross of Gallantry.

All of this dispiriting charge-countercharge was secondary to the real—and secretive—campaign. On July 14, Vice President Al Gore had met with Doug Wilder in the White House. On September 15, Wilder dropped out of the race just two days before the legal deadline. It was his second withdrawal in eight months. On October 19, Presi-dent Clinton met with Wilder in the White House and mentioned that he might name him as a roving ambassador to Africa.

Of course, there probably was no specific talk of a tit-for-tat deal. The Washington establishment long ago mastered the sophistication to avoid operating so crudely. Although the circumstantial evidence is strong, the dangling of a high federal post before Wilder has never been documented. Tom Lehner, Robb's chief of staff, calls it an "urban leg-end" spread by Republicans. In any case, Wilder received no White House appointment after the election.

During the high-level courting of Wilder, the Robb campaign pri-vately suggested that the senator might help the former governor—his political foe since 1977—retire the campaign debt from Wilder's brief

run for the 1992 Democratic presidential nomination. Here was yet another example of the establishment putting aside enmities and closing
ranks when facing a serious challenge. On October 21, Wilder, two days
after meeting with Clinton, endorsed Robb outright at a Democratic
fund raiser in Alexandria, Virginia, attended by the president. Wilder
thereupon decamped to Bobby Scott's Third Congressional District.
North had been slightly leading in the polls in a four-way race. Now it
was just North, Robb, and Coleman.

Even before Wilder's expected withdrawal, North's pollster flew
down from suburban D.C. to meet North, his wife Betsy, his son Stu-
art, and two top campaign aides in a hotel suite. The pollster had bad
news.

He solemnly handed out computer printouts of poll results. As
North recalled, he said, "Here's what the tracking polls showed last
night, and you're behind, and you won't be able to close this thing as
long as there are three people in the race and one of them is Marshall
Coleman, 'cause he's going to take ten to twelve [percentage] points
from you, and you will lose the race by two and a half to three points."
(This prediction turned out to be accurate within two-tenths of a point.)

The pollster continued, "It's going to take something to polarize the
electorate to get them out to vote for you. What it's going to take is an
ad that's racially divisive. Because you are going to lose that [black]
vote. [Jesse] Jackson and Robb are campaigning heavily in Bobby
Scott's district, which you are going to lose, and you've got to close the
margin with enough votes that will bring [whites] aboard instead of going with Coleman."

The pollster had obtained some ABC News video footage, never
broadcast, of an interview with the foreman of the jury that had convicted North in 1989. The foreman said something to the effect, "He
was white, we were black, they would have thought we were stupid if
we didn't convict him of something." Focus groups promptly con-
vened by the pollster revealed that white Virginia voters did not realize
that North had been tried before an all-black jury.

Overnight, the pollster's firm hastily produced a bare-bones, thirty-
second TV ad that opened with "Did you know?" followed by the jury
foreman's candid remarks. This spot was cued up on the hotel suite's
VCR and played for North and the others.

"It was a very straightforward ad," North remembered. "The campaign guys said, 'If you run this ad you'll probably win. Without this ad
you can't, unless Marshall Coleman gets run over by a truck.'

"They put that in front of me. I told them no. I did not want to be a United States senator so bad that I would run as a racially polarizing and divisive person. That's not who I am. Thirty-one days later I lost the election. I [still] don't know if they were right or not."

North said this matter-of-factly, not presenting it as a decision wrought by a personal dark-night-of-the-soul moral crisis. He had grown up in small-town upstate New York amid the 1950s northern trumpeting of racial "tolerance," had fought alongside blacks in Vietnam in the quite successfully integrated armed services, and was unschooled in the depths of southern racial politics.

However ideologically polarizing North was, racial polarization indeed did not represent "who he was." But North received no credit for this restraint; the proposed ad has never been disclosed.

The pollster shrugged—these guys pay you to give them your best advice, and if they do not want to take it, well, that is their prerogative. Perhaps North, so constrained by handlers, also felt the small thrill of telling a hired expert that he is way over the line.

After this incident, North suspected the race might be lost. But, just as in the Romney-Kennedy race, the final weeks saw a frenzy of campaigning by both sides. Robb, Wilder, and Jesse Jackson preached from black pulpits in the Third District. Clinton and Gore stumped with Robb. Senator Warner, Coleman's campaign chairman, was elbow-to-elbow with him at campaign events. At the Norfolk airport, North chanced upon Reverend Jackson and impishly wrote on a campaign brochure, "Jesse Jackson—I want your vote—Oliver North," and thrust it over like a quarterback handing off the ball, which Jackson politely folded and placed in a jacket pocket.

In the campaign's final two weeks, North directed his attacks against Clinton more than Robb. This probably was a strategic mistake, considering the aphorism that "all politics is local"—even though both sides did their utmost to nationalize the Virginia election. In many jurisdictions, the Republican strategy to make 1994 a referendum on Clinton and the GOP "Contract with America" worked well, but not in Virginia, with personalities as dominant as Ollie North and Chuck Robb.

Bob Dole and Republican Governor George F. Allen of Virginia stumped with North. On the day before the election, Robb, mouthing words seemingly written by a speechwriter on dexedrine, called North a "document-shredding, Constitution-trashing, Commander-in-Chief-bashing, Congress-thrashing, uniform-shaming, Ayatollah-loving, arms-dealing, criminal-protecting, resume-enhancing, Noriega-coddling, Social Security-threatening, public-school-denigrating, Swiss-banking-law-breaking, letter-faking, self-serving, election-losing, snake-oil sales-man who can't tell the difference between the truth and a lie"—an im-pressive wealth of invective.

Election day, November 8, was sunny and mild—62 degrees—across Virginia. Good weather boosts voter turnout and a high turnout nor-mally is good news for Democrats. In the Washington suburb of Fair-fax, lines at the polling places were up to three hours long. That night, in a Richmond hotel ballroom across the street from the Coliseum where he had won the nomination in June, North made the obligatory phone call to concede to the winner.

The electorate was unaware that the two men had known each other for years. In fact, there are unconfirmed oral reports that during the Iran-contra hearings, North sometimes asked Robb for advice on how to handle this or that senator on the investigative panel. In 1989, Robb cast a Senate vote against stripping North of his Marine Corps pension because of Iran-contra—why punish a fellow Marine for following or-ders from his superiors? When North called on election night, Robb said, "Ollie, from one Marine to another, you gave as good as you got." North said only, "You won. Govern well," and hung up.

Later, appearing before his supporters in the ballroom, North did not offer the traditional congratulations to the winner or even mention his name. He merely said, "I share the hurt you feel. That I did not win this contest is in no way your fault or your failure." Then he hugged his wife, and they walked away.

Robb's chief of staff, Tom Lehner, said, "North really thought he was going to ride this into the White House. He really believed, and his followers believed, that he was capable of that."

Robb won by just 56,000 votes out of 2.1 million cast. North lost the Third Congressional District by 60,000 votes. Obviously, the 91 percent of black voters who went for Robb provided the incumbent's victory margin. But then, the challenger did not get all the votes of the Christian right, either. He barely carried Chesapeake, base of the Christian Coali-tion, and actually lost Lynchburg, home of the Reverend Jerry Falwell of the late Moral Majority. Coleman got 11 percent of the statewide vote.

Robb spent $5.5 million, including $1.3 million from PACs and none of his own money. North spent an amazing $20.6 million, but the sum is smaller than it appears because much of it was continuously recy-cled into ever more direct-mail solicitations. Direct mail is an expensive medium that on a good day might return about fifty cents on the dollar.

Incredibly, Virginia did not have the costliest Senate race of 1994. Representative Michael Huffington spent $30 million in a failed effort to unseat Senator Dianne Feinstein of California, who spent $14.4 million. As a rule, challengers cannot raise enough cash to prevail, but another axiom is that, when they can, money alone does not win elections.

As for North's $20.6 million, only $166,544 came from PACs, and he loaned his campaign a paltry $5,000. Robb got the usual PAC thousands upon thousands, while North's national cadres of conservative true believers donated an average of $19.11. One way to look at this election is as the defeat of rural and small-town voters by gigantic urban partisan and lobbying institutions.

Then again, perhaps North was just too notorious to win a statewide election, even in a Republican year. Maybe the Democrats' client groups of public-sector unions, minorities, and southern "yellow-dog Democrats"—so loyal that they would vote even for a yellow dog if nominated by the party—simply outnumbered the GOP constituencies of country-club economic conservatives and Christian-right social conservatives. It could be that North was an anomaly who does not belong in this study of the systemic advantages held by incumbents.

But consider that the Democratic president and vice president engineered the withdrawal of a minority Democratic "independent" candidate (Wilder) who threatened the Democratic incumbent (Robb); and that a Republican senator (Warner) arranged an independent Republican candidacy (Coleman's) that ensured the splitting of the opposition vote, and thus the re-election of the Democratic incumbent. Now consider that the partisan alignments were reversed: that the president and vice president were Republicans, North a Democrat, and John Warner a Democrat who put up an independent Democratic candidate to split the opposition and guarantee the re-election of the incumbent Republican senator. Would the outcome have been any different?

North said, "If my recollection serves me correctly, there were thirty-four or thirty-five U.S. Senate seats open. I was one of the challengers. Only one full-term incumbent was defeated. And if that isn't a statistic that sends a chill through the heart of any challenger who wants to run against an incumbent, I don't know what would."

North's memory was accurate, but only technically so. Thirty-five Senate seats were contested in 1994, the year of the Republican takeover of Congress, which set all the punditry hounds to baying. "Full-term" Democratic Senator Jim Sasser of Tennessee was defeated, but so was Senator Harrison Wofford of Pennsylvania, elected to a partial term to fill a vacancy in 1991. Although the GOP recapture of Congress in 1994 was believed to be earth-shaking, the incumbency re-election rate still exceeded 90 percent.

5

VIRGINIA

JAMES C. MILLER (R) v.
SENATOR JOHN WARNER (R)

James C. Miller III was not the only Virginia Republican who remained disgruntled with Senator John Warner for having torpedoed Oliver North's campaign in 1994. Actually, Warner's transgressions against conservative rectitude predated 1994. He had voted against President Ronald Reagan's nominee for the Supreme Court, Robert H. Bork, in 1987. In 1989 he cooperated with Senate Democrats in rejecting President George Bush's nomination of former Senator John Tower of Texas as secretary of defense. In 1993, Warner opposed Michael P. Farris, a hard-liner of the Christian right, for lieutenant governor.

So Miller challenged Warner in 1996 and the Washington press could not resist portraying the contest as "a battle for the soul of the Republican Party." It was not. It was a battle of a challenger against an incumbent.

Still, for the record, these were the candidates' differences on issues: Miller was for tax cuts, a flat income tax, term limits, and against abortion except when the mother's life was endangered; Warner supported selected spending cuts and tax increases to reduce the deficit, opposed term limits, and was against abortion except in cases of mothers' endangerment, rape, or incest, although he had voted for Medicaid funding of abortions on demand.

Miller launched his campaign on December 5, 1995, and the incumbent-protection machine whirred into action immediately. Although Miller had the tacit support of the officially neutral Virginia Republican Party organization, this was nothing compared to the power of the national GOP hierarchy. Among the prominent Republicans who rallied to Warner's side via endorsements or outright campaign appearances were former President George Bush, former Vice President Dan Quayle, Senate Majority Leader Bob Dole, Senate Majority Whip Trent Lott (who later that year became majority leader when Dole resigned to work full time on his presidential campaign), and retired General Colin Powell.

"I knew that there were probably at least ten members of the United States Senate who strongly preferred me over John Warner, but they would not go so far as to endorse me over their colleague," Miller said. The Republican National Senatorial Committee also kept its hands clean by not endorsing or giving money to either candidate until after the nominee was decided, as the committee's by-laws stipulate. But the organization still provided soft money and "in-kind" help to Warner. He received office space, research assistance, a fund-raising plan, and staff scheduling of fund-raising events. The committee chair that year was Senator Al D'Amato of New York, a hard-bitten pol of the old school from the Long Island Republican machine.

From Warner's point of view, he had good reason to feel anxious about re-election, for he had made powerful enemies including Miller, North, Farris, Bork, and the Christian Coalition. Accordingly, he exercised his right to decree that Virginia Republicans select their Senate nominee by a primary election, not a party convention.

He could do this because Virginia—like all states—writes its election code to benefit incumbents over challengers and the two established parties over third parties. An odd provision in Virginia essentially allowed incumbents to choose their method of seeking renomination: by primary or convention. The GOP state chair went to court to try to overturn this provision to no avail. Warner was wise to go the primary route because when the state party eventually held its convention, Miller won a straw poll over Warner by a three to one margin.

In 1994, Republicans nominated by convention and Democrats by primary; in 1996, the situation was reversed. Warner would run in an "open" primary not restricted to Republicans and independents—voters of any party could take a ballot, especially Democratic government employees in the District of Columbia suburbs and African-American Democrats in the Tidewater.

In September 1995, Warner moved from the Watergate complex in Washington, a politically unfortunate address, to suburban Alexandria, Virginia. He had sold his estate in Middleburg in the Virginia horse country and thus had no Virginia voting address. "One of his campaign themes was that he was a real Virginian, whereas I was an interloper. Living in the Watergate didn't quite fit," Miller said.

After the move to Alexandria, Warner soon learned he had perhaps less to fear from Oliver North than he had believed. In January 1996 at a GOP prayer breakfast in Richmond, North said, "The person that we elect ought to be a resident of Virginia, someone who lives with the people of this commonwealth, not in some ivory tower on the other side of the Potomac." However, he never mentioned Warner's name, nor did he specifically endorse Miller, who was at the breakfast, although Miller had promptly endorsed North after losing to him in 1994. North's detractors saw this as petulance, just as he had refused to name or congratulate Robb in 1994.

Within weeks of announcing his candidacy, Miller faced formidable odds. He was challenging a three-term incumbent backed by the national machinery of his own party. His opponent was running in a primary open to Democrats, who had no primary of their own in which to vote. North, probably the most popular Republican in the state, would not stand foursquare behind him.

Still, Miller believed that he was the better man, that he had better ideas for the country, that Warner's campaign of clout-and-pork-touting had worn thin with the public, and that the conservative Republican tide of 1994, rather than receding, had not yet crested. On the plus side in terms of campaign mechanics, North did agree to rent Miller his mailing list of supporters. Further, Miller enjoyed the support of the Christian Coalition, which promised to circulate 750,000 "voter guides" favoring him, but only implicitly, so as to protect the group's tax-exempt status. Moreover, Miller thought he could tap into major Republican donors with access derived from his service as director of the Office of Management of Budget (OMB) under President Reagan. He learned differently.

Aside from fund-raising dinners and receptions, known in political circles as "funders," candidates spend much of their time—an outrageous amount of time made necessary by the federal limit of $1,000 on personal contributions—calling prospective donors, known as "dialing for dollars." Like many challengers, indeed like many members of Congress, or so they say, Miller found such solicitations to be personally degrading. But it was part of the job and he did it, only to encounter unexpected resistance. Not even the U.S. Chamber of Commerce, which had enjoyed much clout in the Reagan administration, would support Miller. The chamber explained that, under its rules, an incumbent who scores above a certain level on legislative votes deemed critical to the chamber is automatically endorsed. The chamber's national president told Miller, sorry, you're a good guy, you would be more effective than Warner for the causes we think are important, but that is our rule. Miller said sardonically, "As Reagan's budget director, people begged me for millions and billions of dollars. Now I beg people for hundreds."

A maneuver by the Warner campaign further impeded the challenger's fund raising. Miller had a "leadership PAC," a political action committee set up not to fund his own race but to provide policy and legislative help as well as contributions to other candidates, thus winning their gratitude and support. All big-name pols and presidential aspirants have these leadership PACs; they can amount to millions of dollars. Miller's was a modest "Commonwealth PAC" for Virginia state legislative candidates. Warner, through his campaign manager, filed a seventeen-page complaint with the Federal Election Commission, a toothless regulatory agency, alleging that Miller illegally was spilling money from his state PAC into his federal candidacy. (Such a sloppy overlap of state and federal PAC spending led in part to the House ethics sanctions against Speaker Newt Gingrich in 1997.) Warner was chairman of the Senate Rules Committee, which has jurisdiction over the FEC, the officials of which were aware of this circumstance.

Filing ethics complaints with the FEC has become routine in campaigns. The damage to Miller was that several of his contributors and contractors had to hire expensive election-law attorneys to file affidavits, an annoying distraction at the least. Personally hurtful was that Warner (technically, Warner's campaign manager) accused Miller's son and staffer Felix of a conflict of interest, merely for being on his father's campaign pay roll.

Miller, like other candidates in similar situations, complained that reporters docilely transcribed the he-said-he-said, charge-defense-countercharge as ordinary campaign fare without trying to get to the truth. But the FEC keeps the case files secret until the issue is resolved. The FEC dismissed Warner's complaint as unfounded in August 1997, fourteen months after the election.

Meanwhile, Warner's forces took the next step of calling major donors and fund raisers—those who assemble $1,000 individual contributions into a large "bundle," people known as "bundlers"—to warn that they had better not give to the challenger or they would regret it; a scandal was about to break, having to do with campaign financial charges by the FEC. Such poison-pen tactics are common in campaigns, although in Miller's case, the potency of the poison might have seemed dubious. He had even released his 20-page Federal Bureau of Investigation file from his background checks when he was named to head the Federal Trade Commission in 1981 and the OMB in 1986. The FBI report was so dull that probably even Warner's aides were burdened to read it through to the end.

Speaking of dullness, Miller knew he was an unexciting candidate. An economics professor at George Mason University, he was apt to give long-winded answers to simple questions. Not that this is a character flaw, but it is a frequent and unhelpful trait of political amateurs going up against professional incumbents.

To appear folksy, Miller toured the state in a red pickup truck. (The same ploy had been used successfully in Tennessee in 1994 by Senate candidate Fred Thompson, another Washington insider running as an outsider.) Miller acknowledged that his truck was in part "a statement," but he insisted it was a natural part of his lifestyle. Both he and his wife owned red pickups with four-wheel drives to get to their cabin in the Virginia mountains.

In another bow to political imagery, the challenger entered campaign events with speakers blaring "Friends in Low Places" by country music star Garth Brooks. Miller had been startled after a radio interview when his young traveling aide asked the disc jockey to play it. Miller knew the song, but his his musical taste ran more to Henry Mancini's "Baby Elephant Walk," which he hummed between engagements. Anyway, the Garth Brooks opus became the campaign theme song.

Not about to be outdone on the imagery front, Warner took care always to refer to his opponent as "Doctor Miller," code for "out-of-touch intellectual." By June, standing with Bob Dole and General Powell in McLean, Warner took to saying, "He's impersonating a Bubba." Miller's retort showed some wit: "He's impersonating a U.S. senator."

Warner was no stranger to artificial imagery of either the Washington or Hollywood varieties. From 1974–76, he directed the American Revolutionary Bicentennial Commission. By all accounts, he did a good job superintending the hoopla and displaying some talent for oratory, if a bit on the sonorous side (a "foghorn," Miller said). Then Warner married actress Elizabeth Taylor. The predictable divorce came in 1982 after six years.

In 1978, party leaders selected Warner as the Republican candidate for the Senate after the original nominee was killed in a plane crash— Warner had been the runner-up for the nomination at the Virginia GOP convention. He won the Senate seat, was re-elected in 1984, and in 1990, Democrats did not field an opponent.

In 1996, Warner strolled through courthouse squares in a Panama hat and khakis. Before plunging into a crowd, he would ostentatiously unknot and remove his tie. Impersonating a Bubba indeed. Neither candidate's behavior did much to allay the cynical belief that the public relations industry has overwhelmed national politics.

Born in Washington in 1927, Warner was a son of privilege. He earned a law degree from the University of Virginia in 1953, clerked for a federal appellate judge, and was appointed secretary of the navy by President Richard Nixon. Warner has an aptitude for official ceremony and pageantry; besides the bicentennial post, as Senate Rules chairman he presided over President Bill Clinton's second inauguration in 1997. But in 1996, he was a southern good old boy.

This review of the Warner-Miller race has concentrated on campaign mechanics, tactics, and imagery because policy differences between the candidates did not decide the election. If there was a cutting issue, it was which candidate could preserve Virginia's naval shipyards in Nor-folk and Newport News, threatened with closings after the end of the Cold War. Warner claimed that if re-elected he was in line to chair the Senate Armed Services Committee. This was disingenuous as long as Senator Strom Thurmond of South Carolina was alive—admittedly an uncertain prospect; Thurmond was ninety-three. (In fact, Thurmond retained the Armed Services chairmanship in 1997 at least in part to punish Warner for having opposed defense secretary-designate John Tower in 1989; Warner would finally assume the seat in 1999.)

The Warner campaign also subtly put out the word that Miller, age fifty-three, had dodged the draft in the Vietnam War, during which he had held student deferments. In contrast, Warner had volunteered for the Navy at age seventeen in 1944 and later served as a Marine in Korea from 1950–52.

Facing these attacks, Miller was a perfectionist with a consequent tendency toward pessimism. Yet an air of unreality descended on the challenger's campaign, as it does for underdogs' efforts from city coun-cil races up to presidential hopefuls. Miller liked to wear a necktie bear-ing the portrait of Adam Smith, author of *The Wealth of Nations* in 1776 and father of laissez-faire economics. Surely the contemporary conser-vative ascendancy would put him over the top. Mike Farris, the defeated lieutenant governor candidate and now a leader of the Christian Coalition, assured Miller that the coalition would deliver at least 200,000 votes. He miscalculated, for Miller barely broke 170,000 votes.

The challenger also was handicapped by staff ineptitude. Too much could easily be made of this. All candidates in all major races attract volunteers, hangers-on, and paid staffers of doubtful expertise. These folks actually are the unsung heroes of American electoral democracy. They work night and day, subsisting on cold pizza, tepid soda, and—alas— lukewarm beer. Telephones are all but surgically implanted in their ears. They forsake personal lives, snub lovers and spouses, sometimes even break up with them, all because they are so emotionally invested in a candidate and his or her cause. They live on adrenalin and instantaneous reponses to contingencies, the rush of confronting a crisis a day. If their candidate wins, they are geniuses, and if he or she loses, they are fools.

They also gossip, backstab, jockey for power, and compete for prominence, exactly as in corporate office politics, except that these activities are compressed and intensified by the pitiless deadline of the election. Disregard all media reports of campaign aides fighting for access to the candidate's ear: of course, they are. Likewise beware of assertions that candidates and their staffs know what they are doing. All "well-oiled machines" creak and clash from the inside. These folks are winging it. They are feeling the undertow and thrashing their arms to catch the onshore wave. And some of them are simply incompetent.

The first indication of such ineptitude came in Miller's drive to collect the necessary number of voters' petition signatures to gain access to the ballot. Miller had hired a field director who blithely promised between 30,000 and 60,000 signatures. The legally mandated minimum was 15,312. The staff tallied the petitions on the campaign computer and with alarm eyed a total below 10,000. Frantically the volunteers—the young cold-pizza and warm-beer subsisters—fanned out to shopping malls and courthouse squares and garnered the requisite number before the deadline. In fact, they filed earlier than Warner did, thereby gaining the first spot on the ballot. Political experts believe the top-name position can entice perhaps two or three percentage points of the vote.

Meanwhile, Miller's initial chief of fund raising was at first uncertain of the federal limits on personal and PAC contributions, an inexcusable ignorance. Miller also demoted his first "communications director" as incompetent. Still, she stayed on staff at the campaign office in Falls

Church and spent the days watching C-SPAN and making personal phone calls.

None of this information came from the gentlemanly Miller, but he did speak with irritation of the time he tried to override a media consultant and got snookered.

The direct-mail firm he had hired in Richmond presented a campaign brochure that said, "John Warner would rather have lunch with his New York girlfriend Barbara Walters at the Palm than visit with people in Martinsburg, Virginia." Miller red-penciled the sentence out as invidious and returned it to the consultant. The consultant left it in anyway and sent out the mailing. Warner made the expected, aggrieved response about dirty pool and so forth. As to whether the slur won Miller any votes, who knows?

Another time, a supporter suggested that Miller exploit the endorsement of Warner by the *Blade*, a gay newspaper. The man who suggested this was himself homosexual. "I'm not a hate monger," Miller said, and that was the end of that.

Warner, hopscotching the state in airplanes while the challenger navigated winding and narrow country roads in his red pickup, slickly arranged other apparent endorsements. The senator's camp faxed a news release to media outlets headlined, "Bob Dole and Gov. George Allen Attend Endorsement Ceremony for John Warner." In reality, the governor carefully made no endorsement and merely showed up at a Dole-Warner event in support of a nickel reduction in the federal gasoline tax. Allen made such a fuss that Warner was constrained to fax another release clarifying the record.

Then, Warner invited former British Prime Minister Margaret Thatcher to a tea in Williamsburg, the historic colonial capital. Thatcher is a figure revered by American conservatives second only to Reagan. Upon arrival, Thatcher was dismayed to learn that the "tea" was 400 people attending a $1,000-a-head Warner funder. Warner's media people quickly edited a videotape of the event for a TV ad implying an endorsement. "I happen to know privately Mrs. Thatcher was somewhat upset about that because the videotape with him was out of context and did not constitute an endorsement on her part," Miller said. Probably so, but the point is that the challenger probably could not have attracted Thatcher even to a tea that really was one.

Warner's TV ad slogan was "Thoughtful, Conservative Leadership with Integrity." He did not mention his partisan identity.

Miller advocated privatizing the U.S. Postal Service. Warner seized on this seemingly radical idea and touted his own one-time employment by the Postal Service. What he had done was work during a college Christmas break as a postal helper. He went to the national meeting of the postal workers union as a fellow traveler and got both their endorsement and PAC donation, a rarity for a Republican.

But the Miller campaign was not above its own sneaky little tricks of disinformation. Campaigns routinely dispatch staffers to attend every public appearance of their opponent. These workers, sometimes called "quote boys" because they record the rival's words, instantly relay to campaign headquarters intelligence of what the other side is saying and doing. Thus a response can be vouchsafed to the media within the same morning-or-afternoon news cycle (a technique perfected by the Clinton campaign of 1992 and adopted by every smart politician since). Miller's college-age staffer Tyrus O. Cobb liked to scam Warner's quote boys. He would bark campaign "secrets" into a cellular phone within their earshot. "It is amazing what the Warner staffers would believe when I would talk loudly into a cellular phone that wasn't even on," he remembered.

Miller volunteers drove around the state to post ten-by-twenty-eight-foot "Miller for Senate" banners, sometimes trespassing on public or private property to put them up. In reaction, Warner made a public relations miscue. "I don't need a banner; the people of Virginia know me," he declared numerous times, thus appearing petty and pompous. All consultants try to pound into their clients' heads the necessity of staying "on message." By making the banners an issue, Warner was getting "off message" and publicizing his opponent.

It hardly mattered, for the stolid Miller was not igniting the right wing, and Warner, honoring page one in any political consultant's campaign handbook, refused invitations to debate. Why should a front runner give his challenger free publicity?

In the final stages, the campaign was a gruesome contest of the candidates trying to "out-Reagan" each other in appealing to conservative Republican voters—Reagan, who by that time was afflicted with Alzheimer's disease, endorsed nobody—while Warner also tried to attract Democrats as a moderate. Warner spent $1.5 million on TV ads while Miller barely ponied up $100,000 for radio spots.

On June 1 at the GOP state convention, Oliver North finally explicitly endorsed Miller. North insisted that he was not just seeking revenge against Warner for having sunk him in 1994. Miller was grateful for North's backing, but it came too late to induce significant numbers of what counted, dollars and volunteers, even though North sent out a fund-raising letter and signed it, "Semper Fi, Ollie." Demonstrating anew that a cult of personality is not transferable, Ollie's supporters printed bumper stickers saying, "Dump Warner," but they could not bring themselves to add, "Vote Miller."

On primary election night, June 11, at a Holiday Inn in Richmond, Miller knew the race was lost when returns from Arlington, Alexandria, and Fairfax came in. These heavily Democratic bedroom precincts near Washington, packed with federal government workers, reported voter turnouts as high as 35 percent compared to the statewide turnout of an abysmally low 16 percent. The black Tidewater region, as expected, went heavily for Warner also. Exit polls indicated that many Democrats and Republicans alike wanted to send another message of, "Screw you, Ollie North." As a result, Warner outpolled Miller by a two to one margin.

The Christian Coalition, as well as the Virginia-based National Rifle Association, which endorsed Miller outright, took a beating in their own backyard. Ralph Reed, at the time the head of the Christian Coalition, blamed Miller. He said, "In the end, it's about the candidate, stupid. Jim Miller, while he was an affable guy, just didn't light the fire under conservative activists." Reed ignored the fact the coalition also had not elected Oliver North, who did indeed "light the fire."

Here are some factors aside from Miller's lack of charisma that cost him the race. Through the primary, Warner spent $2.3 million. Miller spent $1.5 million, including $31,450 from PACs and a personal loan of $110,000. The incumbent's contributions from special-interest PACs exceeded the challenger's by a ratio of five to one.

Afterward, Miller drove his pickup to the old log cabin he had restored as a vacation home in the Blue Ridge Mountains. In the general election, Warner defeated Democratic nominee Mark R. Warner (again, no kin), who had made $100 million in the cellular telephone business and spent $11.6 million on his campaign ($10.3 million of it from his own checkbook). Senator Warner, for the entire election cycle, spent $5.6 million. This was the most expensive election of 1996, and Senator Warner also was the top PAC recipient in the nation, collecting $1.6 million. His winning margin was a narrow 52 to 47 percent.

The Warner-Warner race was still another example of the entrenchment of incumbency. The senator, a purveyor of pork, attacked his challenger for using Democratic Party connections to win cell-phone licenses, as if the senator were innocent of the manipulations of power. All the while, he touted his own clout as the guardian of Pentagon spending in Virginia.

In October, Senator Warner's media consultant ran a too-clever-by-half TV commercial that placed Mark Warner's face over a picture of Charles Robb shaking hands with Doug Wilder in the company of Bill Clinton. Senator Warner ostentatiously fired the consultant and apologized, thus gaining a double whammy as an upholder of clean politics even as the ad subtly got out the message that his challeger was of the ilk of the liberal adulterers Robb and Clinton and the liberal African American Wilder.

The voting returns were no surprise: The senator swept the District of Columbia suburbs and the military precincts around Norfolk and Newport News, whereas Mark Warner ran well in the conservative "yellow-dog Democrat" areas of the south and west portions of the state. Probably the challenger would not welcome this analysis, but his support came from the same localities that had backed the conservative Ollie North and Jim Miller against the civil and military government workers with a stake in the status quo. Democratic teachers, government, and defense workers—as well as Republicans of all stripes—all had an interest in keeping the Republican incumbent on the job.

A year after the election, Jim Miller was asked whether he would advise anyone to challenge an incumbent. He gave a typically convoluted answer. "If you're willing to run against an incumbent with the almost certainty that you are going to lose, but that you're going to have an interesting experience, and you're going to run on whatever money you can raise and not dip into your savings, and that's a discipline that's very hard to follow, I would say, yes, go ahead. Or, if you happen to be independently wealthy and have a lot of money and want to throw a lot of money at the race, with an expectation of losing though with some prospect of winning, but to be able to write off the loss as being the price of doing your own thing, then I'd encourage them to run. But if you have any notion that you're going to be able to, one, get your message out if you don't have any money, or two, that people are suddenly going to latch on if you have a good message, that they are going to choose your good message over the power and influence that an incumbent will claim he has . . . it isn't going to happen."

Or as Oliver North put it: "Incumbents have awesome, scary political power, and they're very difficult to knock off."

Late in 1998, Miller said, "Arguably, I—or we—have not learned my—or our—lesson. This past election cycle, my wife, Demaris, took on three-term incumbent [Democratic Representative] Jim Moran, and lost two-to-one after winning the Republican primary. Moreover, she is inclined to run again in 2000!"

In a thank-you letter to supporters, Demaris Miller wrote, "We could not get the press to pay attention to issues or even to Virginia races. Whenever I spoke with them, I talked about education, taxes, traffic, social security, health care, and national defense—but all they wanted to write or talk about was MONICA! And they rarely printed or mentioned anything except my responses to their direct questions about impeachment [of President Clinton]."

She noted that "as the incumbent congressman, Jim Moran was able to get on TV and in the papers almost daily, but when I was mentioned at all, it was as an asterisk in the last paragraph." (The ways in which the press covers—or fails to cover—congressional races will be examined in later chapters.) Demaris Miller went on to express the public-spiritedness and optimism that keep democracy healthy: "Next time, it will be more difficult to ignore me."

6

SOUTH CAROLINA

Elliott Springs Close (D) v. Senator Strom Thurmond (R)

In 1932, Democrats at their national convention in Chicago first nominated New York governor Franklin D. Roosevelt for president. Among the Roosevelt delegates was an ambitious twenty-nine-year-old South Carolina politician who was a candidate for his state legislature. Both he and Roosevelt won their elections in November.

In 1996, Republicans at their national convention in San Diego nominated former Kansas senator Bob Dole for president. Seated among the Dole delegates was a ninety-three-year-old senator from South Carolina, a forty-two-year Senate veteran running for the seat for the ninth time. Dole lost in November but the senator won. Voters were aware that he would be 100 years old when his term expired in January 2003.

In both instances, the South Carolinian was Strom Thurmond, the longest-lasting public figure in the United States. Often a subject of derision, a staple of late-night television humor with his pronounced Piedmont accent, rust-colored hair implants, and young wives, he has navigated both the civil rights revolution and the media politics era as skillfully as anyone—more so, considering his durability.

Still, if any incumbent could be considered vulnerable, it would seem to be a ninety-three-year-old man. Thurmond's triumph was the result of a number of factors. Some were specific to South Carolina and others followed the pattern of systemic incumbency protection.

In the 1920s, Thurmond was a teacher, coach, and school superintendent while he studied law under his father. In the South at that time, the requirement for formal professional credentials was not as rigid as it is nationally now. A graduate of Clemson University, Thurmond never earned a law degree. But following his filial apprenticeship, he practiced law and won election as a state senator and circuit judge.

Past draft age in World War II, he obtained an age waiver and parachuted behind enemy lines in the D-Day invasion of Normandy at age forty-one. It must be understood that Thurmond is a creature both of the Old South, with its tradition of military glory and racism, and the New South, with its globalized economy and elimination of legalized racism.

Despite this progress, South Carolina was and is more stereotypical of the Old South than the Virginia of Ollie North and Jim Miller. Thurmond, elected governor after World War II, led an anti-civil-rights walkout of the Democratic National Convention in Philadelphia in 1948. The convention had adopted a civil rights plank, pressed by Minneapolis Mayor Hubert Humphrey, while dithering over the nomination of the unpopular Harry Truman, president since Franklin Roosevelt's death in 1945.

Thurmond then ran for president against Truman as a "States' Rights Democrat." The Democrat in the appellation is important—just as Alabama governor George Wallace, nominally the American Independent Party candidate, campaigned for president in the South in 1968 as "the other Democrat"—that is, besides the party's official nominee, Vice President Hubert Humphrey. Indeed, Thurmond actually had been listed under the Democratic column on his 1948 home-state ballot. In 1948 and even in 1968, the South despised the Republican Party for its oppression of the region in the post–Civil War Reconstruction. In any case, Thurmond collected thirty-nine southern electoral votes for president while Truman won the election.

Thurmond ran unsuccessfully for the U.S. Senate in 1950, the only statewide election he has lost. In 1954, he was elected to the Senate as a write-in candidate; then he resigned to run for the seat properly in 1956 and, sure enough, was re-elected. In 1964, he switched to the GOP to support the presidential candidacy of conservative Senator Barry Goldwater of Arizona over President Lyndon Johnson.

With the perspective of thirty-five years, an effort is needed to appreciate what a radical step this party switch was at the time. Republicans had trouble finding enough warm bodies to fill all their county chairs in South Carolina, let alone town and precinct leaders. Thurmond was nearly clairvoyant in perceiving that Republicans eventually would win over the South. President Johnson privately shared this prescience, fretting to friends that his far-reaching civil rights bills eventually would hand Dixie to the GOP. And so it came to pass. In 1968, Thurmond was instrumental in delivering much of the South to Richard Nixon, both for his Republican presidential nomination and election.

Thurmond also was—the phrase sounds strange, and yet apt—ahead of his time on civil rights. After Johnson's Civil Rights Act of 1964 and Voting Rights Act of 1965, the senator endeavored to attract blacks into his constituency far earlier than other white southern segregationists eventually did, for example, long before George Wallace. Thurmond was the first southern senator to hire blacks on his staff, and he even placed a black on the federal bench (district judges formally are nominated by the president but in fact are selected by senators). He voted to renew the Voting Rights Act and to create the Martin Luther King Jr. holiday. Meanwhile, Thurmond's efficient staff made sure that black voters received the customary courtesies of a small-state senator's office, such as condolence letters when a spouse died.

Democrats calculated that they could stay in power in South Carolina with a black voter monopoly and enough working-class whites to form a majority. But Thurmond and his Republicans turned the tables. They brought together newly middle-class whites in the Sun Belt boom along with just enough blacks to win elections.

The small town of Edgefield lies about midpoint between the Low Country coastal plains and the Up Country foothills and mountains of Appalachia in South Carolina. As in other southern coastal states, South Carolina's Low Country, location of the storied antebellum plantations, and Up Country, home of independent mountaineer small-farmers and textile mill workers, are different regions with disparate politics and had even different loyalties during the Civil War. Thurmond has been prodigiously successful in bridging the two areas.

In October 1996, the driver for Strom Thurmond took Exit 5 off the Strom Thurmond Highway and headed for the Strom Thurmond Appreciation Day festivities at Strom Thurmond High School in Strom Thurmond's hometown of Edgefield. Thurmond, chairman of the Senate Armed Services Committee, erect but stiff-legged and shambling, walked to the podium in the high school auditorium and spoke of military glory. He celebrated the heroes who hailed from Edgefield

County, starting with Colonel William Barret Travis, defender of the Alamo against the Mexican army in Texas in 1836.

Thurmond said, "He's the guy that with 3,000 Russians threatening to attack. . . . " This was exactly the sort of geriatric lapse that inspired people in both parties to conclude that Thurmond was overripe for retirement, even though he always had labored to delay the aging process with daily fifty-minute physical workouts and healthful habits. His first wife was twenty-three years his junior. After her death, the senator married a former Miss South Carolina who was forty-four years younger than Thurmond. He was sixty-nine years old when the first of their four children was born; Thurmond gleefully challenged fellow senators both to push-up contests and, tongue in cheek, fathering contests (he and his wife later separated).

The age issue was significant enough that Thurmond attracted opposition in the the GOP primary. Party leaders on both sides generally hate contested primaries because they consume money and stir up hard feelings, both of which could better be turned against the other party. For a Republican to run against Thurmond in South Carolina, with its lingering veneration of tradition, hierarchy, and of Thurmond himself, took a lot of nerve.

The hard-right secretary of state, Jim Miles, made noises about a possible challenge. The popular former governor, Carroll A. Campbell Jr., endorsed Thurmond, but his supporters suggested that he might run if Miles jumped in, hoping for a plurality win in a three-way race. In the end, Thurmond was challenged only by Harold G. Worley, a wealthy contractor and state legislator from North Myrtle Beach, and by an unknown third candidate.

The Myrtle Beach area had become a favored vacation spot for Appalachian Yankees from Ohio, West Virginia, and Pennsylvania. In previous decades, South Carolina had been accustomed only to selling gas to northern motorists en route to Florida and catching them in small-town speed traps. Worley was part of the new economy, including tourism, that was transforming the traditionalist Low Country.

"Simply too old," Worley said of Thurmond. Presenting himself as a representative of the New South, he gave Thurmond a well-funded primary challenge for the first time since 1964. The challenger's TV ads featured old people thanking Thurmond for his service while urging him to retire. "I don't have nothing against him, but he's old enough to retire and rest hisself up," one man said.

Worley spent $600,000 of his own money, but in the June 11 primary, Thurmond thrashed him, 61 percent of the vote to 30 percent.

"Those who would believe that my age is a handicap or even a reason not to vote for me have been silenced," Thurmond proclaimed.

Evidently, Worley was not a student of history. South Carolina had not ousted an incumbent senator since the popular election of senators, replacing their selection by state legislators, began there in 1914. Even though Thurmond had become dependent on Reaganesque cue cards and his staff controlled him like a puppy on a leash, he still appeared to be invincible. His longevity rested on layers of southern traditions, including a paradoxical strain of antipolitics.

In the ancient stew of southern class and racial conflicts is a heavy spice of contempt for politicians. Denigrating them is a national sport, but in the Deep South, politicians were regarded as especially lower-class—again, a bitter residue from Reconstruction, when white "scalawags" joined African American officials installed by federal troops to rig provisional state governments that oppressed the former supporters of the Confederacy. This ancestral attitude is a major reason why Dixie voter participation often was woefully low. Of course, the historical disenfranchisement of African Americans was another factor. But even today, turnouts remain low. The electoral process is seen as the lowbrow business of scalawags, and an undercurrent of scorn for those who voluntarily throw themselves into the dirty business of politics survives.

Despite this disdain, nearly every southern state has clutched to its bosom a champion of the southern way of life—a populist white supremacist—and re-elected him for a lifetime to accrue the patents of seniority and authority to wield against the evil-doers of the North and West. (It was precisely to counter the power of southern seniority that Dan Rostenkowski persuaded Chicago mayor Richard J. Daley to send him to the U.S. House in 1958 and then keep him there.) The many exemplars of Dixie seniority include Governor and Senator Huey "Kingfish" Long of Louisiana and his son, Senator Russell Long; Governor and Senator Harry Byrd Sr. of Virginia; Governors "Big Jim" Folsom and George Wallace of Alabama; Governor Eugene Talmadge and his son, Senator Herman Talmadge of Georgia; Senator William Fulbright of Arkansas (mentor of the young Bill Clinton); Governor and Senator "Pitchfork Ben" Tillman of South Carolina—born in 1847 and an acquaintance, incidentally, of Thurmond in his youth—and Thurmond himself. He had achieved a historical ranking with Kingfish and Pitchfork Ben and personified the traditional South Carolina. The minority of eligible voters who actually did vote habitually marked their ballots for Ole Strom.

Unlike Huey Long, Folsom, the Talmadges, and others, Thurmond was untainted by charges of personal corruption. Also unlike them, he had moved adroitly from the Jim Crow era to the civil rights era. Moreover, for generations he had done official favors for hundreds of thousands of families in his state. He was a master of casework. Charlie Gerow got a taste of this incumbency advantage in Pennsylvania; Thurmond's opponent simply was overwhelmed by it.

For example, in the Appalachian town of Union, the husband of Esther Hunter died in 1993. Thurmond's office sent her a form letter of sympathy. Mrs. Hunter, then eighty-one years old, went to Gene's Restaurant in Union in 1996 to greet the senator at a campaign stop, clutching the wrinkled note in her hand.

She told a reporter, "He sent me this fine letter when my husband died. You can't pay attention to everything you hear. People say, you know, he didn't like black people. But he knows I'm 100 percent black and he sure did pay me respect."

This was the incumbent whom Elliott Springs Close decided to oppose as a Democrat. Yet, even in retrospect, his was not a fool's errand. A newspaper poll indicated in 1995 that two-thirds of those questioned thought that Thurmond should retire. In June 1996, another poll showed Thurmond leading Close by 49 percent to 31 percent, with 20 percent undecided. On its face, the survey gave Thurmond a healthy 18–point margin, but the numbers actually exposed his vulnerability. Politicians understood that any incumbent who could pull less than half the potential vote against a little-known opponent was in danger. Worley's "simply too old" campaign had inflicted some damage.

Like those of many other challengers, Close's campaign showed meaningful promise in the summer but was destroyed by late October. He was a centrist, but right-leaning, millionaire political novice, recruited by his party to run (although he was not among the five such men enlisted that year by Democratic Senatorial Campaign Chairman Bob Kerrey of Nebraska). Close was a lifelong South Carolinian, a political bonus as the state party was tiring of getting clobbered by putting up New South immigrants such as Charles "Pug" Ravenel, who had two fatal Dixie demerits—he had gone to Harvard and held a seat on the New York Stock Exchange obtained through his wife's family connections—and had been beaten by Thurmond.

With his high forehead, long sunken cheeks, and wrinkled chin, Thurmond looked like he was scowling even when smiling, but Close was a young everyman with a ready smile and the sort of bland personableness encountered at any Rotary Club or Chamber of Commerce meeting. If the state had entered the media age, then the challenger was more mediagenic. A native of the mid-state buffer between the Low Country and Up Country, Close, like Thurmond, was poised to span the regions. As a newcomer, he had no heavyweight political friends but, perhaps just as importantly, no enemies. He won the Democratic primary easily against a little-known candidate.

Close had not reached his first birthday when Thurmond first went to the Senate. His family controlled Springs Industries, Inc., a major textile manufacturer. Close was a director of the Springs Company, a diversified holding firm, and the CEO of Island Harbor Development Corporation. With other investors, he brought the National Football League to the region with the Carolina Panthers franchise. His resume included the usual necklace for someone of his status of memberships on educational, civic, and foundation boards. He and his wife Laura had three children, including a girl born in April of the campaign year. On paper, Close was an outstanding citizen-politician.

But like Mitt Romney in Massachusetts, he found himself widely regarded not just as a candidate for public office but rather as something like an infidel in the temple. The religion issue was never made manifest, but for what it's worth, Close was an Episcopalian—the denomination of the Yankee elite—while Thurmond was a Southern Baptist, a religious affiliation nearly mandatory for Dixie politicians. The Thurmond campaign did not touch religious matters but still succeeded in portraying Close as an upstart and a liberal and therefore alien to South Carolina's interests.

The first dilemma that confronted Close was how to handle the delicate question of Thurmond's age. "Simply too old," the Worley approach, obviously had not worked, and another precedent likewise was less than encouraging. In 1984, Thurmond's Democratic opponent had made an issue of Thurmond's age and was beaten two to one. The challenger died of a heart attack two years later at age forty-six.

At first, Close approached the matter gingerly, calling the senator a "living legend" for whom he had "tremendous respect and admiration," while suggesting that his time had passed. In the final days, the challenger attacked the age issue directly—"Is Strom Thurmond up to the job?"—but by that time, the incumbent-protection establishment had closed ranks and it was too late.

Kevin Geddings, Close's media consultant from Columbia, South Carolina, said that Thurmond's response amounted to, " 'I'm not dead yet, why change? You don't even know who this Close guy is.' It's much easier to communicate a simpler message." Or, to quote the senator directly, he told the press, "It might have been more in order for him to run for the town council of Fort Mill. It would take my opponent sixty years to catch up with what I can do in the next six years."

Close started out by challenging Thurmond to town-meeting-style debates, hinting that only then could the senator put the age issue to rest. Thurmond refused—he had not debated an opponent since 1950—but at least he was candid about his motives. He said he would not give Close free publicity.

Thurmond forked into some fried chicken at a Baptist church festival in the town of Ruby one day when Close, arriving at the event, saw him sitting alone. The challenger sat down next to the senator and asked if he would ever participate in a debate. Thurmond replied that he would not provide his opponent free publicity. At that moment, Close began to suspect that Thurmond did not realize who he was. Then one of the senator's aides hustled over, and she certainly recognized Close. "He doesn't want to give you free publicity," she declared.

For the media, Thurmond said, "I'm a conservative and he's a liberal, from all I hear about him. He's got the money, but I've got the experience." Republican Governor David M. Beasley put it more bluntly, calling Close "an absolute liberal left-wing Clinton-type Democrat." The painting of Close as a leftist ideologue illustrates how incumbents have the resources to control the campaign message, even based on flimsy evidence. (Close's brother-in-law was Erskine B. Bowles, a North Carolina businessman and a top aide to President Clinton who later became Clinton's chief of staff.)

Close never ran as a supporter of the Clinton White House. He backed term limits, a balanced budget, a proposed half-billion-dollar cut in federal pork, campaign finance reform, and an end to dumping nuclear waste at the federal Savannah River Site plant in Aiken County. Close had given money to Clinton's campaigns but also had donated to Republicans.

As for "he's got the money," the challenger torpedoed his own personal financial advantage. He refused to take PAC funds, a common stance for citizen-candidates. More to the point, Close pledged to pay no more than half his campaign expenses from his own wallet—that is, he would put up 50 percent matching funds but no more. He disdained to "buy the office" without grass-roots support. This "good government" scruple was a tremendous break for Thurmond. The Close family fortune was estimated to be worth more than $435 million. Meanwhile, Thurmond gathered PAC dollars freely. The defense in-

dustry, for example, was generous to the chairman of the Senate Armed
Services Committee. The nuclear power industry chipped in as well.

Close "went up positive" with his first ads, which mentioned that
Springs Industries, founded by his grandfather, kept its textile mills
running during the Depression to save workers' job. But weeks later,
Springs announced that it would close three plants and lay off 850
workers. Like Mitt Romney with the stationery plant in Marion, Indiana, Close protested that he was just a shareholder and had no voice in
the company's operational decisions, an excuse that did not placate voters or the media.

A shrewd campaign might have turned the issue against Thurmond
for his failure to protect thousands of defense-related jobs in the
Charleston area, which had seen three major military bases close since
1980 despite Thurmond's purported clout on the Armed Services
Committee. But the Springs action was a setback that put Close's campaign weeks behind schedule as he struggled, with a political novice's
inexperience, to make Thurmond and not himself the issue. Voluntarily
ignoring the age question, he had trouble otherwise formulating a coherent message for replacing the incumbent. Like many challengers,
Close was affable enough but not a natural-born campaigner; he did
not know how to "work a room" or "work a ropeline." The enfeebled
South Carolina Democratic Party was of little help either. Close, his
campaign faltering, fired two campaign managers, hiring the third less
than a month before the election.

Thurmond ran ads depicting his opponent as a Springs company
trust-fund baby. At his own appearances around the state, Thurmond
did little but recite remarks typewritten on cards labeled "Stump Speech."
He even broke his tradition of riding a horse in the Ridge Peach Festival
parade. His spinners said it was only because the mare he usually rode
was pregnant.

Close's media man Geddings said, "The South Carolina press corps
is hardly known for its aggressiveness. . . . [They] regularly allowed
Thurmond's handlers to engage Elliott Close in verbal sparring rather
than insisting that such exchanges be between the candidates." The
New York Times and other national media described Thurmond's "ob-
vious inability to meet the rigors of the job for which he was campaigning," Geddings said. "Unfortunately, one good story from *Newsweek* is
not enough to educate every voter in South Carolina."

Growing desperate, Close finally went negative. Taking a tip from
Worley, he ran an ad of a group of senior citizens discussing Thurmond.
"You know, Ole Strom Thurmond's done a pretty good job, but don't

you think at ninety-three it's about time he retired?" one man asked. "Yeah, it's time to let a younger man fight for us," another replied. An unflattering photo of Thurmond appearing ancient, his sunken cheeks looking especially cadaverous, stayed on screen for long seconds to end the ad.

In yet another parallel with Romney, whose TV spot showing Kennedy sitting down painfully on a park bench might have backfired, Close's ad did little to turn public opinion around. The voters seemed determined to let Strom die with his boots on. A political scientist at Clemson, Thurmond's alma mater, called the Close campaign "a colossal failure."

Comfortably ahead in the polls, the Thurmond camp succumbed to an unnecessary, inexplicable, and petty dirty trick, a syndrome that seems to afflict campaigns with too much hubris and too much money—for example, President Richard Nixon's re-election drive against the hapless George McGovern in the Watergate year of 1972. Thurmond supporters circulated a flier printed on pink paper, highlighting a Close fund raiser held at a reputed gay person's home. There was no excuse for this. The Christian Coalition was behind Thurmond anyway.

The challenger also came up short on both "free media" and "paid media" exchanges; he was opposed by the organization of Governor Beasley and former Governor Campbell, by the Christian Coalition, and by the business community, with organized labor hardly even a player. Thurmond won the election, 53 percent to 44 percent. Thurmond spent $2.6 million to Close's $1.9 million—nearly half of it his own money. A third of Thurmond's funds came from PACs.

The voting returns told the story of the newly Republican South. Thurmond swept the metropolitan areas—the Up Country cities of Greenville and Spartanburg, a thriving Sun Belt metroplex which recently had won a giant new German BMW auto plant; the mid-state capital city of Columbia, and the colonial seacoast city of Charleston. Thurmond also won 30 percent of the African American vote, a proportion that North and Miller could not hope to approach in Virginia. Close carried low-income white rural counties, home of ancestral post-Reconstruction Democrats. Voter turnout was 42 percent of the voting-age population, traditionally well below the national average in a presidential election year.

Close's adviser Geddings, whose livelihood depends on finding political clients, said, "I doubt I could urge a close friend or family member to place their lives, marriages, and finances at risk taking on a system that is stacked against ordinary citizens."

When the new Congress took office in January 1997, Thurmond and his South Carolina colleague, Democratic Senator Ernest F. "Fritz" Hollings, had a combined total of seventy-two years in the chamber. On May 27, 1997, Thurmond became the longest-serving senator in American history.

7

GEORGIA

MICHAEL COLES (D) V. REPRESENTATIVE NEWT GINGRICH (R) AND SENATOR PAUL COVERDELL (R)

"He's just a guy," Michael Coles shrugged. Newt Gingrich, just a guy? The same Newt Gingrich who was the Speaker of the U.S. House of Representatives and was regarded—at least in his own mind—as a historical figure of world importance? One thing about political novices such as Coles, they can be fearless.

Coles perceived that Gingrich, like many incumbents, was less entrenched than he appeared at first glance. Yet he was *more* entrenched than he appeared at a second glance. In the end, the Speaker defeated Coles in 1996 after his PAC contributions exceeded his Democratic challenger's by a ten to one margin, and he falsely branded Coles as a liberal.

Georgia's Sixth Congressional District race that year illustrated the hollowness of party labels. Coles, as a Democrat, was a better personification of Republican bootstrap, free-enterprise values than was Gingrich. Indeed, in many other districts in the country, Gingrich might have tried to recruit Coles to run for Congress as a self-made, moderate GOP businessman.

"I've seen a zillion guys like Newt in the private sector," Coles said in the summer of 1996. "They're flash-in-the-pan guys."

Coles's life story explains why Gingrich did not intimidate him. His mother managed to escape from Poland and the Nazi death camps of

World War II—most of her family did not. His father first started as a rag merchant. Coles, born in Brooklyn in 1944, grew up there and in Buffalo, New York. His father fled Buffalo for Miami to evade creditors of his bankrupt small business, even though young Coles had worked three part-time jobs to help pay the bills. At age eighteen, he left Miami to live with an older brother in Rockport, Massachusetts, and finish high school in anticipation of going to college.

But when Coles graduated from high school, he was enticed back to Miami by the owner of a clothing store where he had worked part-time as a boy. His employer was so impressed by the young man that he made him store manager with a one-third ownership. Soon Coles was selling men's clothes in Chicago, Detroit, and Atlanta.

While living near Atlanta, he attended a trade show in San Diego in 1977. There he strolled into a cookie boutique, whose owner volunteered that his profits were spectacular. At once, Coles went to a grocery to buy the makings of chocolate chip cookies, then picked up a postal scale at a drugstore and returned to his hotel suite. Meticulously measuring ingredients in the kitchenette, he computed that a cookie selling for 30 cents cost only 6 cents to bake.

Back home, Coles told this news to his wife Donna and another couple, who held a cherished, three-generations-old family recipe for chocolate chip cookies. In June 1977, the two couples opened the Great American Cookie Company at a mall in Dunwoody, north of Atlanta. The debut was not auspicious. The entrepreneurs had forgotten pot holders to retrieve trays from the oven and the first batch of cookies burned so badly that local firefighters were summoned. Still, the cookie shop, an $8,000 investment, made $18,000 in profit in the first six weeks.

In September 1977, a rock locked up the rear tire of the motorcycle Coles was riding home from work. He smashed into a telephone pole. Regaining consciousness in a hospital, Coles was informed by doctors that his legs were so mangled that he might never walk again without canes or crutches. "It's better than not waking up at all," he thought.

In June 1978, Coles's three-year-old daughter Taryn challenged him to a race to the mailbox. Hobbling on two canes, Coles decided in angry frustration to overcome his handicap. A muscular five-foot-six, Coles invented his own rehabilitation, furiously pedaling a stationary bicycle and lifting weights. He eventually began to make painful bike rides over the low hills of the Piedmont area north of Atlanta. These were followed by coast-to-coast bicycle races.

In 1982, Coles pedaled from Savannah, Georgia, westward—against the prevailing winds—to San Diego, setting a new national record of fifteen and a half days. The next year, he tried to beat his own record for that course, but fractured his collarbone just 379 miles from the finish. Then, in 1984 at age forty, he broke his record, making the same trip in eleven days, eight hours, and fifteen minutes. In 1989, he took the "easy" way east as part of a four-man team that biked coast-to-coast in a record five days, one hour.

By 1996, the Great American Cookie Company had 400 stores in thirty-eight states and Coles was worth an estimated $30 million. "I've always managed to do a lot more than people expected of me," he observed. After he announced his candidacy for Congress, a partner in the 1989 cross-country race wrote him, "Always remember: This is a hell of a lot easier than sitting on a skinny saddle for 11 days." Maybe, or maybe not.

Newt Gingrich would have believed it was easier. Ignoring Coles, he spent most of 1996 campaigning for Republicans in about 140 districts around the country, while opposing GOP conservatives such as Joe DioGuardi in New York and Ron Paul in Texas.

Forgotten now, after the House rebuked Gingrich for ethical missteps in 1997, is that he launched his political career on the ethics issue, running against Democratic Representative John J. Flynt—who, in another cheap congressional irony, chaired the ethics committee while fighting ethical problems of his own. Gingrich lost to Flynt in a south suburban Atlanta district in 1974 and again in 1976 (the year of Georgian Jimmy Carter's presidential triumph), finally defeating him in 1978 to become Georgia's lone Republican congressman. The state's current congressional lineup is eight Republicans and three Democrats, due in large part to Gingrich's ambition and savvy, even though Gingrich resigned his seat following GOP losses in the 1998 elections.

Gingrich fancies himself an intellectual, to the derision of the liberal classes, but in fact he holds a doctorate in European history from Tulane University and maintains an always active, if quirky, mind. Once during the late 1970s, Elizabeth Taylor, then the wife of Senator John Warner of Virginia, went to Atlanta for a Republican fund raiser. Thousands of middle-age suburban women thronged the large old Fox Theater, twittering like teenagers mobbing a rock star while approaching Taylor, seated regally on the stage. When a reporter remarked on the odd spectacle, Gingrich responded with an impromptu lecture on the culture of mass-mediated celebrity—delivered solely for the benefit of a single newsperson.

Gingrich was sometimes mocked for putting on airs for merely teaching at backwater colleges in Georgia such as Kennesaw State and

Reinhardt. He famously told one class that war is the business of men because they want to go out and "hunt giraffes," whereas women in foxholes only "get infections"—but what professor is immune to stupid utterances over the course of hundreds of lectures? In any case, Gingrich masterminded his escalade of the House Republican leadership in the late 1980s and early 1990s, besting the moderate Bob Michel of Illinois, and then engineered the Republican capture of the House in 1994. Both of these endeavors had been considered highly improbable.

Meanwhile, the Speaker of the Georgia House was Tom Murphy, a gruff, crude, vain "cracker" Democrat of the old school. Murphy plotted to get rid of Gingrich by way of a political process that rarely appears on ballots or Federal Election Commission financial reports and seldom makes the front pages or newscasts—the remapping of district boundaries, or "gerrymandering." (The term dates to 1811, when Massachusetts Governor Elbridge Gerry conceived a district so deformed that somebody likened its shape to a salamander, inviting the retort, "Call it rather a Gerrymander.")

Ordinary voters have little notion of how deadly seriously politicians take the redistricting process—it has been known to provoke actual fisticuffs on the floors of state legislatures. Legislators are charged with redrawing both congressional and state legislative district lines after each decennial census. Shifting the lines by only a few blocks in a big city, or by a few townships in rural areas, can determine whether a jurisdiction trends Democratic or Republican, depending on the socioeconomic status of its voters. Gerrymandering thus is necessarily a primary technique of incumbency protection. Also, like many of our political processes, redistricting has been taken over by computers and—far more often than is healthy for a representative democracy—the federal courts.

Anyway, Speaker Murphy noticed that Gingrich had won re-election in the south suburban Sixth District in 1990 by just 974 votes. As boss of the Democratic-controlled Georgia legislature, he remapped Gingrich out of the Sixth District, putting him in the Third District with an incumbent Democratic congressman who presumably could beat him. The old Sixth District migrated to the northern suburbs. Gingrich thereupon moved his residence to the northwest suburb of Marietta so that he could continue to run in a Republican-leaning district. In the 1992 GOP primary, Gingrich, burdened by twenty-two overdrafts in the House bank scandal, won renomination by only 980 votes (which prompts "what-if" speculation: If 488 Georgia voters had changed their minds in 1990 or 491 in 1992, would Democrats still control the U.S. House?).

Unwittingly, Murphy had done Gingrich a favor, for Marietta is the home of a huge Lockheed defense plant. Lockheed welcomed Gingrich's efforts in delivering military contracts, such as orders for C-130 Hercules cargo aircraft that the Pentagon did not want or need. In 1994, Gingrich outspent his Democratic opponent by nearly six to one and was re-elected with 64 percent of the vote. He expected the same result in 1996.

Early in 1995, the national media portrayed the new Speaker Gingrich as tantamount to a co-president with Bill Clinton. In December 1995, following a temporary federal government shutdown, which Clinton adroitly contrived to blame on the Republican Congress, a Democratic poll revealed Gingrich's lack of popularity in his home district. His job performance rating there was 51 percent positive but a chilling 47 percent negative. Large majorities thought that Gingrich was "arrogant" and "talks too much" (criticizing a politician for these attributes is like condemning a zebra for having stripes).

The poll heartened Michael Coles, who sneered at Gingrich as "a guy who's never had a private-sector job in his life . . . who's clearly been at the taxpayers' trough his entire career." He attacked Gingrich's shoveling of pork to the defense, mining, and timber industries (mainstays of the Republican base in the South and West), while noting wryly, "No one's subsidizing cookies." He told campaign audiences, "No matter what level of success I've achieved, it wasn't that long ago that [my wife] Donna and I worried about making the mortgage payment." During a break between jetting to other districts, Gingrich called his challenger a "liberal millionaire."

Coles anticipated spending $2 million of his own money—in the end, of course, he spent more—and refused help from the Democratic Congressional Campaign Committee, not that the committee was eager to give any. "I want to keep this a very local race. I don't want to get tied up in any party," Coles said. Again, in most southern districts, he might have been recruited by Democrats as a self-made "pro-growth" centrist to appeal to middle-class white voters who had defected to the GOP. But national Democrats were not swayed by Gingrich's high negative ratings in his home base. They knew that he would outspend his opponent with national PAC and partisan money, that he was a ruthless schemer, and that the Sixth District was heavily Republican to boot.

Within the memory of many voters in the area, the Sixth District was a lower-middle-class expanse of farms, small farm-to-market towns, and mom-and-pop operations such as making tufted bedspreads. Now the area north of the Interstate 285 beltway around Atlanta is known as the Golden Crescent, site of corporate office towers and shopping malls identical to those outlying Chicago or Los Angeles. Voters who grew up without running water and indoor plumbing now have hot tubs and home saunas. The district actually ranks among the top 5 percent of the most affluent and best-educated in the nation—Gingrich, by the way, is no southern "good old boy." He was born in Harrisburg, Pennsylvania, in 1943 and followed his adoptive father, an army officer, to postings around the world.

Coles was a superb candidate for this new southern bourgeoisie except that he was a Democrat challenging the state's most powerful politician. Aware of his obstacles, Coles campaigned fifteen hours a day with the same zeal he had devoted to learning to walk again. Impishly, he challenged Gingrich to a winner-take-all bicycle race: "Instead of both of us spending a lot of money on TV ads, we could ride across the district." Gingrich did not deign to respond. So Coles began running TV ads as early as September 3; Gingrich did not follow suit until October 1.

Gingrich's first spot was positive—"He kept his promises"—and then he went negative, per standard campaign-consultant procedure. He accused his opponent of violating child labor laws. In fact, Coles was fined in 1993 when a Department of Labor inspector found a sixteen-year-old and a seventeen-year-old operating a freight elevator. Although the irony went mostly unnoticed, here was Gingrich, the champion of lifting the yoke of oppressive government regulations from business, attacking a businessman for a minor transgression against big government. Appearing at a school in Alpharetta, Gingrich was asked by a seventh grader, "Why would a person running for office tell bad things about your opponent?" The Speaker's reply: "Because it works."

Coles did not dwell on Gingrich's ethical problems in turn. Gingrich had taught his course, "Renewing American Civilization," at Kennesaw State, a public college, for two years. The faculty there refused to renew the course in 1993 for fear it was politically tainted by subsidies from a dummy foundation set up by Gingrich. Republicans interpreted this action as an expression of the liberal control of academia. Gingrich took his course to Reinhardt, a private college, in 1994, then dropped it after becoming Speaker.

Gingrich, ironically, had taught his course at Kennesaw State in the Michael Coles School of Business, which his challenger had endowed. "That was the last straw for me," Coles said. "That literally was the primary motivation that got me to run, because he had put the school in such jeopardy."

Meanwhile, Gingrich's GOPAC was under investigation for funding federal, instead of just state and local, campaigns. Coles ignored these matters to run simply as an antipolitician. "I am not looking for a career," he said. "I want to be the guy who holds a press conference on the steps [of the Capitol] every day and says, 'Let me tell you what's really going on inside.' I will be the least popular guy there, but I'll be popular in my district."

But at the candidates' sole debate, for just thirty minutes, on October 25, with polls showing him losing, Coles knew he would have to make his challenge personal. At a public television studio in Atlanta, Coles charged that in December 1995 Gingrich had "shut the government down, costing taxpayers $1.4 billion, because he didn't like his seat on an airplane." The reference was to Gingrich's complaining that President Clinton had snubbed him by keeping him in the back of Air Force One during a flight home from a state visit to Israel. This notorious tantrum had demonstrated that Gingrich, like Clinton, was a politician of immense talents with commensurate immaturities.

Coles scored some points in the debate, and afterward, Democrats held some hope of an upset, for—after all—none of the "experts" had foretold the election defeat of the previous Speaker, Tom Foley of Washington state, in 1994. But on election day, Gingrich won 58 percent of the vote to 42 percent for Coles.

It was the most expensive House race of 1996. Gingrich spent $5.6 million, including more than $1 million from PACs and none of his own money; 64 percent of his funds came from out of state. Coles spent $3.3 million, including $2.4 million in contributions and loans from his personal bank accounts and just $102,000 from PACs; only 24 percent of his funds came from outside Georgia. Although Gingrich outspent Coles by a ratio of 1.7 to 1, he outpolled him by just 1.4 votes to 1. Among the common run of incumbents against challengers, Gingrich's showing actually was poor. He ran behind presidential candidate Bob Dole in his own district.

The next January, the Republican House reprimanded its Speaker and fined him $300,000 for ethical lapses with GOPAC and the Kennesaw State course. Gingrich agreed to pay the fine by January 1999, possibly with help from a loan offered by Dole.

Coles took little note of this event, for he had resolved to run for the U.S. Senate in 1998. "I decided to run because the issues did not go away," he said. Having lost in a single district "that is well over 70 percent Republican," Coles felt that "running in a statewide race, I'd have a much, much better shot at getting the job."

Governor Zell Miller named Coles to chair the Georgia Democratic Party. Meanwhile, Nebraska Senator Bob Kerrey, chair of the Democratic Senatorial Campaign Committee, and President Clinton both tried to persuade the highly popular Miller to run against Senator Paul Coverdell. After Miller declined, Coles announced his candidacy in September 1997.

Coverdell, a small, thin figure who speaks in a reedy montone, is not an imposing presence, but he is a tough infighter. As a first-term senator he sought out the cloakrooms and the party hierarchy rather than the news cameras. He and Representative John Boehner of Ohio (who had urged an IRS investigation of Joe DioGuardi) were made chairs of the "Thursday Group," weekly strategy sessions with GOP client organizations such as the Christian Coalition, U.S. Chamber of Commerce, and the National Federation of Independent Business. Then, though a freshman lawmaker, Coverdell was elected secretary of the Republican Conference, a spot in the Senate leadership.

Coverdell's focus on internal Senate processes instead of publicity formed one-half of a challenger's dilemma. Incumbents like Gingrich are hard to beat because they have such high profiles. But incumbents like Coverdell are difficult to unseat because they have such *low* profiles.

"Coverdell's the worse, harder to beat," Coles said after the election. "One of the things I've learned, the power of incumbency is extremely high, especially when you're running against someone who has not really made anybody angry in any kind of a public way. They haven't made anybody real happy, either, but in a year of the incumbent, which it was [in 1998], it makes it very, very difficult to defeat them."

Coverdell was born in Iowa in 1939, grew up in Kansas City, graduated from the University of Missouri, and served in the Army in the early 1960s. After joining his parents' insurance business in Atlanta, he was elected to the Georgia Senate in 1970. Those were lean years for Georgia Republicans; Coverdell became the minority leader of exactly four fellow Republicans in the fifty-six member Senate. President Bush plucked him from the legislature to head the Peace Corps in 1989. In 1992, Coverdell narrowly won the U.S. Senate seat in a run-off election.

Six years later he ran a traditional, sit-on-your-lead front-runner's race designed to avoid mistakes, while Coles struggled to gain traction for his campaign. In July 1998, President Clinton accepted Coles's invitation to speak at an Atlanta fund raiser for him. The biggest contributors were shunted into a separate room to line up for photos of handshakes with the president, a tradition known in the trade as "grip and grins." Then Clinton went to the hotel ballroom, where Governor Miller lavishly praised Coles, who would introduce the president.

When he stepped up to the podium, Coles paused a few moments to blink away tears. "I got choked up because of what Zell said about me," he told a reporter later. "For a man like me to introduce the president of the United States, and to have the governor say the things he said, you'd have to be stoic to have it not affect you."

Appearing with Clinton was a gamble for Coles because the president was in the midst of the Monica Lewinsky sex-and-lying scandal. Typically, Coles took the risk. He now brushes off analysts who said it alienated Georgia voters. "I've always believed that there is only a certain amount of impact you get out of an endorsement from anybody. Again, it's more about firing the incumbent than it is about hiring you. And that was hard to make a case for." Besides, Coles added, the Clinton appearance, "if anything, had a positive effect. At least it let people understand that I would not agree with him on every issue, but at least you've got the ear of the president if you're in the minority party [in the Senate]."

Both before and after Clinton's visit, Coles said, "our head-to-head [polling] numbers, from the very beginning of the race, were very close. . . . But the one number that was very frightening was that he had over 70 percent job approval rating. But if you asked anybody why, they couldn't answer.

"We ran an above-board, issue-oriented campaign. We didn't run a single personal attack. By the time it was over, after we started exposing his record, we had his job approval rating down to 52 percent. And that's exactly what he got of the vote."

While Coles chipped away at Coverdell's approval rating, the establishment closed ranks. Democrats such as Griffin Bell, who had been President Carter's attorney general; former Senator David Gambrell; and four former congressmen all endorsed the GOP incumbent. Coles dismisses them as closet Republicans—but that observation only serves to underline the secondary importance of party labels when incumbency is at stake.

Late in the game, Jimmy Carter taped a TV spot for Coles, only his second such ad for a candidate since leaving the White House. Carter's support might have come too late because an October 3 *Atlanta Journal-Constitution*/WBS-TV poll showed Coverdell leading by 22 percentage points. Constant polling influences elections not just by the horse-race numbers indicating who is ahead or behind, but moreover in the all-important effort to solicit campaign contributions from the race track railbirds. The 22–point spread inhibited Coles's fund raising. As Merle Black, an eminent political scientist at Emory University in Atlanta, said, "If he's out raising money, you can't raise a dime with this."

Frustrated, Coles urged his media consulting firm to attack Coverdell more directly. "If we made one mistake in the campaign from my standpoint, I just don't think we went after him hard enough," he said. "I wanted to start calling him 'Pinocchio Paul.' I wanted to run an ad, basically just a caricature of him with his nose growing, basically saying, 'You're a damn liar.' " But sophisticated consultants normally counsel against such frontal assaults (as a later chapter will demonstrate).

For his part, Coverdell brought back the "granny ad." One of the most effective ads of the 1992 elections was Coverdell's TV spot featuring a seventy-three-year-old actress, sitting on a porch swing and singing a campaign jingle she ostensibly had written. In 1998, Coverdell's campaign hired another elderly actress to gesture with a bar of soap while saying, "Michael Coles, you better start telling the truth, because you're going to have your mouth washed out with this soap." The supposed issue was that the Great American Cookie Company had required employees to "pay to take leave to care for a dying relative," a standard political half-truth: The rule was never enforced before it was erased by a later health plan.

The Republican campaign also bested the Democrats in the advertising medium of direct mail—this GOP advantage is generally true in elections across the country. Republicans have a stronger stable of mailing lists and better-funded mailing houses. As the political analyst and author Howard Phillips said in an interview, "You cannot, in the space of a single campaign, run profitable direct mail. It takes two years, really, to build up a house file for prospect mailing. These boys [incumbents] are in business forever, and as a result, they can profitably use direct mail to strengthen their position."

Coles said, "We didn't do any direct mail. It takes a lot of money, and you can't do direct mail effectively unless you do a lot of it. Coverdell did a lot of very misleading and pretty diabolical direct mail. One piece went to veterans, saying basically that he had served and I had not, and that I had taken $2,000 from Jane Fonda."

In response, Coles secured the endorsement of the head of Disabled American Veterans and circulated letters of support from a general and other "military people who knew me." But these counterattacks lacked the impact of a well-funded direct mail effort. For one thing, Coles's message was not scoring with "free media" news reports.

In challenging Gingrich, Coles had won a fair amount of national news exposure. In opposing Coverdell, he scarcely could obtain even local coverage. Part of the explanation is that the media were concentrating on a fierce election battle for governor of Georgia and the Senate race seemed to be a sideshow. Another factor is that the local and national media were fixated on the Clinton White House scandals.

"The public didn't care that much about it," Coles said. "I would say, 'Look, I'll answer your [a newsperson's] question about how I feel about what the president did. But can we talk about public education, can we talk about health care, veterans issues?' The bottom line is, they would talk about it, but they would never report it.

"Paul Coverdell has a zero environmental voting record for six years in the U.S. Senate. We sent out press release after press release after press release—never got a single story. There was an incredible lack of [media] interest, which made it very difficult, especially when you're being outspent."

Excepting the Clinton fund raiser and two later televised debates with Coverdell, Coles reckoned that "we got less than two minutes" of Georgia television news coverage. "That's just unbelievable."

Coverdell spent $6.9 million, including $1.6 million from PACs and none of his own money. Coles spent $5.2 million, including $237,000 from PACs, $3.9 million in personal loans, and $72,000 in personal contributions. In two election campaigns, Coles had put up more than $6.5 million of his personal finances. Yet, not even that impressive sum matches the amount that the incumbent Coverdell was able to raise in a single campaign. Coverdell won 52 percent of the vote to 45 percent for Coles.

"I don't know that I have all the answers," Cole said, "but certainly for someone who's run now twice as a challenger against an incumbent, we're not going to fix this system until we have term limits. I just can't imagine that any one of the Founding Fathers, bright as they were, ever imagined that we would be where we are today in terms of politics. If they were writing the Constitution today, they would have term limits.

The power that people have in these jobs makes it impossible, almost impossible, unless they just really messed up, to be defeated."

Actually, he reflected, he indirectly accomplished his initial goal of defeating Gingrich. "I think we moved Newt somewhat more to the center and ultimately that was not acceptable by the right wing of his party. In some ways we had a delayed reaction, but he will not be my congressman any longer."

However, Coles's ultimate outlook on his campaign experiences takes in much larger matters than any election win or loss. He continues to express the bedrock strength of American democracy: "It's very important for whoever reads this to understand that this is an incredible country. The fact that a guy like me has had the opportunity to run against both the Speaker of the House and the fifth-ranking senator in the United States Senate speaks very well for the country that we live in. And the opportunities available for its people, regardless of the [election] outcome, that's the message.

"Tomorrow, I'm going to speak to ninth graders and tell them the whole story. About my accident. And how you can't win if you don't run. And there's no shame in being defeated.

"For my kids to see their dad, who they know came from a very poor family, go out there and have the president of the United States, the governor, the mayor of Atlanta, all stand on the same stage—what an incredible place this is to live! When I ran against Gingrich, someone taking on the third most powerful figure in the whole country. . . . In most countries, you'd have to go out and get an army to do that."

8

OHIO

CLIFF ARNEBECK (R/D) v. REPRESENTATIVES CHALMERS WYLIE (R) AND DEBORAH PRYCE (R)

Previous chapters have examined challengers who played by the rules—challengers who raised and spent large sums of money, only to learn that the rules are rigged. Clifford O. Arnebeck, an experienced and well-regarded reformer, undertook to break the prime rule of modern electioneering: He refused to solicit money and explicitly ran against the incumbency-preservation system, believing the media would applaud his effort. He was dismayed by the outcome.

Arnebeck's races for Congress were not so much election contests as nonevents. In this respect, they were typical. Take away the Ted Kennedys, Ollie Norths, and other celebrities, and Arnebeck's campaigns in central Ohio can stand as a part for the whole, the archetype for the fate of committed citizens who oppose congressional incumbents. Arnebeck ran in an ordinary congressional district, Ohio's Fifteenth, comprising most of the state capital of Columbus and the suburbs on its west and south flanks. It is an entirely average white middle-class urban/suburban district, the sort of place where advertising executives from New York and Los Angeles go to market test the launch of new consumer products. Like many inland cities of its size, Columbus boasts of having a cultural life that unfortunately is still obscured by its old cowtown image.

The district is dominated by a locally owned monopoly newspaper, the *Columbus Dispatch*, whose owners also control the local CBS-TV affiliate, two radio stations, and a suburban newspaper. Arnebeck came to believe that these media were key defenders of incumbency.

Born in 1945, Arnebeck Jr. grew up in the Washington suburb of Silver Spring, Maryland, and earned a law degree at Harvard. He practiced law in Cleveland and Canton, Ohio, before moving to the Columbus suburb of Upper Arlington in 1980. Upper Arlington is seen across the Olentangy River from the locally sacred Ohio Stadium when blimps televise aerial shots of Ohio State Buckeyes football games.

One of Arnebeck's legal clients was the Senate Republican Campaign Committee in Ohio, while his law firm represented EDS, the computer services firm founded by Ross Perot. Arnebeck came to know and admire Perot and John W. Wolfe, head of the *Dispatch*. Indeed, Wolfe became the financial partner in a home services company launched by Arnebeck and a friend.

After visiting his dying father in 1989, Arnebeck returned home "determined to change my life by acting on the basis of what was important to God. That would be world peace." He helped organize an ecumenical peace celebration on New Year's Eve of 1989 to honor the sweep of freedom across eastern Europe after the collapse of Soviet Communism. Later, "I decided I might accomplish something for peace and freedom as a reform candidate for Congress."

Accordingly, he went to talk with his local party chairman. "He said there was not anything of interest to talk about, because the guy I was challenging was a twenty-four-year incumbent, the ranking Republican on the Banking Committee. I told him, 'If a client of mine proposed this, I would tell him he was nuts.' But I said I was running to make a contribution in the dialogue with Wylie, not to win. I said I had no intention to raise any money, but I felt that by running in a Republican primary in a Republican district, I could address national issues."

Arnebeck then won tacit approval for the race form one of the area's top Republicans, *Dispatch* publisher John W. Wolfe, by clearing it with a Wolfe associate. In response, Representative Wylie "acted as if this was an indignity, to have a primary challenge." Wylie not only refused to debate, he never even left Washington to appear in the district before the primary. Arnebeck resorted to "town meeting" debates with the Democratic candidate prior to the primary—forums that drew a fair amount of local news coverage.

Arnebeck deliberately spent the barest minimum for a campaign because he was trying to deliver his message through public forums. He wrote personal checks to pay campaign bills of $3,500. Two persons made unsolicited contributions totalling $2,000, but no PAC offered, or was asked, to chip in a single dime. Meanwhile, Arnebeck also went into debt by lending his campaign $15,000. In sum, his entire campaign cost only $20,530, chump change next to Wylie's standard six-figures budget.

Yet there was just enough of a stir through Columbus, just enough of a breeze of voter disaffection with the status quo, to capture the notice of the White House. "I did an unscientific poll the week before the primary, and it showed me beating the incumbent," Arnebeck said. The White House would not have been moved by an unscientific poll commissioned by a little-known challenger. Still, perhaps concerned by the publicity gained by Arnebeck's forums, Wylie asked President George Bush to intervene in a House primary, which presidents rarely do. Weighing costs against gains, presidents normally keep away from taking sides and fomenting hard feelings in a local jurisdiction. Indeed, a presidential endorsement in a contested primary violates National Republican Committee rules, unless there were first a formal, written request and exceptional circumstances. In this case, there was neither.

Wylie had been essential in implementing the Bush administration's bailout of the savings and loan industry. The president "weighed in with a heavy endorsement of the incumbent, all weekend long before the primary," Arnebeck said. "Bush was on all forms of media asking the voters to return the incumbent, that he depended on the incumbent. It was like it was the voters' patriotic duty to vote for the incumbent. The commander in chief ordered it."

Despite Arnebeck's landslide defeat, he believed that Bush's last-minute intervention had proved that his barely funded campaign of town hall debates had been successful. "The next proof of the potential of free campaigns was Ross Perot's candidacy for president in 1992. He achieved the leadership position in the national polls in June 1992 without ever having run a paid commercial. It was all free advocacy covered by the media as news."

Arnebeck was the counsel for the volunteers who put Perot on the Ohio ballot. After Perot withdrew and then re-entered the race, Arnebeck was one of many former supporters to turn against him. He appeared on C-SPAN for a half-hour calling Perot unworthy to head a democracy, followed by a half-hour with Perot's spokesman Orson Swindle of Hawaii (the subject of chapter 14 in this book).

Arnebeck was winning some name recognition as a spokesman for congressional term limits and campaign financial reform. He was the legal chair for a coalition of reform groups that filed a lawsuit in May 1992 to limit the congressional frank. The suit was successful in August, when the U.S. Court of Appeals for the District of Columbia agreed that House members could not send taxpayer-funded mail to areas they did not represent. Also in 1992, Ohio voters approved term limits.

When Republicans surprisingly won a congressional majority in 1994, Arnebeck made an odd decision. The new GOP hegemony inspired an appreciable number of local and federal Democratic office holders to switch parties. Arnebeck made the opposite move: He changed from Republican to Democrat. "I ran in 1996 feeling that the Democratic Party had been wiped out in 1994 and would now be more friendly toward campaign reform and would become the party of campaign reform. That's where my ideas were," he explained. This perception was, if not apparent in 1996 then certainly in hindsight, misguided. Both parties spurn campaign reform because both draw their sustenance from the same overlapping pool of PACs.

Arnebeck said later, "Newt Gingrich had written a book about the 'imperial Congress.' He certainly understood all of the dynamics, the excessive staff, the abuse of the frank, the PAC money. . . . Then he gets in a position to do something about it, and he doesn't. I could not stomach Newt Gingrich because he's a blatant hypocrite." Although Arnebeck was now a Democrat, this was the same complaint voiced in 1996 and thereafter by Republican conservatives who felt that Gingrich and his troops had "gone native" inside the Beltway culture.

After his party switch, Arnebeck won the endorsement of the Democratic Party in Columbus and easily defeated an opponent in the Democratic primary. He thought he would be helped out in November by the party, perhaps even by the Clinton White House.

Wylie, implicated in the House bank overdrafts, had retired in 1992. The new incumbent was Representative Deborah Pryce. An Ohio native born in 1951, she graduated from Ohio State and earned a law degree from Capital University in Columbus. She tried cases as senior assistant city prosecutor before winning election as a Franklin County Municipal Court judge in 1985.

In 1992, she took Wylie's former seat with just 44 percent of the vote in a three-way race against a Democrat and a hard-line, pro-life independent. In 1994, she was re-elected with 71 percent of the vote against a Democrat who did not raise enough money even to meet the minimum $5,000 threshold required for FEC financial filings. Gingrich rewarded her with a coveted seat on the powerful Rules Committee. At the same time, Representative John R. Kasich of the neighboring Twelfth District was named chairman of the Budget Committee. Columbus was well situated to gain federal pork.

By her own account, Pryce had little understanding of what serving in Congress entails. "Totally a child in the dark," she reminisced to a *New York Times* reporter. She thought life in Washington would be "chandeliers and limousines" because as "a regular normal American, I thought everybody elected to those positions had more of a glamorous life." In reality, she lived in a Capitol Hill studio apartment with an empty refrigerator, dashed around every day to committee meetings and personal and party fund-raising receptions, struggled with constituent casework, and on weekends sped to the airport for a seventy-five minute jet flight home—always bumpy because of air currents roiled by the intervening Appalachian Mountains—to see her husband and daughter. (One wonders why the life of a backbencher congressman attracts so many people to seek it.) Still, Pryce was a Gingrich favorite, and her future looked bright.

Arnebeck announced his candidacy on February 12, 1996, repeating his bold—even radical—pledge not to raise money. "Gerrymandering, lobbying dollars in campaigns, and abuses of office have turned representatives into quasi-royalty," he said. Assailing "dollar democracy," he called on the media to cover candidates' forums as news. The Wolfe family's *Columbus Dispatch* now became a critical factor.

Few cities have a paper as locally powerful as the *Dispatch*. The newspaper building sits across the street from the grey, flat-domed state Capitol. The *Dispatch* offices are topped by a garish red neon sign: "Ohio's Greatest Home Newspaper." The huge sign stands higher than the Capitol dome, almost as if the newspaper and the seat of government house a kind of co-legislature for the state.

Inside the *Dispatch* lobby are framed portraits of brothers Robert Frederick Wolfe and Harry Preston Wolfe, both men wearing grim scowls in the style of Victorian-era photos. After making a fortune in shoemaking factories, the two obtained control of the *Dispatch* (founded in 1871) early in the twentieth century, then went on to make another fortune in banks, followed by more riches in real estate and broadcasting. Their local radio and television outlet was WBNS, standing for Wolfe Banks Newspapers and Shoes. The family dominated the city's economy and communications for decades. Arnebeck's friend John W. Wolfe had died of a heart attack; the current president, publisher, and CEO of the *Dispatch* is another descendant named John F. Wolfe.

Family-owned newspapers with an overt political bias used to be common, the personal hobbyhorses of individual press titans or their heirs. Thus, Robert McCormick published the *Chicago Tribune* as a propaganda sheet for isolationists and conservatives, Dorothy Schiff ran the *New York Post* as a liberal Democratic organ; Robert Chandler used his *Los Angeles Times* to help crooks obtain water rights for the city; William Randolph Hearst supposedly sparked the Spanish-American War to increase his papers' circulation, and so forth. All of these legends are gone with the wind. Their newspapers now are published by faceless conglomerates that provide for the entertainment and consumerist needs of upscale readers (with the exception of Rupert Murdoch's low-brow *New York Post*).

Critics scorn the new conglomerate-owned chain newspapers—the "chain gang"—as superficial and bland, but they also condemned the old press-titan-owned newspapers as biased and idiosyncratic. Newspapers are businesses and will serve their owners in any case. As for the Wolfes, they have never published their *Dispatch* with the flair of a McCormick or Hearst. Rather, the paper expresses a Midwestern GOP banker/bourgeois stolidity. The city's Republicanism goes back to Abraham Lincoln.

Like most unsuccessful candidates, Arnebeck complains that he could not get a fair shake from the press. He has a case, but so does the newspaper.

A political reporter's drill when a challenger announces his candidacy is to ask three questions:

1. Have you taken a poll?
2. How much money can you raise?
3. Who is your media consultant?

If the answer to the first question is no, the second ambiguous ("as much as we can"), and the third unimpressive, the candidacy is not taken seriously. Unfortunately for Arnebeck, he satisfied none of the three criteria. In these instances, reporters dutifully will write the candidate's stand on the issues, but thereafter they pay little attention. There is usually nothing personal in this. With multiple campaigns to cover and limited space in which to print political stories, and considering how entrenched incumbents are, reporters simply lack the time. In Arnebeck's case, he still was $13,800 in debt from his 1990 personal campaign loan of $15,000, and also he refused to raise money. Under the circumstances, the news of his candidacy was placed on page six of the paper's second section. Journalist conventions simply did not accommodate such an unorthodox campaign.

Societal trends also are behind such scanty coverage. Politics used to be a major civic sport in cities across the country, abetted by aggressive newspaper coverage. With the public increasingly turned off by politics, readership polls and TV viewer surveys persistently show that consumers do not want to hear about it. As the public has drifted away from politics, the media have followed it out the door (excepting the Boston-New York-Washington prestige media axis). The result is ever more political ads but less news coverage and fewer voters in a ceaseless spiral. Despite all the hand-wringing by good-government types over this sorry state of affairs, the fact that incumbents are all but permanently fixed in office is often slighted. From a stay-at-home voter's viewpoint, voting apparently accomplishes nothing except to ratify the status quo.

Arnebeck would argue that the media situation in Columbus was more insidious than such trends would indicate—that he was deliberately portrayed as a noncandidate because he presented a threat to the incumbency system. He and other Democratic candidates met privately with John F. Wolfe at Wolfe's request. The publisher made the case, in so many words: "We're doing very well here; we've got John Kasich on the Budget Committee and we've got Deborah on the Banking Committee [actually, she then was on a health and financial services subcommittee of the Rules Committee] and a significant leadership position in the House structure. This is like, in terms of the financial community, having your own personal lobbyist in strategic positions. Why would you want to change that?"

Arnebeck quickly concluded, "The press wouldn't want me to win." He may well have been correct. Indeed, the situation in Columbus typifies the joint venture between the local establishment and an incumbent—GOP or Democrat—in any jurisdiction in the United States. Pryce was a fairly conservative Republican, supporting term limits and a balanced-budget amendment to the Constitution, but she bucked the party leadership and the Clinton White House alike on a matter of banking interest. In April 1996, she helped to defeat a measure, opposed by banks, to strengthen a thrift-industry insurance fund.

However, none of this explains the day-to-day news coverage of the campaign. Contrary to popular suspicions, reporters almost never hear from high-level executives of their employing corporation about their work, one way or another. Those execs have higher concerns than the dreary news cycle of charge/countercharge, news conference/party rally. An outside press critic might conclude that the *Dispatch*, led by its statehouse reporter James Bradshaw, covered Arnebeck's race with routine competence and that he got at least as much ink as his meager campaign chest warranted.

Tim Miller, who reported from Columbus for the *Dayton Daily News* at the time and thus was Bradshaw's competitor in the state Capitol press room, said, "It was pretty much the standard coverage. Cliff was known to the press corps from the early Perot campaign and was a very credible guy. I never sensed any kind of bias or anything against him. And I didn't feel that Pryce was getting any more [coverage] than any other incumbent would get."

Of all things, a Native American issue was one that Arnebeck promoted. The 1978 Indian Child Welfare Act granted Native Americans priority in adopting Indian children and made the tribes, not state agencies, arbiters of Indian adoption disputes. Ensuing litigation was a predictable by-product of the federal government's zeal to regulate nearly every facet of society. A Pomo Indian couple in Long beach, California, placed their twin girls for adoption at birth. They were adopted by a Columbus couple. Then the children's grandmother sued to take them back on the grounds that they had a tiny amount of Pomo blood and therefore were subject to the federal law. The Columbus couple had had no knowledge of any Indian lineage.

Pryce, herself an adoptive mother, went to bat legislatively for the Columbus couple, who were, after all, her constituents. She moved to amend the 1978 law to shorten the time in which Native Americans may file adoption appeals and limit the amount of Indian ancestry covered. Her effort failed in a conflict with Republican Senator John McCain of Arizona, who considered himself the Capitol Hill expert on Native American matters. In any case, this human interest story caught the notice of the Columbus media.

Arnebeck saw in the adoption controversy a nexus between "Indian sovereignty" and "voter sovereignty." He accused Pryce of trying to undercut both. On October 25, he called a news conference to say he had received a $3,000 donation from the National Congress of American Indians and would take part in a Native American demonstration downtown. He had not filed an FEC form disclosing his personal finances because he had not yet raised the $5,000 minimum that triggers mandatory FEC filings. The $3,000 would push him above the $5,000 floor, but he would refuse to report it. In an effort to entice TV coverage, Arnebeck issued a press release saying he would rip up the FEC form. Even so, no TV cameras showed up. Arnebeck said his refusal to file was an act of civil disobedience meant to protest restrictions on free speech that keep incumbents in office forever. The maximum FEC fine for failure to report is $5,000, "which I wouldn't pay," Arnebeck vowed. If the government tried to collect, then litigation might settle an important constitutional question, he said. But a *Dispatch* editor rewrote a reporter's account of this event "to make me sound like a scofflaw, like a nut."

Rodney Grant, the actor who played "Wind In His Hair" in the movie *Dances with Wolves* was scheduled to attend the Indian demonstration. Grant did not make it, and the celebrity on hand on October 30 was "Buddy" Apesanahkwat, a chief of the Menominee tribe in Wisconsin and a leading actor in the TV series "Northern Exposure." A couple dozen people staged a brief Native American ceremony in front of city hall, then marched past the Capitol and across the Broad Street bridge over the river, intended as a metaphor for the Democratic "bridge to the twenty-first century," to Veterans Memorial Auditorium for a rally. Besides the adoption issue, Apesanahkwat appealed for the release of Leonard Peltier, serving two life terms for the shooting deaths of two FBI agents in South Dakota in the 1970s. The Indians maintained he was a political prisoner, not a killer. Whatever the merits of their claims, they were not a voting bloc in the Fifteenth District.

The *Dispatch* ran an advance notice of the event on the third page of the fifth section and a report on the incident on the seventh page of the third section—about where any conventional news editor would have placed them. For one thing, protest demonstrations by aggrieved minorities were hardly novel happenings by the 1990s.

Local TV cameras videotaped the march, but the stations aired no footage of it. When viewers have a choice among hundreds of cable stations, local stations desperate to hold an audience for their advertisers take heed of viewer surveys documenting their lack of interest in politics. Even when producers decide that a political story is important enough to put up, they have only a minute or so in the "news hole" after sports, weather, and ads are subtracted from a half-hour newscast. Then, if they cover one candidate, standards of balance require getting a response from the other side, which takes staff time and news-hole time. After all that, if they do show something about the Fifteenth District, then the Fourth, Seventh, Twelfth, and Eighteenth districts—also within range of Columbus broadcast stations—might press for coverage. Best just to touch on the races for governor and senator, if anything, and leave the congressional races alone.

Where was Representative Pryce during the Indians' demonstration in her hometown? She was on a "fly-around" to other Ohio cities with Ohio House Speaker Jo Ann Davidson and Attorney General Betty Montgomery, campaigning for presidential candidate Bob Dole and other Ohio congressmen. This procedure is known in the trade as a "tarmac campaign" because its major purpose is to stage news conferences on airport tarmacs long enough to appear before local TV cameras before winging off to the next city. While airborne or in airport "holding rooms," the politicians also make fund-raising calls.

Pryce's fly-around illustrated two iron laws of incumbency protection. First, incumbents are in position to raise money for themselves and others. Second, they have an automatic claim on media attention, merely by virtue of incumbency. (After back-to-back appearances by the Fifteenth District candidates at a civic forum, one Columbus station violated journalistic standards by airing tape of Pryce but not Arnebeck.) Ill-funded challengers are reduced to stunts or, if they are willing to play the game, scurrilous attacks as ploys to gain publicity.

While Pryce basked in the approval of the Republican establishment, Arnebeck learned another lesson in how the system treats challengers with little money. The day before the Native American march, President Clinton campaigned in Columbus but provided no place on the stage for Arnebeck. The omission was noticed because two other House candidates and even the candidate for Franklin County recorder of deeds not only were on hand with the president, but were given a turn at the microphone to address the crowd.

A few political operatives approached Arnebeck when he appeared at the event on the Ohio State campus to ask him not to complain about being excluded. When he was undeterred, the operatives told reporters that the candidate simply had not requested podium space prior to the rally. "They're lying. I did ask in advance," Arnebeck said. "They left me out because I haven't bought into the politicians' big-money system." According to Arnebeck, a *Dispatch* editor altered the quote to say that he had not "bought into the Democrats' big-money system"—a subtle but significant shift in meaning.

"I was running an essentially nonpartisan campaign for reform in the public interest and the *Dispatch* crafted me as anti–Democratic Party, anti–Republican Party, and anti-independent," Arnebeck said.

And so it went. *This Week*, a weekly paper in suburban Arlington owned by the *Dispatch*, ran a profile of Arnebeck back in the paper's "Homes and Gardens" section. An Arnebeck TV ad was canceled and the money returned without explanation. By the Sunday before the

Tuesday primary, the *Dispatch* reported that Arnebeck "has raised little money and is barely campaigning."

In the end, Arnebeck spent only $9,631, including a $3,500 personal loan, on his campaign. He said he was conducting an experiment in whether the media would fairly report a campaign as a contest of ideas when one of the candidates conscientiously spurns the campaign financing system. The attempt was not successful.

On election day, Pryce won 71 percent of the vote to the challenger's 29 percent. Pryce spent $384,780 on her campaign and retained $299,202 in the bank *after* the election, thus hoarding a treasury big enough to scare off most future challengers in advance. Arnebeck never did file the FEC personal disclosure form. He said the agency never has contacted him about it.

Arnebeck said, "The real threat to the system is that the challengers of both parties might get together and sound a common theme which connects with the public." A year and a half later, Arnebeck was interviewed again and asked, with wounds having healed somewhat, whether he might consider another run for office. "In running twice, each time I learned something," he said. "What I learned in '96 was that I was too idealistic about the media, perhaps due to my friendship with John W. Wolfe. Now my attention is focused on, how do you get around media censorship of the election process? If a candidacy could facilitate that, I would not rule it out. But it is not my heart's desire."

For Representative Pryce, the 105th Congress brought both a stirring professional success and a personal heartache. After House Republican Conference Vice Chair Susan Molinari of New York resigned to take a job with CBS News, Pryce sought a spot in the leadership. She was a popular member, chosen in 1992 as interim president of her Republican "freshman class." In July 1997, the GOP caucus elected her as conference secretary over three other candidates on the second ballot. Both Pryce and Molinari's replacement as vice chair, Jennifer Dunn of Washington state, were favorites of Speaker Gingrich.

In mid-1998, Pryce took an authorized leave of absence from the House to care for her seven-year-old daughter, Caroline, who suffered from a form of leukemia. Despite her withdrawal from the public stage, Pryce was re-elected in November 1998 with 60 percent of the vote.

9

ILLINOIS

Dick Simpson (D) and Michael P. Flanagan (R) v. Representative Dan Rostenkowski (D)

Political insiders and media pundits presumed that Representative Daniel D. Rostenkowski of Chicago was unbeatable—even after he was indicted for stealing public money in 1994. This presumption underscored the political establishment's belief that incumbents not only are entrenched but in some cases are invincible, even if under indictment. Journalists habitually described Rostenkowski as "the powerful chairman of the tax-writing Ways and Means Committee" and "the last of a breed"—a hulking, straight-talking, high-living, and indestructable survivor of the old Mayor Richard J. Daley machine of urban ethnic politics.

But two men had the nerve to take him on. Dick Simpson, a college professor, challenged "Rosty" in the Democratic primaries of 1992 and 1994. Mike Flanagan, a young law school graduate with exactly one suit to his name, ran against Rostenkowski as a Republican in 1994.

Both challengers heard, even from many wellwishers, that Rosty was invulnerable. He had entered Congress under Mayor Daley in 1959 at age thirty-one and was re-elected seventeen times, sometimes without opposition. He regularly brought home federal pork such as the massive Deep Tunnel flood control project, single-handedly scooping it out like some political Paul Bunyan.

Rostenkowski took big campaign donations from interest groups and often slipped special tax breaks for his friends and contributors into the tax bills drafted by his committee. However, he avoided any involvement in the perennial congressional scandals—Abscam, the savings and loan fiasco, the House bank check bouncings, and sexual indiscretions. By 1992, though, there were murmurs that he would be implicated in the House post office scandal.

In the zoology of Chicago politics, Dick Simpson was of the species "lakefront liberal." Rostenkowski was a Northwest Side "white ethnic," a Polish American partner of the local Irish American oligarchy. His congressional district had been redrawn after the 1990 census to encompass outlying city precincts and nearby suburbs unfamiliar to him. Simpson figured that Rosty had lost touch with his home base, succumbed to "Potomac fever," and could be defeated in the 1992 primary.

Actually, whether the incumbent even would seek re-election in 1992 was a question. He could personally pocket his million-dollar campaign fund if he retired, but a new law prevented members of Congress elected that year and after from doing so. Republican President George Bush, Republican Governor Jim Edgar, and Democratic Chicago Mayor Richard M. Daley, the late mayor's son, asked him to stay on for the good of the country, state, and city. Rosty and Bush had been close friends since both men sat on the Ways and Means Committee in the late 1960s. It is hard to say no when your president, governor, and mayor all appeal to your ego. Moreover, as Rosty realized, if he retired, "the obituaries will say, 'He kept the million bucks.' "

Still, Simpson posed enough of a threat that Rostenkowski was impelled for the first time to run a modern campaign, making media appearances and hiring a pollster and media consultants—technicians of the new politics, which he disdained. "The cameras come on, you go from a frown to a smile," he grumbled.

Simpson had been a lakefront alderman in the 1970s, one of the few independent Democrats who always nettled the elder Mayor Daley but never could defeat him. Simpson left the city council to teach political science at the University of Illinois at Chicago and lead the Illinois Coalition Against Reaganomics. Personal ambition aside, he resolved to challenge Rosty in 1992 out of a civics-textbook, good-government conviction: The people of the Fifth Congressional District were poorly represented and deserved better.

Unfortunately for Simpson, he had a hangdog, plodding, professorial manner that turned many voters off. Nevertheless, his campaign against "congressional deadlock and corruption" might well have won had he been able to raise more money.

In May 1991, a House post office clerk was fired because his cash drawer was short of funds. Surprise audits by U.S. Capitol police found that most of the other twelve clerks were missing funds, too. The U.S. attorney in Washington took notice. Some of those implicated offered to identify higher-ups in exchange for leniency.

In Chicago, the House postal probe sparked the softest of whispers that Rostenkowski would be tainted. Voters paid little mind to such inside-the-Beltway developments, but they were alienated by politics in general.

The Democratic machine's precinct captains—city hall patronage workers in their uniform of windbreakers, khakis, and Chicago Cubs caps—perform a winter ritual of circulating their candidates' ballot access petitions block by block. In December 1991, something unprecedented happened. Some voters slammed doors in their faces. The Daley/Rostenkowski troops started to worry seriously about the public's anti-politics, anti-incumbents mood.

Despite all the obituaries that have been written for the Chicago machine, it survives on the Northwest and Southwest sides of the city. On primary election day, March 17, 1992, hundreds of machine workers invaded Rosty's district, all but yanking targeted, promachine voters out of their homes to escort them to the polls.

Simpson had calculated he would need to collect $350,000 to win. He raised only $215,500. Rostenkowski raked in $1.7 million. Simpson's base, the affluent lakefront with its enclave of good-government types known in Chicago parlance as "goo goos," had only 17 percent of the district's population. Despite all that, Simpson's campaign against Rosty as the lord of "honorariums and free travel and free lunches and backroom deals and payoffs" won 43 percent of the vote.

At the time, Mike Flanagan was ending his second stint in the U.S. Army. A captain in the 1980s, he had rejoined to write the official history of the Third Army's operations in the Gulf War. Now he was looking for a job practicing law. Flanagan's hero was Ronald Reagan, but he took no particular interest in politics.

With timing that did Simpson no good, the U.S. attorney investigating the House post office subpoenaed Rostenkowski two months after the primary. In previous months, four clerks and a mid-level manager had been indicted, the House postmaster resigned, and the Washington press reported that House officials apparently had tried to thwart the investigation.

The House tied itself in knots trying to deal with the scandal. In July, a House Administration Committee task force on the postal mess, deadlocked on party lines, issued two different reports. Democrats blamed postal managers, not members of Congress; Rosty claimed vindication. Republicans insisted the case was far from closed: Key witnesses had refused to testify.

The House then voted to turn over the task force records to the Justice Department and the House ethics committee. But it would not even think of making the information public. The House takes care of its own.

Meanwhile, Rostenkowski refused to honor the subpoena, asserting his Fifth Amendment right against self-incrimination, deploring a "political witch hunt."

In the November general election, a Republican nobody who listed his ballot name as Elias R. "Non-Incumbent" Zenkich held Rostenkowski to 57 percent of the vote (normally he won by three to one margins). Zenkich spent only $83,000 to Rosty's $1.4 million for 1991–92. Still, the political establishment continued to believe Rosty was unbeatable.

For the next eighteen months, Rostenkowski was mired ever deeper in the House post office scandal. A Democratic patronage sink, the post office in effect had provided a money laundry for Rostenkowski and at least two other (little known) congressmen to convert stamp vouchers and campaign funds into personal cash.

The *Chicago Sun-Times* published a series of stories detailing Rostenkowski's alleged misuse of funds. His campaign had paid himself and his twin sisters money to rent office space that the family owned and that was little more than a mail drop. He leased cars from taxpayer funds and then took personal title to the vehicles when the leases expired. His congressional payroll included no-show "ghost" employees. Although members of Congress mail their official correspondence for free, Rosty had claimed $55,000 in postage costs over six years. The U.S. attorney in Washington took these findings to the grand jury.

There was much speculation over why—when Rostenkowski was in a position to steal millions of dollars if he wanted—he would get himself in trouble over pilfering some stamps. The head-scratchers did not understand the legacy of machine politics. As for Rostenkowski's attitude: The pickings were easy, he was entitled to them, and nobody except a few goo goos ever cared anyway.

A CEO in the private sector expects his firm to provide a top-floor corner office, a luxury car and parking space, expensive luncheons, country club dues, weekend retreats, and shoe shines. In like manner, Rosty believed the chairman of Ways and Means deserved taxpayer-paid employees to cut the grass at his Wisconsin vacation home, keep the books for his sideline insurance business, photograph his daughter's wedding, and so forth. He made no apologies, not even after he went to jail.

Bill Clinton, the new Democratic president, wanted Rosty to assemble a House coalition to pass his national health care plan, in the same way as Rosty had won passage of the monumental tax reform law under President Reagan in 1986. In March 1993 Clinton's attorney general, Janet Reno, fired all U.S. attorneys. If this maneuver was intended to protect Rostenkowski, it failed.

In July 1993, Clinton visited Chicago and praised Rostenkowski lavishly. That same summer, Flanagan, who was drawing unemployment because his law practice was going nowhere, hung out at neighborhood bars, playing darts.

An old friend from high school ROTC and a few other companions joined him one night at Ray's Chili and Suds on Lincoln Avenue. The ROTC fellow had just returned from a trip to Washington, where he was stunned by the immensity of the federal establishment. "The Department of Agriculture is three buildings that look like the [Chicago] Merchandise Mart," he said.

So while they tossed darts, the friends griped about Clinton and big government. Flanagan was the only lawyer, and somebody suggested he might do something about it, for instance, run for Congress. Two weeks after walking out of Ray's pub, Flanagan decided to do so. The candidacy was kept quiet for a time, not that anybody would have noticed.

Simpson, meanwhile, regarded 1992 as a dry run for 1994. A shift of 7,000 votes would have beaten Rostenkowski, and "that's less than it takes to elect an alderman in Chicago," he observed.

The critical question was whether Rostenkowski would be indicted before or after the March 1994 primary. The investigation, in the tradition of Washington probes of official wrongdoing, seemed to be taking forever. Private individuals and Common Cause President Frank Wertheimer had written the House ethics committee (formally, the Committee on Standards of Official Conduct) demanding an investigation of Rostenkowski. But the ethics committee had handed off the scandal to the Administration Committee, which followed precedent by dillying and dallying. Later the U.S. attorney asked the ethics committee not to investigate lest any public hearings jeopardize his case, as had happened in the Iran/contra scandal of the 1980s, in particular the case against Oliver North. The committee—dreading the fall of a titan such as Rosty—was happy to comply.

Anyway, once indicted, Rostenkowski, under House Democratic rules, would have to abandon the Ways and Means chair. In that case, he might resign forthwith, or else spurn a re-election fight to concentrate on his legal defense. Then, Simpson reasoned, "I would be the front-runner and could more easily raise the necessary resources, including money."

Two events he had not counted on cropped up. First, Rostenkowski appeared so imperiled that other Democrats were enticed to run against him, thus splitting the opposition vote. Second, the political establishment in the persons of President Clinton and Governor Edgar rallied to Rostenkowski's side. Edgar depended on Rosty to deliver pork to Illinois.

A forty-five-year-old Democratic state senator, John J. Cullerton, a member of a family that had held political offices in Chicago since 1871, announced his candidacy. Cullerton thought he could not lose. If Rosty dropped out, he could beat Simpson. If Rosty ran, Cullerton would cut into Simpson's vote, thus ensuring Rosty's renomination and earning the gratitude of the machine, which thereby would slate Cullerton for Congress in 1996.

Accordingly, Cullerton aimed his attacks against Simpson, not Rostenkowski. In fact, he claimed at first that he would leave the race should Rostenkowski decide to run.

But then ambition got the best of him. Emboldened by polls showing Rostenkowski's weakness, Cullerton started running against the incumbent, which angered Daley and the White House. Two weeks before the primary, Clinton stood at Rosty's shoulder at a Chicago school and all but showered him with rose petals, stopping just short, for the sake of protocol, of an explicit endorsement (presidents normally do not intervene in primaries).

Simpson kept hammering away with a "Cancel Rostenkowski" message, a play on the stamp scandal. The incumbent's campaign "countered essentially with, well, he may be corrupt or he may be a crook or whatever, but he's ours, and he can do good for us," Simpson said. Clinton cabinet members shuttled to Chicago for photo-ops at federal projects Rostenkowski had secured. Although Rostenkowski never engaged Simpson personally, his campaign put out the word that Simpson was a liberal flake. Cullerton joined in with gusto.

In 1989, Simpson had published *The Politics of Compassion and Transformation*, which his opponents now derided as the ravings of a New Age whacko. Cullerton sent mailings to voters ridiculing the book. One mailer, headlined "The Twilight Zone," featured the book's jacket photo of Simpson in a clerical robe (he is an ordained United Church of Christ minister) in front of a large "Nuclear Weapons Free Zone" sign. Another piece highlighted out-of-context quotes such as, "I tried various techniques of self-discovery from psychotherapy and Progoff Life Context Journal to past life regressions." Neither brochure mentioned Cullerton, except for a tiny "paid for by" statement required by law.

Simpson was not surprised to learn how rough and nasty Chicago politics can get, but he was dismayed at the lack of a clear shot at Rostenkowski. "When they did the direct-mail attack on me so my [poll] numbers started dropping, [Cullerton] actually thought for a while there that he could win. He then got over-enthusiastic for his own good."

Simpson charged that Cullerton was an apprentice Rostenkowski, another backroom wheeler and dealer. He also tried without success to run on women's and seniors' rights, term limits, and other issues. But the only real issue was Rostenkowski. In the end, Cullerton and Rostenkowski fired away at each other in TV ads while Simpson could afford only a few radio spots.

A week before the election, Rostenkowski spoke at a Pulaski Day celebration at the Polish Museum of America near his home, a gathering of the tribe. "Your support and your faith in me is more valuable than any political victory could be," he said, choking back tears and adding, "In the final analysis, the sum of a person's life can be found in who their friends are. . . . I say to myself, 'Danny, you're a lucky son-of-a-gun. You're a darn lucky son-of-a-gun.' " Mayor Daley was there; so was Governor Edgar.

On election day, March 15, the machine went pedal-to-the-metal for Rostenkowski, deploying as many as 800 precinct workers. Rosty helped his own cause by spending $1.05 million. Cullerton spent $412,000. Simpson spent $261,000. The vote: Rostenkowski, 50 percent; Cullerton, 30 percent; Simpson, 14 percent. Two minor candidates got the rest.

Then there was the Republican primary. Despite Rostenkowski's lackluster showing in his primary, Flanagan's nomination for the GOP ballot spot in November was regarded as a formality. "Feeble" is too strong a word for the Chicago Republican Party. In the Democratic primary, 93,246 votes were cast (a relatively low turnout); in the Republican, 10,108.

There was no GOP primary campaign to speak of—no debates, rallies, phone banks, polls, news conferences, or commercials. Flanagan had four opponents, including "Non-Incumbent" Zenkich and three other nobodies. They campaigned by visiting Republican ward committeemen—some of whom were ringers for the Democratic machine—and enlisting family and friends as volunteer workers.

The Fifth District was a mix of Poles, Italians, Irish, Asians, and others, with almost no blacks, and most of the Hispanics shunted off into an adjoining district gerrymandered expressly for them. The good Irish name of "Michael Patrick Flanagan" on the ballot no doubt attracted voters, even though the Irish composed only 15 percent of the district. Throughout Chicago, voters are accustomed to selecting Irish names—another leftover from the old machine of Richard J. Daley.

Flanagan spent about $5,000 and won a plurality of 38 percent of the vote to 21 percent for Zenkich (a Bosnian). Flanagan lived three blocks outside the district but moved in after winning the GOP nomination.

The morning after the primary, a *Sun-Times* reporter called Cook County Republican headquarters seeking a phone number for Flanagan. They did not have it. The county chairman had never even met the man. "He's the candidate in the Fifth, isn't he? He's the congressional candidate, isn't he?"

Simpson, at age fifty-three, went back to teaching at the university. On May 31, again with timing unhelpful to Simpson, Rostenkowski was indicted on seventeen counts of mail fraud and misuse of public campaign funds.

The seriousness of the charges suprised even Rostenkowski's enemies. He was accused of converting to personal use $688,000 in public funds and $56,267 in campaign funds through various schemes such as making phony stamp transactions, scamming car leases, and hiring fourteen no-show "ghost" payrollers.

The indictments were vivid and personal in their details. One of the "ghosts" was a former Rostenkowski son-in-law who allegedly kicked back his unearned government pay to the congressman. Another count accused Rostenkowski of tampering with a witness. He had given crystal models of the Capitol, engraved with personal plaques, to fifty friends. Allegedly, Rostenkowski told the engraver not to testify that he did the private work at public expense.

Having relinquished his committee chair, and having rejected frantic efforts by his lawyer to win a plea bargain, Rosty proclaimed his innocence and vowed to fight to the end.

There followed one of the oddest general election campaigns in Chicago memory. Both candidates almost vanished from the public stage. Presumably, Rostenkowski was hoarding his campaign funds to pay legal bills. Also, in the language of political consultants, they feared that campaign publicity would only "drive up his negatives." As for the Republicans, they accepted the prevailing wisdom that voters loved pork so much they would re-elect Rosty, indictments or no. The National Republican Congressional Campaign Committee wrote Flanagan off. Nor did any conservative GOP front groups target the district, although Rostenkowski was exhibit A for the national movement to limit congressional terms.

The campaign was a silent contest of generations as much as a clash of issues, including even the ethics one. Rostenkowski, born in 1928, was politically formed by the New Deal and World War II. Flanagan, born in 1962, was politically molded by the resignation of Nixon in 1974, the fall of Saigon in 1975, and the humiliation of the Iran hostage crisis of 1979–80. The two men had vastly differing attitudes toward the federal governnment.

Flanagan was a lawyer but hardly a yuppie. The son of "Roosevelt Democrats," he spoke in the "dese-dem-and-dose" idiom of the Northwest Side. He was single, chubby, an unabashed chain-smoker, and nearly broke. Other than his army years, volunteer work at a local AIDS clinic was his only record of public service. With his unfashionable nerdy glasses and bushy moustache, he presented himself as an ordinary guy from the neighborhood, fed up with the rottenness in Washington.

Flanagan made the circuit of neighborhood coffees, civic club luncheons, and "free media" appearance on public affairs programs. He assailed the excesses of big government but not Rostenkowski personally. He realized there was no need to spotlight his opponent's ethic problems—the media would take care of that job.

Rostenkowski stayed away from the media, paid or free. During the primary campaign, he put out ten mailings to voters, slickly printed in vivid blue, green, and red. He sent only one mailer against Flanagan. Its stark cover with contrasting white and red type portrayed Flanagan as a dangerous, radical conservative. On the back, Rosty appealed for "the chance to clear my name."

The *Chicago Tribune*, the dominant newspaper, endorsed Rostenkowski, of course, but so did the *Sun-Times*, sneering at its own reporters' revelations of the incumbent's wrongdoing. Both papers portrayed
him as an indispensable civic asset.

Newsweek and other national publications reported that Rosty was a
shoo-in. In the high traditions of pundrity, none of these "experts"
later explained how they got it so wrong, or even admitted that they
were wrong.

Larry P. Horist, a combative, maverick conservative political consultant who advised Flanagan, is the unsung hero of the Republican
campaign. He understood the vulnerability exposed by Rosty's defeat
of a weak "Non-Incumbent" challenger in 1992 by just seven percentage points, followed by the fact that fully half the Democratic primary
voters in 1994 did not want him. The Flanagan campaign lacked
money for professional polling, so Horist pressed for a telephone poll
conducted by volunteers.

The results indicated that Rostenkowski was doomed. Through an
Illinois congressman, Horist forwarded the poll to the National Republican Congressional Campaign Committee. The incredulous committee commissioned its own scientific poll, did not believe it, and
ordered another.

Convinced at last, the committee dropped $55,000 into the district
for a last-minute Flanagan TV buy. The sum (the legal maximum) was
not impressive but the mere fact of its arrival made a media splash.

By the Friday before the Tuesday election, Democratic ward committeemen knew the race was lost. It told in their faces and body language, though for the record they said otherwise. They had seen the
private Democratic polls. Rostenkowski said after the election that his
polling support once was as low as 29 percent and never exceeded 40
percent.

In the final days, at the groceries and shopping malls and senior cen-
ters and block clubs of the Fifth District, Democratic precinct workers
were nowhere in sight. The disappearance of the machine still remains
somewhat mysterious. Probably the explanation is that Rostenkowski
personally was devastated by the indictments. "Jesus, this is awful, my
stomach is hamburger," he told a friend. "What [is history] going to say
about Danny Rostenkowski?"

"When the heart goes out of the candidate," said former Illinois
Governor James R. Thompson, a Republican and long-time Rostenkowski friend and supporter, "the heart goes out of the organization."

Flanagan spent $113,000 and won 54 percent of the vote. Rostenkowski spent $695,000—not a large amount next to his eventual $3 million in legal fees—and got 46 percent of the vote. Flanagan was part of the Republican resurgence of 1994, which took control of Congress for the first time in forty years.

On election night, Rostenkowski was dignified and stoic in defeat. At Flanagan's victory celebration, when his supporters started jeering Rostenkowski, the congressman-elect scolded, "Hey, nunna dat, nunna dat."

Weeks later, Rostenkowski held a private fund raiser for his legal and campaign costs. Much of the Illinois political hierarchy and many heads of the Chicago Loop boardrooms showed up to deliver heartfelt tributes to a legislator of historic importance, brought down in their eyes by ambitious prosecutors and the scandal-mongering press.

Congressman Flanagan promptly moved into the cramped bachelor apartment that Rosty had vacated in a seedy area of southwest Washington (Rosty had almost never stayed in Washington on weekends and, on the rare events when his wife, LaVerne, visited the capital, he rented a hotel suite). "I'm working very hard to deflate this myth that he's an arrogant, overbearing son of a bitch, because he's not," Flanagan said. "I have found him to be affable. His advice was to take care of the people."

In April 1996, Rostenkowski pleaded guilty to two counts in a plea bargain and was sentenced to seventeen months in prison. Jail turned out to be "just like the army except you don't have to march," Rostenkowski, a private in pre-war Korea, told friends.

Flanagan strived to establish himself as an "urban Republican," sometimes bucking Newt Gingrich's House leadership. As a challenger he had spent $113,000; as an incumbent he was able to raise and spend six times that much for his 1996 re-election campaign. Nevertheless, he still was not part of the Chicago Democratic establishment and his Democratic opponent was in effect a shadow incumbent. The Democrat, Rod Blagojevich, spent $1,552,000, more than doubling Flanagan's outlay and ranking number thirty in expenditures among all House candidates that year. Blagojevich beat Flanagan with 64 percent of the vote.

Blagojevich was the thirty-nine-year-old son-in-law of a Democratic ward boss who had helped put Cullerton in the 1994 primary. The canny ward boss had calculated that Cullerton and Simpson would be defeated, and then Rostenkowski either would lose in November or else resign, thus clearing the path for his son-in-law in 1996. He was right.

He also had understood that thirty-six-year incumbent Rostenkowski was going down only by a series of flukes. His home base had been redistricted; it was going to be a Republican year; and moreover an investigation of a few low-level House postal workers somehow had exploded into the exposure of Rosty as a major thief.

Rostenkowski was released from prison in the fall of 1997 and developed a consulting business in Chicago instructing business and labor lobbies in the ways that Washington works. *Newsweek* and the *Chicago Tribune* published articles lionizing him as an elder statesman.

Flanagan considered running for the U.S. Senate in 1998 but then bowed out. He still is seeking an occupational niche.

10

TEXAS

RON PAUL (R) v. REPRESENTATIVE GREG LAUGHLIN (D/R) AND CHARLES MORRIS (D)

Challengers sometimes win. It can happen. Almost always, though, there are special circumstances—the challenger was already a celebrity in another field, possessed overwhelming personal wealth, or faced a weak incumbent who was at odds with his party leaders or perhaps mired in an ethics mess.

Thus, Michael Flanagan won in Chicago after Dan Rostenkowski was destroyed by scandal. Also in Illinois, Democratic Senator Carol Moseley-Braun was defeated in 1998 under a personal financial cloud. More typically, Senator Paul Coverdell of Georgia upset Democratic incumbent Wyche Fowler by just 16,237 votes in a run-off election in 1992 after Fowler, a maverick first-termer, committed some political blunders. Once esconced in incumbency, Coverdell easily fended off a challenge from Democrat Michael Coles in 1998.

Sometimes, challengers win in part because they are former incumbents themselves and have learned to walk both sides of the campaign street. One former congressman, Joe DioGuardi in New York, was unsuccessful. Another, Ron Paul in Texas, won.

Paul captured a House seat as a Republican in 1996 by a weird combination of his own appeal as a candidate, local Texas politics, and national politics including hard-core conservatives and their supposed brothers in arms, Newt Gingrich Republicans—who ganged up against Paul just as fiercely as they did against DioGuardi.

Ron Paul is commonly labeled a "right-wing extremist" or "ultraconservative," terms that drives conservatives up the wall with complaints that the media never seem to identify a "left-wing extremist" or "ultraliberal." Paul is a congressional rarity, a true ideologue in the strict sense of the word. Properly speaking, he is a libertarian, a school of thought that does not hang its hat comfortably in either the left or right cloakrooms. Libertarians take an absolutely minimalist view of federal powers, insisting, for example, that the Federal Reserve System of currency regulation is unconstitutional (attacked as beyond the pale, this in fact is far from a novel argument—it was essentially President Andrew Jackson's case against the Second Bank of the United States in the 1830s).

Challengers tend to be aggressive, take-charge types who assume that when they find something broken they should try to fix it. Born in 1932 in Pittsburgh, Paul trained as an obstetrician-gynecologist at Duke University and served as a U.S. Air Force flight surgeon in the 1960s. Practicing later in southeast Texas, he "became very disenchanted with the way government was working," a former aide remembered. Therefore, Paul ran for Congress. It was a suicide mission as a Republican in a "yellow-dog Democrat" district in 1974. Losing two to one but not discouraged, he ran again in a special election to fill a vacancy in April 1976. He upset the Democratic candidate and went to Washington, only to lose the seat in the general election in November.

Despite these setbacks, Paul perceived that the South in due time would go Republican, as did a few other seers such as Strom Thurmond, Lyndon Johnson, Richard Nixon, and—a fact almost never noted—George Bush, a Houston congressman in the 1960s. In 1978, Paul won his House seat back and was re-elected twice.

Paul still sees himself as a physician and only a part-time citizen-legislator. "Even when he was in Congress in the '70s, I think he snuck off to the hospital here in Washington and delivered a few welfare babies," a former aide said. Although he says he has delivered more than 4,000 babies, considering the longevity of his public career, Paul perhaps is fooling himself that he is not a politician.

But as a politician, he is certainly a most unusual one. The heart of his standard stump speech is, "the government perpetually takes our money, lies to us, and makes our lives worse." There probably are no more than a handful of congressional districts in the country that could elect a candidate who says such things. Indeed, Paul's message already had failed at the statewide and national levels. In 1984, he was smashed by Phil Gramm in the Texas Republican primary for a Senate seat, 73 percent to 16 percent (incidentally, Senator Gramm's classmate in the economics doctorate program at the University of Georgia had been Jim Miller of Virginia). In 1988, Paul was the Libertarian Party's presidential nominee and won less than one-half of 1 percent of the national vote in the contest between George Bush and Michael Dukakis. Nevertheless, in 1995, Paul decided to challenge the Democratic incumbent in the Fourteenth Congressional District of Texas. Previously he had represented a neighboring district; the Fourteenth was remapped after the 1990 census.

That district is among the relatively few in the country still classified as rural, a status certain to be changed after the 2000 census counts the new suburbanites surrounding Austin and those in the "edge cities" of Houston and San Antonio. Most of the district is prime cropland in the humid coastal plain, having more in common with the Old South of King Cotton than with the Texas wildcatters and cowboys of worldwide legend. Still, the Fourteenth stretches from the Gulf Coast northwest to Blanco County west of Austin, the storied Hill Country that was the home base of LBJ. Historically the area was yellow-dog Democratic with a small sector settled by immigrant Germans who were pro-Union in the Civil War and still vote Republican. As in Virginia and South Carolina, ancient Civil War loyalties remain a factor, however diluted, in southern elections to this day.

The district's Democratic congressman was Greg Laughlin, an insecure incumbent. He lost a race in 1986 but then won a 1988 rematch against the incumbent, who had lied about his resume and legislative record. In his third term, Laughlin was caught in a minor (by congressional standards) financial scandal. The FBI investigated him for legislatively favoring a moving company that had moved his family to Washington for free and dropped big dollars into his campaigns. Laughlin was not charged with any wrongdoing, and in 1994 he defeated his Republican opponent with 56 percent of the vote.

But Laughlin was shaken by the GOP takeover of Congress that year, a political event of the first magnitude that was misunderstood at the time and still resists definitive analysis. Among its tangible effects, the turnover installed an unprecedented Texan triumvirate of House Majority Leader Dick Armey, House Majority Whip Tom DeLay, and House Ways and Means Committee Chairman Bill Archer. Of the three, Archer might have been the most important. The Ways and Means Committee—writer of tax, trade, Social Security, and Medicare bills—was the locus of Chairman Dan Rostenkowski's power from 1981–94.

During that watershed year of 1994, Newt Gingrich had attacked Laughlin as a Clintonesque liberal, a potentially deadly charge in the conservative South. "Greg Laughlin has a 78 percent voting record with Bill Clinton. That tells you where he stands," Gingrich harrumphed. In fact, Laughlin had compiled a moderate voting record, and Gingrich's statement was an example of how statistics can mislead. Much White House-sponsored legislation is routine and nonpartisan and draws majorities from both sides of the aisle. Only a few critical votes on budgets, defense, judicial appointments, and social issues really tell the tale. Laughlin's 78 percent voting scorecard hardly denoted undying devotion to Clinton.

At any rate, Republican efforts to recruit party switchers escalated when they won a majority of Congress. Bill Archer offered Laughlin a deal: Jump to our side and we will give you a seat on Ways and Means. Some members spend their entire careers angling for a seat on that all-powerful committee, a prime purveyor of pork. The Texas oil industry, dependent on Ways and Means for its depletion allowance and other tax breaks, would smile on Laughlin if he joined the committee. All he had to do was change his party label.

In June 1995, Laughlin took the deal. Archer sealed the bargain with a celebratory cake for the cameras. In Washington, Laughlin had made a smart move. But, in his home district, ordinary voters did not appreciate the significance of a seat on Ways and Means. Party switchers in general, such as former Texas Governor John Connally—LBJ Democrat turned Nixon Republican—tend to lead unhappy lives (except, of course, former New Deal Democrat Ronald Reagan).

Ron Paul had been calculating a race against the Democratic incumbent and now suddenly faced a primary challenge to a Republican incumbent. A signpost of his political constancy is that he did not alter either his tactics or his message. Not even when the national GOP leadership lined up against him.

Meanwhile, Laughlin labored to explain why he abandoned the Democratic ship. "I tried to be part of the Democratic team, but I was miserable on some of the votes I cast," he said. "Since I've been a Republican, I haven't cast one hard vote."

He added, "Conservative Democrats were not getting leadership positions, policy assignments on the committees. We were getting skipped over by more liberal members. If I was the only one that felt that way, I'd be the only one that switched parties. But there's five of us [in the end, seven—five representatives and two senators], and I know several more who retired instead." This was fair enough, but hardly a

ringing campaign slogan. Paul reversed the incumbent-challenger tables. In effect, he was the "pro" with a simple, consistent message,
while the incumbent was a confused "amateur" unsure of whether to
run as a moderate or a conservative.

Paul also functioned as an effective incumbent in his ability to raise
money. He spent $1.9 million for the primary and general elections
without putting up a dime from his own pocket. The funds came largely
from aggressive direct-mail appeals to national conservative mailing
lists, including some obscure ones. What got Paul into politics in the
first place was President Nixon's decoupling of the dollar from gold in
1971. Libertarians hold that the only money allowed by the Constitution is gold, silver, or notes convertible to those precious metals—
"Federal Reserve Notes" not backed by specie are hence fraudulent. So
Paul garnered contributions from so-called gold bugs and subscribers
to the *Ron Paul Political Report*. He was able to match Laughlin, TV
commercial for TV commercial.

Still, Laughlin's campaign assets were formidable. Born in 1942, he
had graduated from Texas A&M and earned a law degree from the University of Texas—certificates of true Texan personhood in the same way
that John F. Kennedy's 1940 Harvard diploma draped over him the
mantle of Boston aristocracy. Also, Laughlin could more than hold his
own with Paul in military epaulette-brushing. He was an army intelligence officer during the 1960s and, as a lieutenant colonel in the army
reserve, volunteered for two weeks of service in the Persian Gulf War of
1991 (Paul opposed that war). Finally, Laughlin was supported by the
national Republican establishment.

As early as January 1996, Gingrich flew to Texas for a campaign appearance with the incumbent, which annoyed local Republican leaders.
That was just the beginning. Former President Bush endorsed Laughlin in April, his first Republican primary endorsement since he had run
for re-election in 1992. This maneuver was arranged by his son, George
W. Bush, elected governor of Texas in 1994. The junior Bush stood
with Laughlin in his home town of West Columbia, saying, "The definition of welcome for this governor is not only to say behind closed
doors, 'You are welcome' [in the party], but to say, 'I have helped you
win our party's nomination in any way I can.' " Later, he reflected, "It
would be the worst message you could send, you know, to say, 'Switch
parties and then lose a primary.' " Texas senators Phil Gramm and Kay
Bailey Hutchison and Majority Leader Armey stumped for Laughlin.
Fifty-four GOP members of Congress sent him money. Gingrich said,

"When they put on the team jersey, they're on the team. As a Republican, he has been an absolute team player."

Voters might be forgiven if they were confused by this rhetoric, which upheld a widespread suspicion that Democratic and Republican, liberal and conservative are just brand names stuck on essentially identical products, like Ford and Chevrolet. (Recall George Wallace's 1968 slogan, "There ain't a dime's worth of difference between the two parties.") In the space of just eight months, from the November 1994 election to his June 1995 party switch, Laughlin somehow had been transformed from a Clintonesque liberal to an "absolute [Republican] team player." In contrast, Paul had a coherent message.

Befuddled about how to challenge Paul on ideas, Laughlin relied—a familiar strategy—on personal attacks. His oppo people dug up a 1992 *Ron Paul Political Report* stating that 95 percent of the black men in Washington, D.C., are "semi-criminal or entirely criminal" and that black teenagers are "unbelievably fleet of foot." This politically unwise and unfounded assertion apparently did not hurt Paul in the Fourteenth District, whose population is only 10 percent African American.

Laughlin's major avenue of attack was the drug issue, with pornography as a parallel path. From a libertarian standpoint, Paul advocated the repeal of federal drug and pornography laws, leaving these matters up to the states. "The [federal] war on drugs has been an absolute failure," Paul said, a view which, antidrug rhetoric aside, can be supported by statistics. But out-of-the-mainstream positions exposed Paul to charges that he was pro-drugs and pro-pornography, forcing him to dodge the extremist label.

Laughlin's side road of attack was "push polling," a dirty trick that warrants examination in some detail. Incumbents have no monopoly on it, but in general, only they have the money to pay for it. Crudely put, a push poller purporting to be conducting an impartial, scientific survey calls voters to ask, "Do you support candidate X?" Yes. "Would you still support X if you knew he was a draft-dodging, wife-beating, child molester?"

The historical father of push polling was the "midnight flier" dropped on voters' doorsteps on election eve, anonymous screeds smearing a candidate with accusations of various misdeeds. As with so many other features of modern electioneering, technology has replaced the midnight flier. Precisely targeted lists of voters, socially and economically classified by Zip code, are handed to staffers at phone banks in what used to be called campaign "boiler rooms" but now are called "war rooms." The callers, paid by candidates, are fakes, impersonating data collectors but assigned to push voters away from challengers. Usually they are employed in House races, but they also have been used by higher-echelon politicians such as Bob Dole against Steve Forbes in the 1996 Iowa Republican presidential caucuses. This is not to single out Dole—the technique is a bipartisan form of corruption. Naturally, the American Association for Public Opinion Research, a typically self-guarding trade group, piously denounces the practice.

Innovative Marketing Solutions, an Austin firm, did push polling for Laughlin against Paul and his other primary challenger, Jim Deats, an ostrich farmer who had run against Laughlin in 1994. The firm called as many as 35,000 households; a real poll would need a scientific sample of only hundreds of respondents. If voters said they favored Deats, they were told that he had lost four elections and had a 1994 campaign debt of $200,000 (actually, $171,000). If they said they supported Paul, they were told he wanted to legalize drugs, pornography, and prostitution.

Innovative Marketing's push poll is exceptional only in that some of its details have come to light, thanks to reporting by the *Austin American-Statesman* and the *New York Times*. The results were sent to the National Republican Congressional Campaign Committee in Washington. The committee's spokesman would say only, "We paid for a poll." The cost was not disclosed but was estimated by industry insiders at between $20,000 and $50,000.

This expenditure was not reported to the Federal Election Commission as a Laughlin campaign contribution. The NRCCC spokesman explained that it was an unregulated soft-money expense and not a hard-money contribution to a particular candidate. Why? Because the polling results were not transmitted to the Laughlin campaign—yet another example of the absurdities wrought by the Watergate-era campaign reforms of the 1970s.

In 1995, the FEC considered requiring pollsters to tell respondents for whom they were working. Real pollsters do not volunteer this information because it could bias the results. However, a pollster might provide this fact at the end of an interview without skewing the responses. The election commission deliberated but took no action. Aside from its financial data reporting service, the FEC is a joke.

Despite the newspaper push-poll revelations, the print media played a scanty role in the district. It includes no urban media markets, except for some spillover from counties close to Austin and Houston. Contrary to the common wisdom that the media are all-powerful in elections, the Fourteenth's votes were driven by the apparatus of partisan and interest group organizations. Tony Payton, Paul's Washington-based campaign consultant, said, "The media had a difficult time covering this race because it is such a scattered district. The media was biased, but it kind of didn't make any difference. . . . I don't think they liked Laughlin too much. I think they just liked the flamboyant charges Laughlin was making, 'cause it was good news copy."

Gingrich, the two George Bushes, and other GOP luminaries were right to fear for Laughlin's seat. During Paul's 1979–85 tenure in the House, he had been rated the "taxpayers' best friend" by the National Taxpayers Union—he refused even to accept his own congressional pension—and could credibly paint Laughlin in TV ads as a tax-and-spending junket taker. Paul also highlighted a video clip from the 1980s of former President Reagan saying, "Ron Paul is one of the outstanding leaders fighting for a stronger national defense. As a former air force officer, he knows well the needs of our armed forces, and he always puts them first. We need to keep him fighting for our country." This tribute was included in a fifteen-minute videotape that the Paul campaign sent to 30,000 households, a new tool of political salesmanship. In another case of turning-the-tables, the challenger was more media-savvy than the incumbent.

The Paul video prompted the GOP establishment to dispatch Reagan's former Attorney General Edwin Meese to the district to insist that Reagan was making no endorsement in the race. In truth, the video attained a level of disingenuousness worthy of an experienced incumbent. "Fighting for a stronger national defense" or no, Paul actually advocated cutting defense spending by $150 billion.

Gingrich and the rest worried that a typically low-turnout primary, dominated by true-believer conservatives, would sink Laughlin. Due largely to Governor Bush's organization, the turnout on March 12 was a relatively high 34,000 voters—an 89 percent increase over 1994. Laughlin finished first with 43 percent of the vote to 32 percent for Paul and 24 percent for Jim Deats.

Because Laughlin had not won a majority, under Texas law a run-off election would be held on April 9. His 11–point lead over Paul looked commanding, but to political insiders, it exposed his weakness. As a rule, an incumbent opposed by a majority of his party constituents loses a run-off because supporters of the losing candidates swing to the remaining challenger. The Republican establishment could not come through a second time and the run-off turnout was just 20,700. "People don't like being told by party officials who to vote for," observed a GOP official in neighboring Louisiana.

Paul won the run-off with 54 percent of the vote. Laughlin was the first House incumbent to be unseated in 1996. He was gracious in defeat. "I'm still proud to be a Republican," he said. NRCCC Chairman Bill Paxon of New York (a leader of the cadre that opposed Joe DioGuardi) praised Laughlin for "the courage, the strength, the tenacity he showed in his decision to join the Republican Party."

Payton, Paul's campaign consultant, reflected, "Greg Laughlin didn't have any issues in that campaign, which is one of the reasons he foundered. I'm not sure that he knew what to say when he was running in the Republican primary. . . . I think his motivation might have been, he thought he might have been able to beat Ron easier in a primary than in a general election."

Payton added, "You have to understand Texas Republican primaries. They are basically low-turnout events. The people who show up at the polls are the true hard-core believers. I mean the John Birchers and the Christian Coalition. The country-club Republicans kind of waited out until the general election."

He continued, "Of the five [House] Democrats to switch parties that year, he was the least conservative. While he was a party switcher, he still had an obligation to prove that he was a genuine conservative. If he had spent half of that money [Laughlin spent about $500,000] showing Republicans how conservative he was, he probably would have won. But he spent it all attacking Ron. . . . [Voters] cared a lot more about who the real conservative was than about the drug issue." (Harry Truman said that given a choice between a real and an imitation Republican, voters will choose the real one every time.)

Meanwhile, Charles "Lefty" Morris, the Democratic nominee, was a delighted spectator of the GOP blood feud. He seemingly had been handed a gift, an opponent whose "extremist" views surely would be rejected by what he saw as "the mainstream form of conservatism" held by the people of the Fourteenth District. Calling himself a "conservative Democrat," Morris sat back and watched the Republican establishment agonize over what to do about the winner of their primary.

Their distress duplicated what followed Oliver North's Senate nomination in Virginia. Party leaders did not want to lose the seat to a Democrat, but at the same time, they did not want to embrace what *Congressional Quarterly* decorously called Paul's "politically quirky" opinions. But the NRCCC spokesman swallowed hard and said that it was a "Republican seat and we will work to keep it a Republican seat."

As it happened, Paul won not so much with official party help as with skill in the TV politics of personal attack. Morris was a wealthy trial lawyer from the Austin area. Paul called him a "liberal lawyer lobbyist"—a devastatingly alliterative triple epithet. Mindful that plaintiffs' attorneys are unpopular, Morris excluded from his campaign literature the fact that he was a former president of the Texas Trial Lawyers' Association. Paul ran TV ads charging that Morris had "made millions on frivolous lawsuits" and furthermore would raise taxes.

Morris was laden with a politically unfortunate boyhood nickname of "Lefty," but he countered with red and white signs bearing the slogan, "Lefty is Right!" He adopted Laughlin's offensive game plan— Paul would legalize drugs, pornography, and prostitution. Paul objected that he merely wanted these matters left up to the states, but Morris's oppo researchers uncovered a video clip of Paul voicing support for legalizing drugs. Morris said the central issue now was Paul's credibility. "Ron Paul wants to abandon the federal government. I want to fix it," Morris said. This election could have been a competition of libertarian against standard conservative ideas in a district hospitable to both schools of thought. Both candidates are at fault for making it a contest of personal attacks.

Morris got a soft-money contribution via "issues advocacy" ads from the AFL-CIO, which criticized Paul's stands on pensions and federal aid to education. Big labor spent $35 million in House races across the country in 1996. At least in the Texas Fourteenth, the money was wasted, for organized labor was a negligible force there.

Paul augmented his media assault with old-fashioned, shoe-leather campaigning, which once took him to the village of Smithville. As late as 1996, the yellow-dog Democratic town had never before witnessed a Republican rally. Paul recited his Washington "perpetually takes our money, etc." line and called Morris a tax-and-spender.

As for Morris, he did not stop with the drugs, pornography, and prostitution issues, but added that Paul also would abolish Social Security, Medicare, the Internal Revenue Service, and public education. In most areas, these charges could have been fatal. In the Fourteenth, they were not, and indeed Paul's libertarian views exemplify how once-radical ideas gradually blend into the American mainstream. The 105th Congress to which Paul was elected seriously discussed privatizing part of Social Security and providing vouchers for parents to choose public or private schools. Scrapping the IRS tax code was a pet project of Majority Leader Armey. (Another Paul plank, term limits for members of Congress, remains adamantly and ferociously opposed by most incumbents.)

Taking a leaf from the campaign handbook of many challengers, Morris advocated campaign financial reform and refused contributions from PACs. But as the *Almanac of American Politics* dryly remarked, "Trial lawyers don't need them; they have lots of money themselves." Morris spent $979,070, including $266,000 in personal loans to his campaign, to Paul's $1.9 million. The election was close—51 percent for Paul, 48 percent for Morris.

Once back in Washington, Paul lost little time in making a sensation. He said on C-SPAN, "I fear and there's a lot of people in the country who fear that they may be bombed by the federal government at another Waco." In 1993 federal agents assaulted the compound of the Branch Davidian religious cult in Waco, Texas, resulting in the death by fire of sixty-two adults and nineteen children. (Whatever one's opinion of this event, it could have been handled better by President Clinton and Attorney General Janet Reno.) Paul's view was that "an irresponsible federal government has innocent blood on its hands."

The Democratic congressman who represents Waco denounced these remarks on the House floor as "sheer lunacy at best." Majority Whip DeLay scolded that congressman for neglecting to notify Paul in advance, so that Paul might have the courtesy of a reply. More than a defense of Paul, DeLay's action illustrated how seriously congressional leaders take breaches of parliamentary decorum, how they often value procedure over substance. Actually, the GOP leadership regarded Paul as an embarrassment to the party. For his part, Paul disdained to explain his Waco opinions on the floor when he later had an opportunity.

The C-SPAN interview invited pundits to associate Paul with right-wing private militias and survivalists and even the 1995 terrorist bombing of the federal building in Oklahoma City. Paul did not back down but instead billboarded the attacks in fund-raising letters to conservative groups. Representative Martin Frost of Texas, chairman of the Democratic Congressional Campaign Committee, called the Fourteenth "our number one challenge race in the state of Texas" for 1998. The Gingrich leadership cast about for respectable alternatives to Paul, secretly offering financial backing to potential primary challengers.

But the effort failed, and Paul was opposed only by three Republican nobodies who spent a combined total of $4,894. In November, Paul's opponent was "conservative Democrat" Loy Sneary, a former county judge. Paul outspent him by nearly two to one and won 55 percent of the vote. However radical his views, Paul now comfortably resides in the Incumbency Hotel.

11

IDAHO

WALTER MINNICK (D) v. SENATOR LARRY CRAIG (R)

Senator Bob Kerrey of Nebraska, a singular figure on the national stage, was jogging in Washington one day in the spring of 1997 with a new friend, Walter Minnick. Kerrey runs with a prosthesis because during a 1969 combat mission in Vietnam a grenade blew off his right leg below the knee. Despite his wound, he led his Navy SEAL platoon out of danger. He is the first senator to hold the Congressional Medal of Honor since the Civil War era. As they jogged, Kerrey and Minnick talked about the recent 1996 senatorial elections.

Five years earlier, Kerrey briefly had challenged Bill Clinton for the Democratic presidential nomination. Then, like President Clinton, Kerrey was stunned by the Republican capture of Congress in 1994. When the news sank in, the Clinton White House feared a possible challenge from Kerrey or other dissident Democrats in the presidential primaries of 1996.

The White House was relieved when Kerrey agreed in 1995 to head the Democratic Senatorial Campaign Committee (DSCC). This post presumably would keep him out of the 1996 presidential race while offering a perch from which to collect political IOUs for a potential presidential run in 2000. (In December 1998, Kerrey decided not to be a candidate in 2000.)

Kerrey was not an entrenched incumbent of the sort who usually gets the DSCC chair. An amazingly popular Nebraska governor in the 1980s, he became a controversial, idiosyncratic senator. As a first-termer, Kerrey had his own re-election scare from a citizen-challenger during the Republican rout of 1994. Although he outspent his GOP opponent by nearly three to one, he won the election by a margin of ten percentage points, a close call by his standards.

His later supervision of the 1996 Democratic senatorial campaigns was shrewd—though in the end ineffective. Kerry's strategy was to re-cruit centrist, wealthy candidates who could help finance their own campaigns and, equally as important, avoid the "tax-and-spend liberal" epithet. He found such candidates in five states. One of them was Wal-ter Minnick in Idaho.

"You know, Walt," Kerrey told Minnick as they jogged along Wash-ington streets, "yours was the race I felt worst about losing."

Minnick mused later, "I don't know whether he felt sorrier for himself or for me. He thought that my life might be a hell of a lot better being in the nursery business than his was on Capitol Hill." Thus did Kerrey, a politician who is somewhat an antipolitician, express his frus-tration with the system. He might have regretted dragging Minnick into it.

Walter C. Minnick was born in Walla Walla, Washington, in 1942. He went east to Harvard to earn degrees in business administration and law. Despite these elite credentials, he maintained an easy-going, boy-next-door manner. Minnick practiced law briefly in Portland, Oregon, then joined the Nixon White House as a staffer in the Domestic Coun-cil and the Office of Management and Budget.

While driving to work one morning in 1973, Minnick heard on the car radio about the "Saturday Night Massacre" in which Attorney Gen-eral Elliott Richardson resigned rather than fire special prosecutor Ar-chibald Cox on Nixon's orders. "I had worked directly and closely with Richardson on drug policy, admired him greatly, and was furious," Minnick said. Upon reaching his office in the Old Executive Office Building, he called his wife and told her, "Start packing, we're heading west. I can't work for that man [Nixon] any longer."

Six months later, Minnick was a management trainee building trusses on a production crew at Trus Joist Corporation (TJI), a high-tech building materials firm in Boise, Idaho. Within a decade, he was its CEO.

In the mid-1970s Minnick abandoned the Republican Party because it was too conservative for him—a party switch he had in common with

Kerrey, who left the GOP to run for governor as a Democrat in 1982. In considering the 1996 senatorial race, neither man underestimated the difficulty faced by a Democrat challenging Republican Senator Larry Craig in Idaho, in recent years a solidly GOP state. As Richard Stallings, an Idaho Democratic congressional candidate in 1998, re-marked, "Republicans could run a cadaver in this state and start out with about 41 percent [of the vote]." Insiders joked that the state's license-plate motto, "Famous Potatoes," should be replaced by, "Relia-bly Republican." Minnick usually introduced himself as "an independ-ent running on the Democratic ticket."

Senator Craig was born in 1945 on an Idaho ranch homesteaded by his grandfather. Craig called himself a rancher, though he entered poli-tics at age twenty-nine, winning election to the Idaho Senate in 1974. He went to the U.S. House in 1980 and ten years later was elevated to the Senate, where he was in the running for the title of the body's most conservative member. The first-termer was perhaps a bit too far to the right even for Idaho. In May 1996, a poll showed his unfavorability rat-ing was 25 percent, moderately high for an incumbent, while Min-nick's—who was scarcely known—was only 8 percent.

Obviously, the senator's task was to "drive up Minnick's negatives." He succeeded. The Minnick/Craig race—even though it occurred in a remote, sparsely populated state—offers a primary illustration of the power of money and media and the politics of personal destruction. Also, it is an example of the secondary importance of ideology, or rather the confusion, both deliberate and incidental, of ideological principles wrought by campaigns. Further, in this age when party organizations supposedly have been eclipsed by the media, it was in effect a proxy fight between the national Democratic and Republican senatorial cam-paign committees. Idaho prides itself on its distance and independence from Washington, D.C. Its Senate contest had no such quality.

Having seen the political process from inside both a Republican White House and a Democratic senatorial campaign, and having now renounced politics, Minnick is more candid than many unsuccessful challengers. He said, "The biggest change we need is campaign finance reform. It is the most important reform we need if we are going to maintain a democracy. We need to dramatically reduce the cost of cam-paigns. We need to reduce the dependence of candidates on special-interest money.

"Democrats are just as bad as Republicans. If you are a Democrat, you have to sell your soul to organized labor, the trial lawyers, and the

Jewish community. If you are a Republican, you have to sell your soul to the cigarette companies and the natural resources industries.

"Anybody who tells you contributions only buy access [to lawmakers, as opposed to outright influence] has not filled out PAC questionnaires." These forms asking about the candidates' stands on special-interest issues are detailed and specific. The PACs are merciless toward those who do not fill them out satisfactorily.

In May 1996, Craig and Minnick won their respective primaries unopposed. At the time, Craig already had spent more than $1 million on his campaign and had another half-million in the bank. Minnick had spent $340,000, had another $300,000 in the bank, and planned to devote an additional half-million of his own fortune to the race. Like other wealthy citizen-challengers, he underestimated the size of the personal check he would end up writing.

Craig, unlike other incumbents who remain somnolent through an election-year summer, understood the magnitude of the challenge from the start. Minnick, a "green" candidate whose corporation used recycled wood products, not timber harvested from clear-cutting of old-growth forests, quickly put Craig on the defensive, a stance that politicians naturally abhor.

In the Rocky Mountain West there are two salient issues—natural resources and energy. On these matters, Craig stood at the far right. Any casual observer can see that the West is overgrazed by cattle, but Craig fiercely opposed the Clinton administration's (failed) effort to increase grazing fees on public lands. He also fought the administration's (failed) attempt to rewrite the Mining Act of 1872, an incredible giveaway to hard-rock mineral extractors.

On these measures, Craig took the popular western position. But in other areas, he was perhaps extreme. Craig despised the Endangered Species Act and also moved to allow the states (with congressional approval) to take over territory governed by the National Forest Service and the Bureau of Land Management. This would be no mere bureaucratic transfer. The federal government holds title to 65 percent of Idaho's land mass. If Boise rather than Washington controlled this immensity, the timber and mining industries might exploit natural resources with the unregulated zeal of the legendary nineteenth-century robber barons.

Wildlife, timber, and mining were important enough concerns, but Minnick thought he also had a winning issue with a modern dilemma, the storage ("dumping") of radioactive wastes from nuclear power plants. The U.S. Energy Department had been collecting many of these materials, which remain toxic for thousands of years, at the huge Idaho National Environmental Engineering Laboratory (INEEL) in eastern Idaho: Republican and Mormon country.

In 1988, Democratic Governor Cecil Andrus, who had been President Jimmy Carter's secretary of the interior, single-handedly refused to accept any more shipments of nuclear waste to Idaho. Predictable lawsuits ensued. Three lawsuits later, a federal judge barred such shipments, in effect upholding the governor's action, until an environmental study might show that they were safe.

Such complex, technical court contests normally take years. Surprisingly, within months the government came back with its analysis demonstrating that the dumping was safe. This was not just a problem for the Department of Energy. The U.S. Navy also was lobbying for congressional support for Idaho storage of nuclear-powered submarine and aircraft carrier wastes so that those ships could get back on patrol.

Facing these two mighty federal institutions, the new Republican governor, Phil Batt, cut a deal with the Department of Energy in 1995. The feds had proposed placing 190 tons of radioactive debris at INEEL in less than forty years. Barr agreed to accept 110 tons over the next forty years, in return for a federal commitment to clean up the site and get most of the waste out of Idaho by 2035. The materials would be removed to a "temporary" site at Yucca Mountain, Nevada, and perhaps elsewhere—with "elsewhere" unspecified.

Of course, the Nevada congressional delegation was not thrilled with this arrangement. Craig and others passed a Senate bill creating the Yucca Mountain dump, but it died in the House with the help of a promised Clinton veto. The president had little to lose by pleasing antinuke environmentalists while snubbing a Republican state, Idaho.

Senator Craig was "for" the Batt plan in the sense that he would support any deal struck by his GOP governor that eventually would get toxic wastes and (in his eyes) part of the equally toxic federal government out of Idaho. Somewhat to both men's surprise, the plan provoked fierce in-state opposition because it allowed too much radioactive debris to sully Idaho over the next four decades.

The movie actor Bruce Willis was one of a cohort of Hollywood entertainers who were establishing residences in Idaho for its scenery and frontier spirit. Willis and other celebrity advocates of the "no nukes" movement of the 1970s and 1980s fought the Batt plan. A group called Stop the Shipments sprang up and managed to place a referendum on the question on the November ballot. Western politics thus is becoming largely a contest of greens against traditionalists. In this struggle,

the historical labels of Democratic and Republican, liberal and conservative, are often unhelpful.

Minnick came out for Stop the Shipments and accused Craig of abet-
ting nuclear waste dumping in Idaho over the years. "All we are doing,"
he said, "is riding the very tracks that Republicans have laid down over
the years. 'Don't trust the federal government,' they say. We don't."

Craig's response was acrimonious. The race was not a case of the incumbent dominating the airwaves with negative ads, for both sides had
the cash to scarf up every available TV ad minute in a small-market
state. Craig's stategy perplexed a Boise State University academic, who
said, "Craig did Minnick a favor in starting to attack him by name in his
ads in late summer. . . . It's one thing to run scared, but it's another to
give your opponent the kind of publicity Craig did in some of his ads.
That doesn't make a lot of sense."

It made perfect sense. By conjoining Minnick with Stop the Shipments, the incumbent in effect nationalized the election, making it a
referendum on out-of-state liberals, funded by green "extremists,"
against traditional westerners, sons and daughters of the timber, mining, ranching, and energy industries. In addition, Craig's maneuver
made the election a referendum on President Clinton, who, while
coasting to an easy re-election over Bob Dole, remained supremely unpopular in Idaho. It was Clinton who said, in effect, that Idaho had to
keep swallowing toxic wastes.

Rendering the state election as a referendum on the president and on
national green endeavors was not just a subtle abstraction. Craig made
sure it was explicit. He ran a radio ad featuring a narrator who imper-
sonated Clinton's voice, saying it was all right for Minnick to falsify
Craig's record on the nuclear dumping issue.

It is a sad commentary on modern media politics that the broadcast
ads in the 1996 Idaho senator's race only compounded voter confusion
on a complex issue: the disposal of nuclear wastes. Each side accused the
other, with some justice, of smear tactics.

Craig, challenged to ten debates, agreed to appear at two. This grudg-
ing acceptance was a telling sign that the incumbent felt vulnerable and
that he needed to fight on every front—a Democratic poll in early October found the race statistically even. During the first debate, Minnick said
the waste should stay where it is—at nuke plants around the country—
until a permanent site is designated, thus sparing Idaho the dangers of an
interim depository. He said, "We should leave it where it is until we can
ship it to a permanent nuclear waste storage site."

Craig's campaign quickly produced an ad that edited Minnick's quote to say only, "We should leave it where it is"—period. This deception enabled Craig to charge that the challenger offered no solution to a troublesome problem.

The senator, one of only two incumbents who agreed to answer questions submitted by the authors of this book, still insists that the ad was fair. "Throughout the campaign, Minnick had no plan for removal of the nuclear waste that has been temporarily stored at INEEL," he said. "He opposed the sites we proposed for interim and permanent storage. . . . His comments during the debate were a clear reflection of his opposition to any proposed plan, while failing to outlilne any proposal of his own, throughout the campaign."

Minnick responded to the ad by becoming the first to directly call his opponent a liar—a political blunder. Maybe the "Lying Larry" alliteration was irresistible. But most political consultants tell their candidates never to accuse their opponent of outright lying. The word is so emotionally charged that it can only backfire against the accuser. In fact, under the mythical "code of the West," calling a man a liar to his face is to challenge him to a fight, by fists or other weapons—the equivalent of a gentleman taking off a glove and slapping it across an enemy's face in the ancient times of dueling. The consultants say to use euphemisms such as gross distortions or misrepresentations of the facts or underhanded falsehoods and so forth, but not, "you liar."

Craig soon assumed the innocent pose taken by Charles Robb and other threatened incumbents. Undertaking a statewide bus tour, he said, "It's always tragic when campaigns go negative." Later, he said in wide-eyed wonderment, "I've never had any opponent openly and intentionally spread falsehoods."

Actually, his own advertising campaign deceptively shifted him ever greener. He abandoned his previous demands to disarm the agents of the federal Fish and Wildlife Service—an emotional issue in the West, where federal agents sometimes need firearms in confrontations with survivalists and private militias. Craig also shelved his "War on the West" slogan about environmental regulations. His TV ad crew featured him white-water rafting down the Snake River—an image as unlikely as Dan Rostenkowski bungee jumping. Craig was far from a rafter, backpacker, rock climber, or other form of yuppie outdoorsman.

The Snake River commercial proved that no state is safe from the professional manipulators of media imagery. In mid-October, a poll found that Minnick's negative rating had risen to 33 percent.

In a parallel to Craig's white-water outing, Minnick produced an ad showing himself with a hunting rifle, an unexpected pose for a leading member of the Wilderness Society. "I was the industrialist on the Wilderness Society board and the conservationist in industry groups," he said in attempting to explain a posture that did not lend itself to easy sloganeering.

The rifle-bearing commercial was meant to counter opposition from the National Rifle Association, which favored Craig, who sat on the organization's board and was a ferocious opponent of gun control. Early in his term, he had derided California Senator Dianne Feinstein's knowledge of firearms, a debating thrust she demolished with the comment that she had learned everything she needed to know about guns when she discovered the body of the mayor of San Francisco, fatally shot in city hall by a city councilman in 1978. On another occasion, Craig told an Idaho audience, "Easterners should stop interfering with environmental issues. It isn't a New York City problem. The only endangered species in New York City is probably a free white human being." He promptly retracted this violation of political correctness, but neither the Feinstein sally nor the "free white" remark apparently hurt him in Idaho.

The same academic who had misunderstood Craig's publicizing of Minnick in his early TV ads commented late in the election season, "The only way a Democrat can win this race is to run as a moderate Republican." Whether this was true or not, Minnick ran to the left of Craig on the environment, but to the right on such red-meat GOP issues as requiring a balanced federal budget and imposing term limits on House and Senate members. Craig was a typical Republican incumbent in that he was "for" these restrictions at some point, but not right away. In the meantime, Craig was supported both by the NRA and the Christian Coalition, which were decisive in Idaho, unlike in the races of Oliver North and Jim Miller—nonincumbents—in Virginia.

Minnick in turn was opposed by the NRA, the Christian Coalition, and even, for what it is worth, organized labor—not a strong force in Idaho, but a national source of campaign cash. Labor spurned the Democratic nominee because he had backed a "right-to-work" initiative in the 1980s, an effort to outlaw closed union shops or what their opponents call "compulsory unionism," even though the GOP incumbent's prolabor voting record was precisely zero. Meanwhile, the heavily Republican Boise business and media establishments were raising money and beating the drums for Governor Batt's campaign against the Stop the Shipments initiative—the issue quickly had turned from technical to partisan. Further, the incessant, warring personal attack ads were turning off voters. Callers to KIDO, the state's major talk-radio station, expressed their disgust with the entire campaign.

On October 24, twelve days before the election, Minnick made a rare, perhaps unique, decision. He announced that he would unilaterally pull off TV all his negative ads that called Craig a puppet of the timber, mining, and nuclear industries. There was no corresponding move by his opponent. Senator Bob Kerrey, the by-now distraught chair of the Democratic Senatorial Campaign Committee, with polls indicating that continued Republican control of the Senate was a certainty, instantly got on the phone and told Minnick he was bound to lose if he did this. The challenger's consultant said the same thing.

Minnick replied, "It's more important to me that I can walk down the street any place in Idaho after the election and people regard me as a man of principle and integrity, that I've run a good positive campaign, even if it should cost me the election."

Later, Minnick said, "Despite what Kerrey and my Washington-based media consultant told me in no uncertain terms about the consequence of pulling my negative ads, I honestly thought it would help my campaign. According to my polling, at that point I was less than 5 points behind Senator Craig with 17 percent still undecided. . . . Based on the feedback I was getting while campaigning—both from 'friends' in the press and ordinary voters—I believed my decision would have a significant positive influence on the 17 percent still undecided."

Minnick said he "steadfastly believed right through election night" that Craig's staying negative "would backfire on him and push me over the top. As it turned out, it was I, not the professionals, who was wrong." His experiment in clean politics ended with the same result as Cliff Arnebeck's effort to run a barely funded campaign on the issues in Ohio.

Craig, asked whether he had considered dropping his negative commercials in turn, said, "Minnick did not pull his negative ads twelve days before the election." (Ads that had already been paid for continued to run for a few days.) "Voters continued to receive, see, and hear negative materials from Minnick or his surrogates up until the last day of the campaign."

Mike Tracy, a top Craig staffer in Boise, said, "To accuse us of dirty tricks is almost laughable. One of his people flipped a lit cigarette into one of our people's faces. Little things like that." Tracy also said that Minnick's campaign manager, "another one of those non-Idahoans," patrolled church parking lots on the Sunday before the election to remove right-to-life brochures placed under parishioners' windshield wipers. "She was forced to apologize for it."

Thus, the pace and emotional intensity of campaigns drive both sides to spend as much money as possible and succumb to practices they might not dream of indulging in other areas of their lives. Back in an early stage of the campaign, Minnick had proposed that both candidates refuse PAC contributions and voluntarily limit their spending to $1 million each. Craig disregarded this, just as he ignored Minnick's withdrawal of negative ads, and continued to campaign negatively and aggressively.

For example, while in the town of Julietta, he came upon a woman wearing a "Hells Canyon Mule Days" T-shirt, who, spying the approach of a despised politician, tried to duck into the back room of a tavern called the First Bank of Pizza. Craig accosted her before she made her getaway, and she said with a nervous grin, "I was just going to clean the cooler." Craig said loudly enough for all the bar's patrons to hear, "I've been known to hunt people down in coolers." The unspoken subtext of this remark was: Your government's incumbency is irresistible.

Craig won 57 percent of the vote to 40 percent for Minnick, who carried just three counties, although their spending was not all that far apart—approximately $3 million for Craig to $2.1 million for Minnick, who spent $945,000 of his own money. Add the soft money spent by national parties and advocacy groups and the tally might approach roughly $4 million for each candidate, or a total of $11 for each registered voter in Idaho.

The surprising aspect of the election is that 497,233 voters went to the polls—71 percent of the registrants. The exceptionally high turnout in this era of low voter participation is explained by factors that do not show up on Federal Election Commission candidate financial disclosures. Hidden, soft-money expenditures were not foreseen by the well-intentioned reformers of the 1970s.

The Idaho race followed the usual pattern of well-funded challengers running competitively in the polls roughly six to four weeks before their primary or general elections, followed by their defeat by a substantial margin at the ballot box after the power structure closes ranks. Minnick said, "We both had polls that showed the race in the single digits . . . I ended up losing by 17 percent. The campaign became nationalized. That was devastating to me."

In a sense, the race was nationalized from the start, when Kerrey recruited Minnick to run. It was nationalized in the end by interest groups tied to the Republican Party (guns, business, the religious right) that were more focused in targeting voters than advocacy organizations linked to Democrats (greens, pro-choice, but—not in this case— labor). The new professional class of campaign consultants, and their technicians who target individual voters by Zip code, precinct, and street address, probably gave the incumbent his victory—or at least accounted for his landslide margin.

In the final ten days, a half-million dollars of Republican funds dropped into Idaho. This was soft money put up by the tobacco industry and other GOP client groups and was used to purchase—not televisions ads—but efforts to identify, register at the last minute, and drive to the polls sympathetic voters. Idaho is one of the few states allowing voters to register on election day. This fact enabled the Craig forces to run an eleventh-hour "stealth" operation that Idaho Democrats scarcely could recognize, let alone counter.

Craig condemned Minnick as the candidate of Hollywood and New York, but his own campaign was propped up by out-of-staters. The GOP retained a Washington-based telemarketing firm to call every phone number in Idaho in order to identify potential Craig supporters. The resulting rosters were handed out to precinct cadres organized into poll watchers, phone-bank workers, drivers, and even baby sitters for voters. "The NRA and the Christian Coalition identified a lot of voters and got them to the polls," Minnick said. "I didn't understand until after the election was over the significance of this field effort."

Like Paul Coverdell in Georgia, Craig also capitalized on the GOP's superior skill in using direct mail. "The Republican Party has very good access to single-issue mailing lists," Minnick said. "Whether it be farmers interested in irrigation water subsidies, or right-to-life activists, or NRA members, or any of a number of others.

"One of the techniques that was used was, I guess half-a-million or a million pieces were mailed to these issue groups early enough to hit before the election, but too late to respond to. It was tailored to the interest group. . . . I was alleged to be in favor of banning all guns, when in fact I scored as well on the NRA [questionnaire] as he did. I was alleged to the agriculture industry to be in favor of dynamiting all the dams, which would have eliminated all of Idaho's water system supply. I was alleged to be in favor of murdering babies and no restriction on partial-birth abortions, which in fact that was the opposite of my position. The content of the mailing was designed to be inflammatory. . . . We ID'd [only] 20 percent of the voters and our get-out-the-vote was pretty haphazard."

A contemporary myth is that negative TV ads determine the outcome of elections, but the Craig and Minnick spots might have just canceled each other out while alienating casual voters and keeping them home on election day. This race was decided by committed single-issue voters, a dominant Republican Party structure, the influence of the Idaho print media, and unforeseen consequences of the Watergate-era campaign financial and disclosure reforms.

"I was the CEO of one of Idaho's largest public companies," Minnick said. "My business friends told me time and again that they couldn't afford to be on my contributors' list. There is a real price to be paid in a Republican state like Idaho if you appear on a Democrat contributor list.

"There were a number of people who crossed over [in 1994] to support the Democratic gubernatorial candidate [against Batt], and there was hell to pay. Our Republican governor was very vindictive. Almost every businessman in the state does business with the state or federal government, or thinks he or she might in the future. . . . I found it much easier to raise money out-of-state than in-state."

He added, "The publisher of the Gannett [publishing chain] paper basically lives or dies on the advertising in the Boise market. I got very little on the front page of the papers, except for the *Lewiston Tribune* and the *Idaho Falls Press-Tribune*, which bent over backwards to ensure that I got a fair shake.

"The business structure was all against me. Most of the newspaper publishers—either because they felt that way or because of the nature of the business—were strongly predisposed to be supportive of the Republican establishment."

Besides Minnick, Kerrey's millionaire centrist candidates in Colorado, Kansas, Oregon, and Virginia also lost their 1996 campaigns.

The issue of disposing of toxic waste—both spent nuclear fuel and items such as irradiated clothing and tools—remains unresolved. The first barrel of a certain form of nuclear debris did not leave Idaho until the end of April 1999. As of early 1999, Congress still had not approved the Yucca Mountain site, although the government continued to spend billions of dollars to develop and test it. Craig warned the Clinton administration that he would hold Yucca Mountain and another site at the southeast corner of New Mexico hostage to Clinton's attempt to win Senate approval of the proposed Kyoto treaty to curb "global warming."

12

OREGON

HARRY LONSDALE (D) v. SENATOR MARK HATFIELD (R), REPRESENTATIVE LES AUCOIN (D), AND TOM BRUGGERE (D)

Challengers have many motivations for running against incumbents. For Harry Lonsdale, it initially was a single Ponderosa pine tree.

Lonsdale was a fly fisherman before the sport came into yuppie vogue. He also was both a wealthy businessman and an ardent environmentalist—a hybrid almost unknown in the East but found here and there in the West, where the management of natural resources is an overriding public concern.

Lonsdale tramped the banks of the Metolius River in central Oregon one day in 1987, heading for one of his favorite fishing holes. The scenery was fit for a Sierra Club calendar shot—icy-blue water, majestic forest—except that an element was missing, something Longdale could not quite identify, a vexing absence. As he neared his objective he finally placed it: A personal landmark, a towering Ponderosa pine, was gone.

He hiked to the stump, sunlit through the hole now bored into the forest canopy, and saw that it was scarred and scorched by chainsaw tracks. How could this happen on public land? Lonsdale was perplexed and troubled.

If he could be faulted for naiveté, consider that this was in 1987, three years before the U.S. Fish and Wildlife Service declared the spotted owl an endangered species and before subsequent court rulings banned further logging in many old-growth tracts of the national forests. The spotted owl quickly became a polarizing symbol in a war between the timber industry and environmentalists.

Unwittingly, Lonsdale was a soldier in this war, for he was helping to lead Oregon away from its dependence on the boom-and-bust cycles of the forestry industry and toward the new high-technology economy of the entire Pacific Rim. Although his campaign was not cast in just this light, Lonsdale represented the high-tech future while his opponent, Senator Mark O. Hatfield, represented the historical exploitation of natural resources.

Lonsdale, born in New Jersey in 1932, earned a doctorate in physical chemistry at Pennsylvania State University in 1957; served as an air force officer stationed in the United States; and worked as a scientist in California, West Germany, and Israel. In 1975, he moved to Bend, Oregon, on the high dry plains east of the Cascade Mountains, and founded Bend Research, Inc. The firm and its spinoff companies now employ more than 200 people. A family man with two grown children, Lonsdale has nearly 100 scientific papers and patents under his name. But in politics, he was unschooled.

After his fishing trip, Lonsdale determined to find out whether that Ponderosa pine had been legally cut down. His ensuing frustrations would be familiar to anyone who has tried to penetrate the federal bureaucracy. The local office of the National Forest Service said the Metolius River woods were being harvested by a huge timber company. On whose authority? Why, the U.S. government, with taxpayers everywhere subsidizing the operation by building logging roads. By whose decision? Well, the Forest Service was a branch of the Department of Agriculture, whose purse strings were controlled by the Senate Appropriations Committee, on which the ranking Republican was none other than Senator Hatfield of Oregon.

In effect, Hatfield alone dictated how much publicly owned Oregon timber could be felled by Georgia Pacific, Weyerhauser, Louisiana Pacific, and other firms. These companies for decades had contributed large amounts to Hatfield's election campaigns. He had been a senator for twenty-four years, governor for eight years before that, and Oregon secretary of state for two years prior to that.

Lonsdale soon educated himself about the forestry industry and concluded that the United States was like a colony that ships a raw material overseas, where developed countries process it into finished goods at a profit. Oregon (and also Washington state and Alaskan) trees were being cut down with taxpayer aid and sent unmilled to foreign powers such as Japan that lacked native forests. The Japanese then stockpiled mountains of cut-rate American timber against future shortages.

Lonsdale wrote to Hatfield seeking an explanation. The reply, probably a staffer's form letter, said—in so many words—that this is an extremely complex issue and do not worry about it because it is being well managed by experts such as Senator Hatfield.

Like any successful entrepreneur, Lonsdale was an aggressive type who believed the best way to get something done was to do it yourself. If the status quo led by Hatfield was wrong, then run against him.

Typically for challengers, Lonsdale's decision was audacious and perhaps foolish. Like Ted Kennedy in Massachusetts or Strom Thurmond in South Carolina, Hatfield was viewed not just as a public official but as a personification of his state, an embodiment of its qualities and the epicenter of its power. Hatfield *fitted* Oregon, one of the most culturally liberal states. Throughout the American foreign wars of his era (1967–97), he was probably the most consistently dovish senator of either party. Perhaps more gratifying to his constituents, he did not let eastern powers push him around. He stood up for what he thought was best for Oregon.

When Lonsdale's tentative candidacy became known, the state's major newspaper, the *Portland Oregonian*, published a long article about Hatfield's U.S. Navy service in World War II. He had been one of the first Americans to visit Hiroshima after the atomic bomb was dropped. The timing of the story was curious because there was no conventional "news peg"—Memorial Day, Veterans Day, Pearl Harbor Day, or even a Hatfield speech to a veterans' group. Understandably, Lonsdale might have taken this as a token of media support for the incumbent.

Still, the challenger envisioned a series of debates with Hatfield thoughout the state. Television and newspapers would cover them, people would make an informed decision on election day, and if Hatfield won, well, Lonsdale would have sacrificed a year of his life for a cause he believed in.

But, of course, Hatfield refused to debate. A reporter commented that Hatfield never "ran" for election but rather, in the stately manner of candidates for the British Parliament, "stood" for office. A venerated figure, the incumbent saw no need to change his ways, especially since the Democratic establishment was turning its back on Lonsdale.

The Oregon Democratic Party, the Democratic National Committee, and the Democratic Senatorial Campaign Committee wished Lonsdale well and invited him to spend lots of his own money on his campaign, but they did not support him, institutionally or financially. It was not his anonymity as such that bothered Democrats. Mileage sometimes can be gained by putting forth a fresh face, a citizen-politician on fire to throw the rascals out. No, what troubled party leaders was that Lonsdale was a gate-crasher, a free agent who owed no favors to anyone. He thus held no passbook account in the political favor bank. He did not even live in or near Portland, the state's Big Apple.

For all his political inexperience, Lonsdale was not totally unacquainted with public life. Governor Neil Goldschmidt named him as chair of his Science Council from 1987–89. Lonsdale also promoted the Great Oregon Spring Cleanup, a roadside litter elimination drive, and the Oregon Rivers Initiative, meant to protect unspoiled rivers such as the Metolius. He also sat on the boards of the Oregon Business Council and the Oregon Peace Institute. In Chicago, he would have been called a "goo goo," a good-government type who adorns civic-betterment boards, which politicians love to empanel for public relations purposes while they go about the real business of politics: jobs, contracts, and egos. As for navigating the political shoals of a Senate campaign, Lonsdale knew next to nothing.

On a TV talk show, an Oregon newspaper publisher wondered whether Lonsdale had "the blood lust" needed to challenge Hatfield, who "can be—if he needs to be—one of the meanest people there is. He's a rough, tough infighter . . . quite a contrast to his public image." This was what, for example, Oliver North learned about Charles Robb, and what Harry Lonsdale eventually discovered about Mark Hatfield.

Naturally enough, Lonsdale first called on his friends. One was a veteran pol who told him, "Harry, you are going to be surprised, because if you do this, people whom you now count as friends will desert you, and people you don't even know will come out of nowhere to stand by you"—another lesson learned the hard way by many challengers. Some prominent names in the Portland power structure formed a Democrats for Hatfield Committee. This was to be expected. But then even organized labor came out against Lonsdale.

Labor held that a "green extremist" such as Lonsdale would create "ghost towns" by shutting down the forestry industry. The situation actually was much more complex. By shipping unmilled lumber overseas, the timber companies were by-passing Oregon mills anyway. Further, once the old-growth stands in the national forests were gone—harvested by "clear cutting" that denuded entire mountains—the industry would be reduced to tree farms. Such farms, with managed and modest annual harvests, would need few loggers. In any event, timber as a mainstay of the Oregon economy was fading. Instead of facing the issue head on, labor spent its energy in futile legislative efforts to prohibit the export of unmilled logs.

Undaunted, Lonsdale rented an empty storefront in downtown Portland, acquired some used furniture to occupy it, and got his campaign under way. Before long, he understood that he needed to hire the technicians of modern campaigns: the oppo researchers, pollsters, media consultants, and fund raisers.

A Democratic fund-raising consultant flew to Portland armed with a list of prominent national Democratic donors. He bullied Lonsdale to call complete strangers to ask for the $1,000 legal maximum, standing over his shoulder and whispering advice on how to "close the sale." Lonsdale found this regimen to be extremely distasteful, but the alternative was to deplete his own life savings.

He easily won the Democratic primary against five nobodies, capitalizing on the public's anti-incumbent mood by saying, "Twenty-four years in Washington has changed Mark Hatfield." Challenging from the left, Lonsdale attacked Hatfield for opposing abortion rights, and he also called him a "timber beast." Asked by a *New York Times* reporter why he was running, Lonsdale said simply: "The trees."

That summer, while Hatfield stayed blithely above the fray, the Lonsdale team went through the familiar internal drill of modern campaigns. The pollster assembled small "focus groups" of typical voters to ask their responses to this or that positive or negative image of the challenger or the incumbent. The candidate and staffers watched from behind a one-way mirror. In accord with the data, the media consultants then produced positive commercials to "get Harry's favorables up," along with attack ads to "drive Hatfield's negatives up."

Per standard procedure, the positive spots ran first to promote the challenger's name recognition and credibility. Then, the first attack ad was of a type known as a "velvet hammer." A mild-mannered Lonsdale mused on camera, "You know, I voted for Hatfield in the past, he's a nice guy and all, but he's been in Washington too long."

By Labor Day, Lonsdale had spent more than $700,000 of his own money for TV commercials. Still, Hatfield was unruffled. On October 4, though, the state's power structure was shocked by an *Oregonian* headline reporting a new poll: "Lonsdale Closing Gap, Just 6 Points Behind."

The establishment instantly closed ranks. The state's other GOP senator, Bob Packwood, loaned the Hatfield campaign his chief of staff to shake things up. The former chief of staff to Governor Goldschmidt—a Democrat—also moved into Republican Hatfield's headquarters. The governor staged joint appearances with the senator. Then on October 23 came another *Oregonian* headline: "Poll Puts Lonsdale Ahead of Hatfield."

Hatfield finally entered the fray, flying back from Washington to hold an angry news conference. Supposedly for the first time in his career, he mentioned his opponent by name. No longer, he said, would he be "a punching bag."

Privately, in a room with his media consultant, Hatfield screened Lonsdale's attack ads. With some justice, he complained, "Now, apparently we have to talk in thirty-second sound bites to survive." If the modern era of negative TV commercials began with the notorious "Daisy" spot in the 1964 presidential campaign depicting Senator Barry Goldwater as a mad nuclear bomber, Hatfield's political career, launched in 1950 with his election to the Oregon House, somehow had by-passed it. "This is the first major election in anybody's memory in which the virus of negative campaigning that we've seen in other areas has invaded Oregon," he lamented.

Not that Hatfield's campaign had been entirely virtuous. His chief of staff, Gerald Frank, wrote a weekly column, "Friday Surprise," for the *Oregonian*. Lonsdale cried foul but Hatfield's office, Frank, and the newspaper insisted the arrangement was perfectly ethical. Frank, then sixty-seven years old, was a millionaire heir of the Northwest's largest department store chain. Known as "Oregon's third senator," he had worked for Hatfield for twenty-three years. He held stock in three timber companies, had sat on the board of a failed savings and loan, and allegedly took personal trips at Senate staff expense. After a Lonsdale oppo person pointed out that several major donors to Hatfield's campaign were being puffed in Frank's columns, the column finally was suspended on October 5—and then only at Frank's insistence, not the paper's.

Meanwhile, Hatfield's oppo researchers found two former employees of Lonsdale's Bend Research firm who signed affidavits accusing the company of dumping wastewater containing toxic chemicals. Actually, the two had approached the senator's campaign weeks earlier but had been turned away. Now they were welcomed. By this maneuver, Hatfield took "his campaign from 1965 to 1990 in the space of three weeks," as one of his aides put it. The incumbent "went up negative" with TV ads spotlighting this allegation. The state Department of Environmental Quality had received no such complaints but, at Hatfield's private behest, investigated the matter. The agency gave Lonsdale's firm a clean bill of health . . . after the election.

Then there was the case of the Bhagwan Shree Rajneesh. The Indian guru had founded a commune, one in a long string in America's history of utopian religious communities, in the central Oregon desert in the 1980s. Conflicts between the commune and local authorities were predictable.

The Bhagwan was an eccentric individual. He had a fleet of personal Rolls-Royce automobiles given by followers, preached sexual libertinism, and mandated that commune members wear only rose or mauve "sunrise colors." Reporters requesting interviews were required first to bathe with unscented soap and shampoo because Rajneesh was ultrasensitive to aromas. The Bhagwan was so mystical that "time means nothing to me," he said, although he wore a diamond-studded Rolex watch.

Some of his disciples were accused of various crimes. In 1985, the Bhagwan pleaded guilty to immigration-law violations and was deported (he died in India in 1990). Lonsdale, in his "goo goo" posture, paid for a personal newspaper ad shortly after Rajneesh left the United States, saying the "harassment and abuse heaped on this gentle man is something that all of us, as freedom-loving Americans, can be ashamed of." Lonsdale said he merely had stood up for religious freedom against nativist prejudice, but Hatfield made the matter a campaign issue.

The Hatfield camp arranged a two-pronged media attack. A county judge who had been poisoned by Rajneesh disciples in an apparent assassination attempt in 1985 staged a press conference to release copies of Lonsdale's newspaper ad. Actually, Hatfield earlier had written Rajneesh a letter expressing much the same sentiments as Lonsdale. But Hatfield called his own press conference in Portland after the judge's. He said, "The issue isn't religious freedom, it's a question of judgment."

Lonsdale, in a challenger's desperate ploy, crashed Hatfield's press conference to demand that the senator debate him. "Mark Hatfield should reflect on his own failings before he criticizes my judgment," he said. The TV cameras loved the impromptu confrontation. The senator stumbled over his words and stalked away without responding.

Hatfield also brought First Lady Barbara Bush to Portland for a $100–a-plate breakfast for 1,100 people. Mrs. Bush lavished praise on Hatfield for pouring federal pork on Oregon, such as the Hatfield Marine Science Center at Newport.

The Democratic Senatorial Campaign Committee, awakened at last, dropped $217,000 on the Lonsdale campaign. Still, the challenger spent well over three times that amount of his own money. He refused

PAC funds, while Hatfield took the maximum $5,000 from groups as disparate as the McDonald's hamburger chain and the Texas Republican Congressional Committee.

Late on the night of October 30 or early on October 31, somebody pried open the kitchen door at Lonsdale's home twelve miles west of Bend and burglarized his office. Files were ransacked; computer disks containing information on Lonsdale campaign contributors and a computer were stolen, along with video and stereo equipment, a typewriter, and a telephone. Deschutes County sheriff's police investigated and found that two threatening phone calls earlier had been placed on Lonsdale's answering machine—far from an atypical occurrence for challengers.

Lonsdale took care to say, "I wouldn't want to accuse anybody of anything." His staffers demanded an independent investigation and the Hatfield campaign deplored any suggestion that it might be involved. On the Sunday before the Tuesday election, two young men who had no apparent connection with the Hatfield camp were arrested and charged with the break-in. Later court proceedings indicated that, despite the burglars' strange interest in Lonsdale campaign documents, it was indeed a routine crime, not politically motivated.

In any case, "the trees," Lonsdale's pet issue, did not decide the election. It turned instead on the familiar politics of character assassination, with the incumbent finding and exploiting two issues—one bogus, the alleged toxic dumping, and the other dubious, Lonsdale's public support of Rajneesh's religious freedom. Plus, as usual, the incumbent was propped up by the state's major media and the powers that be, including the White House. On November 6, 1990, Hatfield won 54 percent of the vote to Lonsdale's 46 percent.

Hatfield spent $2.7 million to Lonsdale's $1.5 million, nearly half of which was his own money. "This was a one-time shot for me," Lonsdale said. "I've lost and it's on to the future."

Not so. Lonsdale had campaigned in 1990 on the issue of saving the trees. He ran again in 1992 on the issue of the corrupt campaign financing system.

In 1992, Lonsdale's opponent in the Democratic primary was Representative Les AuCoin. The winner would challenge Republican Senator Bob Packwood. Lonsdale thought he had the upper hand because AuCoin was caught up in the scandal of the House bank, on which he had written eighty-three bad checks for about $61,000 (technically, they were overdrafts, not bounced checks; the public rightly refused to draw this lawyerly politician's hairsplitting distinction).

AuCoin, then forty-nine years old and a former public relations executive and journalist, was one of the Democratic "Watergate babies" thrust into Congress from traditionally Republican districts in 1974 following the resignation of President Richard Nixon. Indeed, he was the first Democrat to represent Oregon's First District.

AuCoin's campaigns against Lonsdale and Packwood provide perhaps even more lessons about the powers of incumbency than did Lonsdale's race against Hatfield. In an astonishing move, Packwood aired a TV ad against AuCoin even before the May 19 Democratic primary—a gross intervention in the other party's own business, meddling that normally is considered poor sportsmanship at best. Political insiders argued whether Packwood was trying to build up AuCoin in the belief that he would be easier to beat than Lonsdale, or, conversely, tearing down AuCoin because he thought Lonsdale would be a less formidable opponent. There was no argument over the cynicism of the manuever.

Either way, Lonsdale indirectly aided Packwood in the end by hammering on AuCoin's House bank misdeeds. Lonsdale said, "The guy can't balance his checkbook but he wants to play a larger role in balancing the nation's checkbook."

Also, he accused AuCoin of selling his vote on the B-2 "Stealth" bomber. A consistent dove who opposed the Persian Gulf War in 1991, the congressman had voted to fund the aircraft project after taking campaign money and speaking fees from defense contractors. AuCoin's convoluted explanation was that backing the B-2 was the only way to gain support for killing the MX missile program.

AuCoin countered by running TV ads blasting Lonsdale as an apologist for the Bhagwan Shree Rajneesh. Seven years after the commune fell apart, it still was an emotional issue in the state. Lonsdale was a "dangerous" political opportunist, the congressman said.

AuCoin represented Portland and some of the Oregon coast; the Portland Democratic establishment supported him. Still, on election night, the race was too close to call. A recount showed that AuCoin edged Lonsdale by just 330 votes out of 362,000 cast, or one-tenth of a percentage point.

Meanwhile, the Oregon Republican Party was bitterly split by the insurgency of the Christian right, which was pushing an antigay agenda. Packwood took no stand on the gay issue until after he succeeded in neutralizing any potential GOP primary opposition from the right. In the general election race against AuCoin, Packwood ran against the House bank issue and the spotted owl, calling his opponent a friend of "bugs and birds." He defeated AuCoin by 52 percent of the vote to 47 percent. He spent more than $8 million—amounting to $5.38 for each vote cast and far outpacing Senator Hatfield's $2.7 million in 1990—to AuCoin's $2.6 million.

The following years were not kind to either Packwood or Hatfield after their re-elections. On October 29, 1992, *Washington Post* reporters confronted Packwood with charges of sexual harassment from six women. Packwood pleaded for time to review his records and gather information about his accusers. Perhaps such an entreaty from a mere freshman senator or a challenger would not have been so honored. In any case, the *Post* told Packwood on October 31 it would not publish the allegations before election day.

They were made public three weeks later, with the *Post* noting the irony that Packwood, a champion of women's rights, should be so accused. The *Oregonian* had been developing the same story but decided not to publish it on the grounds that the charges were not proven. This situation prompted a local "in joke." The newpaper's slogan is, "If it is important to Oregonians, you will find it in the *Oregonian*." Democrats soon printed bumper stickers: "If it is important to Oregonians, you will find it in the *Washington Post*."

The Packwood scandal dragged out with typical Washington tedium. Ultimately, forty-eight women brought charges of harassment; the details were sordid. Not until September 1995, after the Senate Ethics Committee recommended that Packwood be expelled from the body, did he announce his resignation.

Hatfield, with his own scandal, was more forthcoming. The University of South Carolina had granted a full scholarship to his son. Hatfield had accepted artwork and air travel from the president of the university, without listing the donations on his disclosure statements. As a member of the Senate Finance Committee, Hatfield secured government aid to the school. He likewise arranged federal funds for the Oregon Health Sciences University, whose president personally admitted Hatfield's daughter to its medical school. The listing of the unreported gifts—a $3,875 Steuben glass cross, a $535 Steuben glass eagle, a $3,336 Audubon wild turkey print, $4,415 in forgiven interest on loans, $17,000 to enlarge his bedroom, and so forth—demeaned Hatfield as a senator holding his palm out to rich benefactors.

In August 1992, the Senate Ethics Committee rebuked Hatfield for taking nearly $43,000 in undisclosed gifts, although it found no direct link between the universities' actions and Hatfield's role in legislation. "My mistakes were many and my omissions serious," Hatfield said. It was a sad finale to a long and distinguished life of public service. He retired rather than run for re-election in 1996.

So, in 1996, Harry Lonsdale—perhaps feeling vindicated by the Hatfield and Packwood scandals—thought the third time would be the charm. He filed once again for the Democratic primary. His opponent was a self-made multimillionaire, Tom Bruggere, founder of a Portland software firm, hailed in a trade journal as a pioneer of the "electronic design automation industry." Bruggere was yet one more example of the fortunes made on the Pacific Rim in the go-go years of the 1980s and 1990s. He was an attractive candidate—a Vietnam veteran, he offered day care for working mothers at his firm and donated 1 percent of his company's profits to charity.

Unfortunately for Lonsdale, he could now be painted as a retread, a chronic candidate, and a sore loser. He no longer had a fresh face, forfeiting the media virtue of novelty. Bruggere won the primary, 50 percent to 25 percent. Lonsdale said AuCoin had outspent him by about three to one and Bruggere by about ten to one.

Bruggere lost the general election to Gordon H. Smith, the Republican president of the Oregon Senate. The two nonincumbents were about evenly matched on spending—$3.5 million for Smith, $3.3 million for Bruggere—and on votes—50 percent for Smith, 46 percent for Bruggere. In an "open seat" where no incumbent is running, both candidates have a fair chance. Nonetheless, the practicing politician— Smith in this case—holds the edge.

Lonsdale said, "I am frequently asked why anyone would run for major public office in the present political climate, in view of the vultures of the press, the loss of privacy, the need to raise enormous amounts of money, and all the rest.

"I have thus seen the power of campaign money from both sides [Republican and Democrat]. I have concluded that in elections where both candidates are financially competitive, positions on issues and one's personal background and character matter. However, if one candidate is well financed and the other candidate or candidates are not, none of that matters: money prevails."

Money prevails.

Lonsdale has concluded that the only way to keep special-interest money from controlling elections is through the public financing of campaigns. "I don't like having only millionaires serving in Congress, either," he said, "but between those people and PAC-funded and high-roller-funded ordinary people, I would take millionaires any day. At least they are not PAC-funded whores."

13

ALASKA

DAVID CUDDY (R) v.
SENATOR TED STEVENS (R)

In 1981, a young banker who was also then a state legislator liked to spend off hours jamming on keyboards with his rock band, "Enterprise." The combo enjoyed some local popularity and was invited to play at a wedding reception for a U.S. senator. The band and the guests were full of warm wishes for the senator and his bride, especially when they considered that his first wife had been killed in a 1978 plane crash, which the senator had survived. It was an ordinary scene except that it took place in an exotic locale, Alaska.

Alaskans are few, just 650,000 of them. The solitary big city, Anchorage, has a population of 260,000, roughly the size of Birmingham, Alabama, though the "borough" (county) in which Anchorage sits is bigger than Texas. Other Alaskans live in towns or in rural "Bush" villages or isolated cabins spread out over unimaginable immensity.

The movers and shakers of the Alaska establishment might number only 1,000 people or so, mostly in Anchorage, some in Fairbanks, plus a few leaders of the mostly oil-funded Native American corporations in the Bush. David Cuddy, who was that "Enterprise" keyboards player, was a son of this establishment. He might have believed that it would have treated him better than it did.

In a small polity, the exertions of the power elite to protect itself appear even more naked and raw than, say, those that Cliff Arnebeck confronted in Ohio. In Alaska, the establishment's maneuvers were egregious. At least that is what Cuddy's supporters believe after he mounted a 1996 election challenge against the bridegroom at that 1981 wedding reception: Senator Ted Stevens.

Born in 1923 in Indianapolis, the teenage Stevens went to live with an aunt in California, where he—the image is hard to visualize—learned to surf. In World War II, he flew C-46 cargo planes in China. He went to Alaska in 1950 after working his way through Harvard Law School by tending bar and selling his blood. Nearly his entire career has been spent on the public payroll, starting with the U.S. attorney's office in Anchorage. He received a post in the Department of the Interior during the Eisenhower administration, during which he promoted the cause of Alaska statehood (won in 1959). He was elected to the Alaska House in 1964 and first appointed to the U.S. Senate in 1968. Coming from a remote and tiny constituency, he scarcely is noticed by the New York-Washington media axis, but his fellow lawmakers appreciate him for unabashedly speaking up—as did Dan Rostenkowski—for congressional privileges and pay raises.

Not that he is popular with lawmakers otherwise. A prickly sort given to a break-their-kneecaps style in negotiations, he says sardonically, "I don't lose my temper. I always know where it is." He fervently makes sure that Alaska gets its fair share and more of federal pork.

In 1994, the *Anchorage Daily News* ran a series of articles on "Big Voice for Alaska," a four-day pufferoo which billboarded, "By nearly any yardstick, Ted Stevens belongs in the front ranks of Alaska statesmen." Like Ted Kennedy in Massachusetts, Strom Thurmond in South Carolina, and Mark Hatfield in Oregon, Stevens seemed to personify his state.

Again like Rostenkowski, Stevens was nettled by watching his friends get rich in the private sector while he toiled for decades, feeling inadequately appreciated and undercompensated, serving the public. In 1995, he was dismayed to hear that somebody affluent enough to finance his own campaign was going up against him in 1996.

David Cuddy is a third-generation white Alaskan, a rare species. His grandfather, an attorney, helped to establish the First National Bank of Anchorage. Dave was born in Anchorage in 1952 and pursued a career path seemingly designed to eliminate any suspicion that he was just a pampered rich kid. He worked in a cannery, as a Tastee Freeze clerk, as a placer gold miner, and as an aircraft mechanic's helper. During summers, while in college, he took entry-level jobs at the family bank—teller, accounting clerk. After graduating from Duke University in North Carolina in 1974, he entered the bank's management trainee program and then ran branches in the towns of Palmer, Fairbanks, and Homer.

In 1980, Cuddy won election to a two-year term as a state representative. He flew to Juneau, the state capital located in the southeastern panhandle adjoining Canada, to press for smaller government and more free enterprise just as North Slope oil money was spilling off the legislative tables and lawmakers devoted their energies to contriving ways to spend it. Frustrated, the conservative Cuddy declined to seek re-election.

Cuddy stayed active in the community, serving on the boards of various public-improvement groups, coaching a junior high school wrestling team, raising money for charity, and aiding the Boy Scouts. His wife, Kathy, was a schools reformer and a member of the Alaska Board of Education. Cuddy rose steadily in the bank until by 1992 he was its president. In 1994, he stepped down.

Like many Republicans, he was emboldened by the party's capture of the U.S. House in 1994 after forty years in the desert and the corresponding take-over of the Senate after an eight-year drought. But he read too much into this election. It was time, Cuddy figured, to replace Stevens, who talked conservative but voted for big spending. "If the person with clout isn't taking you where you want to go, what good is it?" he reasoned.

Cuddy endorsed the GOP platform of fiscal and social conservatism, less government, and term limits. In contrast, the *Wall Street Journal* labeled Stevens a status quo senator. Cuddy was heartened when a highly regarded Republican U.S. senator who disliked Stevens—a member of a sizable clan—privately encouraged the challenger to run.

Cuddy then moved Kathy and their three daughters to Fayetteville, Arkansas, for a year while Dave pursued graduate studies in social work, foreign policy, and journalism to prepare for the campaign. By the fall of 1995, he felt ready. He went through the modern campaign drill of hiring a campaign manager, media consultant, and pollster.

The pollster posed to likely voters a hypothetical race between "Candidate A" and "Candidate B." A was "a middle-age businessman with little political experience, who supports less federal spending, less taxes, less control by the federal government, and more control by the state of Alaska, along with more personal responsibility." B was "an older, lifetime politician who has seniority in Congress and the desire and the ability to deliver much federal spending and government programs for Alaska, and supports the present political system."

The result: Candidate A, 53 percent, Candidate B, 35 percent. Cuddy put too much stock in these numbers. Pollsters' so-called blind races are one thing; actually casting a ballot for a challenger against a specific pork-delivering incumbent is another.

On October 16, 1995, Cuddy filed candidacy papers with the Federal Election Commission. Two strange things happened promptly. Cuddy's pollster told Cuddy's campaign consultant that he was leaving—the Republican National Senatorial Committee (RNSC) had called to inform him he would get no more polling work from GOP senators if he continued to work for the Cuddy campaign. Then someone from the same committee called the campaign consultant. The caller said that if Cuddy dropped out of the race, Cuddy would be given a high-level position "of his choice" in the Bob Dole administration, should Dole defeat Bill Clinton in the 1996 presidential election. The consultant soon resigned.

Also during this period, the RNSC sent a person to Anchorage to do opposition research on Cuddy. The oppo was indirectly funded by soft money to the party organization, not directly by hard money to Stevens's campaign. This manuever enabled the Stevens campaign later to complain that while Cuddy did oppo on the senator, Stevens did none on the challenger.

At this point, the average person might have said, "Forget it, I will drop out and hope for a plum from President Dole." But Cuddy was proud, stubborn, and naive about what awaited him. Though of middling height and now a bit pudgy, he had been a wrestler at Duke and retained an athlete's competitiveness.

Meanwhile, Don Young, Alaska's lone congressman, encountered a Cuddy supporter and told him: Dave thinks the race will be about issues but it won't; he has no idea of the forces he is dealing with, and he will have no control over what is said about him. Young was a canny politician and knew the score.

Cuddy formally declared his candidacy on January 17. He said, "Ted Stevens has done his best to represent Alaska. We owe him our thanks. But a new mood of reform is sweeping America."

Late in January, Alaska Republicans held presidential caucuses. The state party had been taken over by social conservatives and gave 64 percent of its straw-poll votes to insurgent candidates Pat Buchanan and Steve Forbes, with only 17 percent for Dole, the establishment's choice. The first-in-the-nation straw poll had been engineered by Fritz

Pettyjohn, an Anchorage lawyer and radio personality who later would play an unhappy role in Cuddy's race.

Anyway, Cuddy was delighted by the caucus results because the GOP Senate nominee would be chosen this time by a "closed" primary in which only voters who declared themselves Republicans or independents could vote, not an "open" primary in which voters of any party could participate. Formerly, many Democrats routinely crossed party lines to vote for Stevens in Republican primaries because the Democratic Senate candidates almost always were nobodies and flakes. The caucuses demonstrated that the state GOP party structure was more conservative than Stevens. The senator regularly affronted conservatives by supporting tax increases, the National Education Association, the National Endowment for the Arts, the Public Broadcasting Service, and the Equal Rights Amendment. Hence, with no Democratic crossovers, Cuddy would have a good chance in the closed August 27 primary.

In February, Representative George Nethercutt of Washington state keynoted the annual "Lincoln Day" GOP dinner in Anchorage. Nethercutt was a Republican giant slayer for having defeated House Speaker Thomas Foley in 1994 after ridiculing Foley for joining a lawsuit to block a 1992 state congressional term-limits referendum. But in just two years, Nethercutt had changed from insurgent to insider. (Later, in 1999, he came out against term limits.) His Anchorage appearance underscored how far the incumbency protection network reaches. He had worked as a Senate staffer for four years for Stevens in the 1970s; at the GOP banquet in 1996, he highly praised the longtime Alaskan incumbent while ignoring Cuddy.

Then, in June, the Alaska Supreme Court voided the party rules and decreed another open primary. State election officials always favor incumbents (recall the rulings for Sue Kelly in New York and John Warner in Virginia). Now Cuddy would have to defeat not just Stevens's forces but that of the Democrats' as well. He faced another should-I-quit dilemma. Press reports estimated his net worth at $23 million, but his actual liquid assets were less than $1.5 million. He had counted on putting only $250,000 of his own money into a closed-primary campaign.

Federal contribution limits foist on challengers a task equivalent to filling a bathtub with a $1,000 teaspoon. Cuddy and his supporters made the rounds of Alaskan CEOs—the challenger's own milieu—only to be told that they would love to help out, but they could not risk Stevens seeing their name on Cuddy's list of contributors for fear of reprisal. Did those who wrote the post-Watergate "reform" laws fore-see this?

One solicitation was especially memorable. An entrepreneur who provided air service to the Bush told Cuddy, "You're right and Ted's wrong, but this country can't be saved. It's too far gone. As long as it's too late to fix, I want a senator who will grab everything off the shelf and give it to me as we go down the toilet. The gravy in my business is postal subsidies to the Bush. You know that Ted is a big supporter of postal subsidies. Dave, I've known you for twenty years, but I'm sorry."

It was Kathy Cuddy who made the decision to keep going. She said, "Dave, if you don't do it, you'll always wonder whether you could have won. We've spent a year preparing and in your heart you know the vot-ers are ready for a change. Go for it." Cuddy worried that he was being unfair to his wife and three daughters, but he committed the couple's "life savings" of $1.2 million to the campaign.

This sum was entered into the budget in the campaign computer and printed out. The next day, the new budget somehow was leaked to the Stevens camp. Politicians are like dogs: They have ears that can pick up things ordinary humans cannot detect. Stevens now was truly alarmed. Cuddy was willing to spend part of his own fortune against him.

However, as the challenger slept in the back of his 1983 Jeep while touring the state, Stevens was whisked from town to town in an ARCO oil company corporate jet. Understand what traveling across Alaska by car means. The distances are staggering and most of the interior is not readily accessible by what Alaskans call "the road system," not even the one-lane dirt paths that spider through some of the Bush. Cuddy was driving for hours to meet handfuls of voters while Stevens was swoop-ing onto Bush runways with the air of a royal visitation.

Also, Cuddy (like Jim Miller in Virginia and others) was no natural politician, no backslapper. He would go door-to-door in Anchorage to hand out campaign literature without trying to engage voters in friendly conversation on the front stoop. "I told Dave several times that the best thing he could do is spend a week at charm school because he's very rigid," said Wayne Anthony Ross, an Anchorage lawyer and GOP leader.

But then, Stevens was hardly in the running for a Mr. Warmth award either. As reported in the Capitol Hill newspaper *Roll Call*, he has said, "I'm a mean, miserable SOB. I want them to believe that I'll make their life miserable if they don't listen to me."

In any case, Cuddy's $1.2 million could buy top-rate campaign tal-ent. He hired Terry Cooper Political Research of Arlington, Virginia, as his oppo person. Cooper scoured Stevens's FEC and Secretary of the Senate filings and, even for a veteran researcher, was startled by what he found. In fourteen years in the business his analyses had never led to the filing of an ethics complaint, until he saw what Stevens had been doing.

Meanwhile, Cuddy's new campaign consultant was Kelley Rogers of the Washington state Republican organization. At a GOP state convention in Seattle, Rogers kept hearing, Don't work against Stevens, he's a good senator, and also he's mean, he'll hurt you. One of the interlocutors was a lobbyist for a major defense contractor. Rogers took these as the normal expressions of incumbency protection. But then on the Monday after the July 4 weekend, he had lunch with that defense lobbyist and a state party boss. The lobbyist said Rogers had to quit as Cuddy's consultant; otherwise, no more defense-firm contributions to the Washington state GOP. Nothing personal against you or Cuddy, the lobbyist said, but Stevens is "our seven-billion-dollar man," and so you have until August 1 to get out. Reluctantly, Rogers gave Cuddy notice. "Ordinarily, I'd tell him to take a flying leap," he said, "but he's my boss's biggest donor."

The challenger's dismay was lessened in mid-July when his new, Virginia-based pollster came back from the Alaskan field with survey results: Stevens led Cuddy by just four points, 37 percent to 33 percent, with 18 percent undecided and six weeks to go until the primary. What was more, Stevens's favorability rating among the undecideds was just 40 percent, low for an incumbent. A political rule of thumb is that undecideds break for the challenger or else stay home. Cuddy felt he could win this thing—Terry Cooper was stoking the fax lines to the campaign as he kept discovering apparent campaign financial abuses by Stevens.

Stevens's Anchorage-based pollster immediately countered with his own poll, sneering that Cuddy had "omitted a digit"—the actual margin was not 4 percent but 45 percent—Stevens 59, Cuddy 14. "Historically, 'outside' research firms have had problems with their accuracy in Alaska," the pollster smugly faxed Stevens.

With Kelley Rogers forced to leave by the end of the month, Cuddy tried to recruit a new consultant. One state legislative staffer turned the job down because he was applying to law schools and feared that Stevens would scuttle his chances of acceptance. After that demonstration of the widespread fear of the senator's reputation—deserved or not—for vindictiveness, Cuddy negotiated with a team that had worked for Oliver North and for a Virginia gubernatorial campaign. The deal was nearly done; the Cuddy campaign booked plane reservations to Anchorage for the hired guns, when suddenly they pulled out, for reasons never explained. (The challenger later was told that the Virginia consultants had been contacted by Stevens's camp.)

In Anchorage, Cuddy's supporters also ran into trouble. Sasha Hughes, part native and part fourth-generation white Alaskan, festooned the bingo parlor she ran—"forty windows"—and her yard at home with Cuddy posters. She also was running for an Alaska House seat. She received an anonymous call. "He said I didn't stand a chance in hell if I didn't get rid of the Cuddy signs." She put up more of them. Hughes lost the election and later her business went broke.

Back in Arlington, Cooper found that Stevens's taxpayer-paid Senate staffers took forty-six taxpayer-paid trips and spent a total of 529 days in Alaska just before his 1990 re-election. This was more than double the average number of trips taken in each of the five subsequent, nonelection years. Some of those 1990 staffers dispatched to Alaska were paid a secondary salary from campaign funds. Using government workers for campaigning is illegal.

Also, Stevens had bought a $32,000 Lincoln Town Car with campaign funds, apparently for personal use. In addition, he had charged his campaign for winter trips to Florida, Hawaii, and elsewhere. Other outlays ranged from the large to the petty; for example, Stevens billed his campaign for multiple copies of *The Social List of Washington*.

Cooper and Rogers were excited by this explosive stuff, but they and Cuddy agreed they should consult an election-laws expert before detonating it. "We did not want to file complaints if they would just be dismissed out of hand," the challenger said. He retained E. Mark Braden, partner in a top-drawer Washington law firm and former chief counsel to the Republican National Committee (and, incidentally, counsel to Oliver North's campaign). Braden reviewed Cooper's material and described Stevens's apparent violations as "of Rostenkowski proportions." He then drafted a letter of complaint, advising his client to file it because "the Ethics Committee and the FEC cannot avoid investigating this."

On July 24, Cuddy held a news conference to say he was sending complaints to the Senate Ethics Committee and the Federal Election Commission. The letters listed 302 questionable campaign expenditures. Cuddy called Stevens's actions "tantamount to embezzlement," strong and, in the end, unwise words that were a long way from the "we owe him our thanks" stance of January.

Stevens struck the customary incumbent's pose of wounded innocence. "It made me lie awake at night," he said. "I've known that boy [Cuddy] since he came into my kitchen."

Since Watergate, the public has regarded the media as scandalmongers, but the Anchorage press recoiled at this potential scandal, accusing Cuddy of *lese-majeste*. How *dare* he attack "King Ted"! On July 28, the *Anchorage Daily News* published an editorial cartoon of Cuddy as a kickboxer with his foot in his mouth.

The *Anchorage Daily News* and *Anchorage Times* are a singular hybrid. The *Daily News* was a liberal paper of the old-fashioned, shin-kicking sort, winning a Pulitzer Prize in 1976, whereas the *Times* was a conservative paper. In 1979, the California-based McClatchey Newspapers group bought the *Daily News* and stamped it with the usual chain brand of broad but shallow coverage. In 1992, the *Times* ceased publishing. Bill Allen, the head of VECO, a politically active oil services company, bought a remnant of the *Times* and cut a deal to publish a half-page of its editorials every day in the *Daily News*. Allen makes no secret of his closeness to Stevens, and one of his editors is a former Stevens staffer.

The *Daily News* often featured Stevens on its front page throughout the summer while slighting coverage of Cuddy. It did not run either its own or an Associated Press candidates' profiles and positions-on-the-issues chart, stock journalistic fare to maintain at least an appearance of impartiality.

Although the local Chamber of Commerce and League of Women Voters traditionally sponsored senatorial candidates' debates, Stevens rejected all offers to debate the challenger. Their only encounter came during a minor public television forum.

Meanwhile, the Senate Ethics Committee supposedly was looking into Cuddy's complaint. If members find an accusation to be serious, they launch an investigation. The results eventually are reported to the full Senate, leading to exoneration or else possible sanctions up to expulsion. If the findings are really serious, they might be forwarded to the Justice Department or the Internal Revenue Service. These are the laborious steps that precede a prosecution of a senator or representative. It is as if the IRS could audit a citizen's tax returns only if a neighbor or another governmental body officially filed a complaint.

The Senate Ethics Committee chairman was Mitch McConnell, Republican of Kentucky. McConnell zealously opposes campaign financial reform, having fought major reform legislation in 1988, 1992, 1994, and 1996–98. Moreover, in 1996, Stevens was in line to become chairman of the Senate Appropriations Committee if the GOP retained control of the Senate. Since McConnell would serve under Stevens on Appropriations, his home-state pork then would be at Stevens's mercy.

Again, it is as if an employee hoping for a promotion from his or her employer were assigned the task of checking whether the boss had padded his or her expense accounts.

During this period, somebody hacked into Cuddy's campaign computer and stole the week's supply of e-mail. The campaign manager later received an explicit, telephoned death threat using her secret e-mail log-in name.

Amid this turmoil, Fritz Pettyjohn, architect of the January presidential caucuses and a Cuddy supporter, invited him to appear on his KENI radio talk show to discuss the ethics charges. "I was told by management that there had been some complaint lodged against the station by someone in the Stevens camp that I was going beyond the bounds of fair political commentary, and when their [Federal Communications Commission] license renewal came up it could be a problem for them," Pettyjohn said. "And so they instructed me to just back off and stay away from it or else they'd have to take me off the air. Anytime you mention the word 'license' around one of these stations, they just freak."

So the station canceled the Cuddy appearance and also relieved Pettyjohn of duty for the next several days. This was a blow to Cuddy's campaign because, while opinion molders for Stevens stayed in place in the print media, the challenger was denied access to the most influential of his supporters in the broadcast media.

As swiftly as August 9, the Senate Ethics Committee dismissed Cuddy's complaint of July 24. Stevens had filed his response on August 1. The committee counsel scorned Cuddy's allegations as politically motivated "mere speculation." Here are some particulars:

1. The 1990 campaign workers were explained away by a Senate rule against spending taxpayers' money on staffers' hotels, meals, and other daily expenses within sixty days of an election. The government paid their airfare because these people were sent home on government business, Stevens said, but then their expenses were covered by the campaign under the sixty-day rule. He did not say why he authorized forty-six such trips to Alaska in 1990 and only eighteen in 1991. (Recall Charles Gerow's dismay at the influx of Bill Goodling's staffers to Pennsylvania.)

2. The Lincoln Town Car had been among three items listed as "purchase of campaign vehicles." Cooper logically inferred that the campaign had bought three cars. It turned out that one of the cryptic phrases denoted a purchase of a vehicle *from* the campaign.

3. Stevens had rented a van in Long Island, where members of Congress often vacation in the summer. The vehicle rental was billed from Long Island but

actually was used to transport Stevens's college and high school summer interns through the mean streets of Washington.

4. Stevens said the Hawaii and Arizona trips were given as rewards to two 1990 campaign workers. He himself had traveled to Florida and San Francisco to give speeches to industry lobbies and—he huffily asserted—had elected not to charge taxpayers for these trips. Lobbies then always paid members of Congress first-class airfare, lodging, and honoraria (speaking fees) to give speeches. Stevens got the dates of one trip mixed up and also he apparently was "double dipping," taking travel reimbursements from the lobbies and his campaign alike. This was legal as long as he reported the campaign money as personal income to the IRS. Whether he did so is known only by him and perhaps by the IRS.

The FEC did not rule until months after the primary. It said allegations predating 1993 were of no matter because members of Congress then were allowed to convert campaign funds to personal use (per the reform law under which Dan Rostenkowski could have "kept the million bucks" had he quit in 1992). As for post-1992 allegations, the agency accepted Stevens's blanket denial of wrongdoing. The remainder of the 302 items listed in Cuddy's complaint never was officially vetted.

The law sets up three Democratic and three Republican FEC commissioners. One might think ethics questions would produce three-to-three partisan splits. In reality, the votes are routinely unanimous in favor of incumbents. As Brooks Jackson noted in *Broken Promises: Why the Federal Election Commission Failed*:

Historically, the commission has consisted mainly of political cronies of party leaders and, more recently, of former employees of the very parties and political action committees the FEC regulates. The FEC is an insiders' club. . . . Even when it wanted to be independent, the commission was faced with the stark fact that some of those it investigated controlled its lifeline to the Treasury. The effect of this over the years has been to take away from the FEC more and more of the tools it needs to do its job. The protective effect works for incumbents of either party. (pp. 10–11)

Congress thus deliberately underfunds and understaffs the FEC. Every four years, presidential candidates blithely ignore the legal spending limits for the premiere New Hampshire primary. They reason correctly that violations will not be cited and possible fines levied for years, by which time, whether they were elected president or no, who would care?

Cuddy's seemingly minor mistakes on the car purchase and the van rental killed him in the 1996 primary. Art Mathias, a leading Alaska Republican, had warned him, "If you are within 1 percent of being wrong on that, they're going to throw the whole thing out. Be careful. Ted Stevens 'owns' all the media in Alaska."

The Anchorage press sledge-hammered the challenger. Early in the campaign, the *Times* editor had happened on the candidate on the street and said, Drop by the office for an endorsement interview, and Cuddy agreed. But the editor never returned the challenger's calls. After the Ethics Committee's pronouncement, Cuddy asked to meet with the *Daily News* editorial board to make his case. His consultant, Cooper, flew up to advise him in person. The meeting occurred, but the editors were unpersuaded. Both the *Daily News* and the *Times* Sunday editorials of August 4 denounced the challenger for smearing the state's senior senator.

Cuddy had made a fatal mistake by taking the fight to Stevens's own turf, the Washington, D.C., political establishment. Like many other challengers, he was an amateur going into the ring with a pro. "I had never been attacked like this," Cuddy said. "I didn't know how to respond. I had never been in this kind of high-pressure, intense situation before. I had no consultants; they were taken away from us." The Stevens forces could do nothing about Cuddy's personal money, so they shrewdly got rid of his campaign talent instead.

Stevens won the low-turnout primary with 59 percent of the vote to 27 percent for Cuddy and 14 percent for fringe candidates. Stevens raised $3.3 million, including $1.5 million from PACs, with 75 percent of his funds coming from outside Alaska. He spent $1.7 million through the primary and an additional $1 million for the general election. Cuddy spent $1.5 million, including a $159,000 personal donation and a $1.17 million personal loan. He took no PAC money, nor was any offered.

Stevens's November election campaign against Democratic nominee Theresa Obermeyer was typically farcical. Obermeyer had spent twenty-nine days in federal prison that summer on a disorderly conduct charge for disrupting a meeting between Stevens and Senator Christopher S. Bond, Republican of Missouri, in 1995. She got 10 percent of the vote.

To Cuddy's surprise, criticism in the Anchorage press continued—especially for his "negative campaigning" through filing the ethics complaints—even after the primary. "I was tempted to respond," he said, "but one political pro told me to roll over and take the beating. It was part of the victory dance and everyone who wanted a favor from Ted would jump on my grave."

In later interviews, editors of both Anchorage papers shook their heads in sorrow rather than in anger against Cuddy. They did not know what had gotten into him. If only he had challenged Congressman Don Young instead of Ted Stevens, which they had wanted him to do, but he would not listen.

Asked whether he might run again, Cuddy was philosophical. "I can understand the power people wanting to keep the perks coming to themselves and to their businesses," he said. "But I can't understand their willingness to sacrifice our systems of free elections and debate to keep their candidates in office, or their desire to resort to smear and personal attacks.

"A challenger must have his own money to finance a challenge campaign. That knocks out most potential candidates. It certainly isn't fun to spend all of your own savings to fight for what you believe in.

"A challenger needs experienced professional advice, even more than an incumbent needs it. Five of our consultants were blackmailed, bribed, or convinced to get out of our campaign. There were no real debates. The controllers worked hard to keep the voters uninformed or misinformed. A United States senator escaped investigation for felony use of staff for campaign purposes."

No wonder that the state's other Republican senator, Frank H. Murkowski, ran virtually unopposed in 1998. Why bother?

14

HAWAII

ORSON G. SWINDLE (R) v.
REPRESENTATIVE NEIL ABERCROMBIE (D)

In November 1966, on the 205th and last scheduled combat mission of his tour in Vietnam, Marine Corps pilot Orson Swindle took off from DaNang in an F-8 Crusader to attack a target a few miles north of the Demilitarized Zone. Earlier that day, two Air Force F-4 Phantoms had been shot down in the same area. As Swindle began his bombing run, his aircraft was disabled by antiaircraft fire. He parachuted right into the enemy's hands and spent the next six years as a prisoner of war.

"Within hours after capture, I found myself subjected to intense interrogation and then, after refusing to answer questions, severe torture," Swindle said. The North Vietnamese tried to keep each POW isolated to break his spirit, but Swindle and others managed to pass messages to their comrades by whispering or by tapping a code on the prison walls.

A quarter-century earlier, Daniel K. Inouye had returned to his native Hawaii after losing an arm while fighting the Nazis in Italy. Inouye belonged to the 442nd Regimental Combat Team, composed of Japanese Americans who signed up to prove their patriotism after Japan attacked Pearl Harbor. Known as the "Go for Broke" regiment, the 442nd was awarded the most combat medals of any unit in World War II.

In the 1990s, these two warriors, Swindle and Inouye, clashed over congressional contests in Hawaii. Inouye, who has been a U.S. senator from the Islands since 1963, twice supported Swindle's election opponent, Representative Neil Abercrombie. Ironically, Abercrombie was an antiwar "dove," a pony-tailed son of the 1960s counterculture who had supported Jane Fonda's mission to Hanoi during the Vietnam War and had called for nuclear disarmament while in Congress. Although the decorated war heroes Swindle and Inouye scorned Abercrombie's leftist positions, that mattered little because Abercrombie was an incumbent and Swindle a challenger. Incumbents almost always protect their own.

Like Alaska, Hawaii is a small state in terms of population, with economic power concentrated in relatively few hands. Such economic power translates into reinforced incumbency protections. Again like Alaska, Hawaii's culture and traditions have made one political party predominant—Republicans in Alaska and Democrats in Hawaii. The combination of incumbency safeguards written into federal laws, and equally potent but unwritten protections in the Islands' one-party establishment, doomed even a candidacy as strong as that of Lieutenant Colonel Orson Swindle.

Born in Camilla, Georgia, in 1937, Swindle became a "haole," the not-very-complimentary Hawaiian term for a white immigrant, in 1989 after careers in the Marines and in the Reagan administration. He graduated from Georgia Tech in 1959 and spent twenty years in the Marine Corps. "I came out of Vietnam saying I wasn't going to be intimidated by anyone," he said. In 1980, President Jimmy Carter remained popular in Georgia, but an undaunted Swindle ran Ronald Reagan's campaign in a congressional district near Carter's hometown of Plains. Not previously active politically, Swindle was enraged by Carter's grant of amnesty to Vietnam draft dodgers.

Swindle got a crash course in federal politics after the Reagan White House rewarded him with a patronage job—Georgia director of the Farmers Home Administration (FmHA). At that time, the FmHA was overwhelmed with delinquent farm loans all across the country. This was especially true in Georgia, whose farmers long had been shielded from FmHA foreclosures by Senate Agriculture Committee Chairman Herman E. Talmadge of Georgia. The 1980 Reagan landslide helped Republican Mack Mattingly to unseat Talmadge, who had been censured by the Senate in a financial scandal.

Swindle moved hard and fast, at the direction of the White House, to install stiffer credit policies. (This federal process inspired Hollywood "plight of the farmer" movies in the 1980s.) Soon Swindle heard from Senator Mattingly, who had been hearing from angry Georgia farmers. When Swindle refused to back off, Mattingly launched a campaign to boot him from office. He succeeded by making Swindle's removal a condition for the White House to win Senate confirmation of a deputy secretary of agriculture in 1985.

Transferred to the Department of Commerce as head of the Economic Development Agency, Swindle started waging another war against federal pork. The agency's purpose was to issue specific grants to impoverished communities, but, in the tradition of government bureaucracies, it had become more of a helter-skelter shotgun of political pay-offs. Among the pay-offs alleged by Swindle were grants by House Speaker Jim Wright of Texas to the Fort Worth Stockyards in his district. Swindle blew the whistle on Wright, which helped lead eventually to the Speaker's resignation under fire in 1989.

The newly elected George Bush and his administration showed no appreciation for Swindle's role in bringing down a Democratic giant such as Wright. As the Washington quip goes, Swindle was "a bull who carries his own china shop with him." A delegate to the Republican National Convention in 1980, he had voted for Jack Kemp for vice president over Reagan's selection of Bush. That was reason enough for the Bush White House to dislike Swindle, but there was more. "They ran him out of town," a former aide to Swindle said. "Someone like Orson, who was so confrontational, didn't fit into the Bush administration. He wasn't 'kinder and gentler.' "

Swindle got as far from Washington as he could while remaining in the United States: He moved to Honolulu, ten hours by jet from the nation's capital, to become executive director of an association of preschools. The job did not satisfy him. In 1992, Ross Perot mounted a third-party candidacy for president and Swindle signed on. "I enjoy the mental combat. I enjoy pressure. I've always thrived on it," he said. "I've had two ulcers in my life, and both times it was because I was bored to tears with what I was doing."

Swindle had never heard of the Texas billionaire until Perot invited Vietnam POWs to a 1973 reunion he staged in San Francisco. Swindle was impressed by the patriotism he saw in Perot; the two became friends, and in 1992, Swindle headed the Perot campaign in Hawaii. Perot's running mate for vice president was Admiral James B. Stockdale—one of the U.S. Navy aviators with whom Swindle had exchanged tapped, coded messages through the prison walls in Hanoi.

Incidentally, this tapping strategem was the subject of an admiring passage in social scientist James Q. Wilson's acclaimed *The Moral Sense*, published in 1993. Wilson said the tapping was instrumental in enabling POWs to uphold a code of honor even under torture. "The standard torture was 'the ropes,' a process in which a prisoner's arms are pulled up behind his back while his head is forced down toward the floor," Wilson wrote.

Swindle described "the ropes" for this book: "My arms were trussed up behind me, hands up my spine below my shoulders, with ropes used in tourniquet fashion above my elbows totally cutting off circulation. Ropes were then attached to my thumbs, now somewhere near the back of my head, and I was hoisted off the ground with ropes over rafters. And then the beating started. The pain was maddening."

Wilson wrote, "No one could hold out indefinitely; sooner or later, everyone submitted. . . . [But] almost all of them resisted, endured much torture, and submitted only after they felt themselves to be at death's door. Why?" The answer was that the wall-tapping communication preserved a sense of duty, comradeship, and shared ideals. The code prescribed that Americans could give in to answering questions and signing propaganda statements, but only after torture. No wonder that Swindle left Vietnam with the conviction that no one could intimidate him.

Years later, Swindle's comrade in arms Admiral Stockdale joined the 1992 Perot ticket. Then, the temperamental Perot abruptly quit the presidential campaign in July.

In anger and despair, many of Perot's allies and consultants abandoned his reform organization, United We Stand, America. Only Swindle and a few other true believers kept the group on its feet. The state coordinators who still hoped to persuade Perot to get back in the race named Swindle as executive director of United We Stand on July 31. He moved from Honolulu to Dallas, where he became the movement's most visible figure in Perot's absence, holding daily briefings for reporters and appearing on network news shows. The telegenic, white-haired, plain-spoken former Marine worked well with the media, far better than Perot did.

Early in October, Perot jumped back into the fray. Swindle understood that Perot's flipflops probably destroyed whatever chance he had of becoming president. "I've told him you cannot believe the damage done to these people. In the conversations I've had with Ross, I'm convinced that in July he did not fully comprehend how deep their feelings were," he said. Swindle, for his part, never wavered in his conviction that the government needed fixing by an outsider. In November, Perot took 19 percent of the national vote, a sensational showing for a third-party candidate.

After the election, Swindle went to work for Empower America, a new conservative organization set up by Jack Kemp and William J. Bennett, who had been Reagan's secretary of education. Swindle was supposed to organize a grass-roots conservative drive, but it soon became clear that the wealthy patrons of Empower America did not necessarily want it to be a grass-roots operation. Plus, Kemp and Bennett were potential rivals for the 1996 Republican presidential nomination and offered no unified vision for the group. Swindle remained on good terms with Kemp and Bennett, but resigned to return for a possible run for Congress. He told the GOP, "We're one of the highest-taxed states. The economy is flat on its butt. Let's do something. Let's run someone for Congress." But nobody volunteered. "They said, 'You can't win.' So I said, 'I'll run. In the state Republican convention in '94, if the poll says I've got a snowball's chance, I'll run.' "

At the convention, the poll showed Representative Neil Abercrombie winning by a margin of eight to one. Swindle interpreted this as a snowball's chance. "If we can get the message out, we can win," he reasoned—the success formula uttered by all challengers before they discover the hardships of getting their message out.

Actually, Abercrombie was not a firmly entrenched incumbent. He was finishing only his second full term, and his political persona is perhaps a tad on the far-out side even for such a paragon of tolerance as Hawaii. He is one of the few politicians who dares to list his religion as "no affiliation," although, for whatever it might signify, a statue of Buddha sits in his home. A bearded and long-haired aging hippie in appearance, Abercrombie was born in Buffalo in 1938 and earned a doctorate in sociology at the University of Hawaii. In 1974, he was elected to the Hawaii House and in 1978 to the state Senate, where he served until 1986. Then he became assistant state superintendent of schools—a powerful post in the Islands, where every school is controlled by a single board.

On the floor and in the cloakroom of the U.S. House, Abercrombie is a tough and zealous debater. In 1994, he was one of a handful of congressmen who racked up perfect ideological scorecards. The liberal Americans for Democratic Action graded his voting record at 100 percent; the American Conservative Union gave him a corresponding "perfect" score of zero percent. Just as the Texas Fourteenth District is one of the only places in the nation that could elect

a Ron Paul, Hawaii's First District is among the few that could elect a
Neil Abercrombie.

Swindle did not minimize his undertaking. "The true heroes of the
Hawaiian military were called *nisei*," he said. "Upon returning from
World War II, these [Japanese American] veterans wanted to participate in Hawaiian politics, which at the time were controlled by the Republican Party. The Republicans said no. These *nisei* then went to labor
and Democrats and took control of Hawaii's politics with the Democratic Party. This Democrat control has lasted since those times."

That is a cogent summary of the Islands' postwar politics. Previous
GOP control of territorial politics dated to 1903, with the party as an
arm of the "Big Five" owners of sugar and pineapple plantations and international trading firms. During the 1930s, the International Long-
shoremen's and Warehousemen's Union (ILWU) organized the
plantation workers with the hard-edged struggles typical of that period.
Some of the classic Depression-era battles of labor against capital were
waged on the shores of a mid-Pacific "island paradise." Many of the
plantation workers were Japanese Americans and others of Asian origin.

Martial law ruled Hawaii during the war, after which the Republicans stepped back into their seats of power. But as early as 1954, Democrats won a majority of the legislature for the first time. Democrats were
energized by organized labor and Japanese Americans—especially
Daniel Inouye, who has held statewide office since Hawaii became a
state in 1959. His former colleague in the U.S. Senate was the late
Spark Matsunaga, another "Go for Broke" combat veteran. The rise to
power of Japanese Americans in Hawaii is one of the great American
political success stories, though scarcely known on the mainland.

Over the years, the influence of the "Big Five" and the ILWU has
weakened with the growth of tourism and of cyberspace trading. Still,
Hawaii maintains a political machine that would be recognized by Chi-
cagoans and a concentration of business power that would be familiar
to residents of Houston.

"They have a machine; we have a tricycle," Swindle said. "The 'Big
Five' are now the banks, media, unions, public employees, and the
Democratic Party. They have Hawaii in an iron grip. I'm running
against all of that. I won't go into debt. I don't have money.

"We've lost 14,000 private sector jobs in the last five years. State employment went up during the same period. Democrats know how to
build a consitutency."

Meanwhile, the supposedly GOP-oriented business community
played ball with the Democratic machine. It has become common for

potential donors to beg off contributing to challengers, lest the incumbent see their name on FEC disclosure forms. According to Swindle, the shunning in Hawaii went even further than that.

"The small players were behind me," he said. "But the big-business people are doing OK. They don't step out of line. Their licenses and ability to do business are controlled by the politicians. Big-business people may quietly support me, but can't give me money or it would show on an FEC report.

"They can't [even] be seen with me at a social event. At one 'nonpartisan' social event celebrating a certain big business's long history in Hawaii, business executives did their best to avoid engaging in even the slightest repartee with me. It was comical."

Swindle was a decorated Vietnam POW in a patriotic state with a large active and retired military presence. He had a measure of celebrity from his association with Ross Perot and a network of potential contributors in United We Stand. He had experience in the federal government. A national Republican tide was building in 1994. Despite all these considerable assets, Swindle ran for Congress with no organization, meager backing from his party, and little chance against Abercrombie—a mere two-termer.

Swindle campaigned hard against Abercrombie for voting consistently for President Clinton's tax increases and defense cuts. But this line of attack was blunted by the fact that every member of Congress, regardless of party or ideology, shovels home the pork. Hawaii's delegation provided millions of dollars for more military housing near Pearl Harbor and Hickam Air Force Base. Although the challenger made inroads into military precincts, they still voted Democratic.

In 1992, Abercrombie had been re-elected with 73 percent of the vote, when his token GOP opponent spent only $1 to every $22 spent by the incumbent. In 1994, against Swindle, Abercrombie raised more than $200,000 from PACs, ten times as much as his challenger. Total spending was $391,451 for Abercrombie and $276,355 for Swindle. Abercrombie won 54 percent of the vote, a relatively narrow victory that surprised the establishment. So Swindle determined to challenge Abercrombie again in 1996.

For the 1996 election, Abercrombie sucked in more PAC money than Swindle by a margin of six to one, even though Democrats no longer held the majority in Congress. This fact alone demonstrates the difficulty of unseating incumbents. Special-interest funds gravitate to incumbents, regardless of party.

Still, the two candidates were fairly even in total spending in 1996. Abercrombie raised $682,898, only $39,044 more than Swindle. The telling point is that 64 percent of the incumbent's money came from PACs, compared to 10 percent for the challenger. The rest he had to raise in infrequent $1,000 dribbles from individuals, with much smaller contributions being the rule.

Abercrombie had a further advantage in the demographics of the First Congressional District. Its population is nearly two-thirds Asian, who are Democratic loyalists in Hawaii. Urban precincts in Honolulu and around the University of Hawaii campus are reliably Democratic and the military voters west of the city tend to be Democratic as well. Only a few higher-income suburbs east of Diamond Head lean Republican.

Despite these obstacles, Swindle held Abercrombie to an eyelash-thin re-election with 50 percent of the 1996 vote. The challenger took 47 percent and a third-party candidate the remainder. Swindle pulled off a near upset by condemning Abercrombie's liberal voting record. Hawaii was two or three steps behind the rest of the country in enjoying the general prosperity of the 1990s, and Swindle portrayed the congressman as an enemy of free enterprise.

"We ran on his voting record. It was perceived as negative advertising. We ran it anyway," Swindle said, referring to print and broadcast ads listing "ten reasons to fire Abercrombie." For instance, the U.S. Chamber of Commerce rated him "the third worst member of Congress" and the National Taxpayers Union listed him as "the eighth biggest spender in Congress."

"We went to great extremes to document everything we said in our ads so that the press would have it," Swindle said. "The press was bad, biased. Abercrombie published ten reasons why I should not win [he would destroy Social Security, and so forth]. Two reasons might be true, eight were not. The press did not challenge it in the least."

Abercrombie did not go hat-in-hand to the press; on the contrary, he opposed a "joint operating agreement" sought by the *Honolulu Advertiser* and the struggling *Star-Bulletin*. These government-approved agreements allow newspapers to combine printing and business operations while maintaining competitive news offices. As in many American cities, the afternoon daily was dying. As elsewhere in the nation, the media slighted coverage of the challenger in comparison to the incumbent. Abercrombie in effect was favored, joint operating agreement or not.

One columnist, A. A. Smyser of the *Star-Bulletin*, defended Swindle's campaign to publicize the congressman's voting record. "When urged to 'give 'em hell,' President Harry Truman is supposed to have

said that he was just telling the truth about Congress—but they considered it hell. The new name for that in Hawaii this year is 'negative campaigning' . . . [but] Swindle had facts to back his claim that one of the
biggest spenders in Congress is Abercrombie," Smyser wrote. He concluded that "1996 was one of the best issues campaign year Hawaii has
seen in a long time—and it worked to the GOP's benefit."

However, the issues debate and both candidates' "ten reasons" may
have affected the outcome less than did the influence of Daniel Inouye.
"As we got close [in the polls], Senator Inouye weighed in with ads saying how valuable Abercrombie was to the Democratic team and how
valuable he was to preserving the military in Hawaii," Swindle said.
"He says he always votes for federal funding of military housing—that
helps the construction industry in Hawaii." The irony of a war hero,
Inouye, helping a 1960s-style peacenik cling to office by raiding the
Pentagon budget somehow escaped notice.

Aside from his solicitude for military housing in Hawaii, Abercrombie not only had voted for Clinton's military spending cuts, he had
joined with the congressional Black Caucus in seeking an additional de-
crease of 30 percent. Nonetheless, "Senator Inouye is literally a political icon in Hawaii," Swindle said. "His words echo with vast parts of the
society and its culture as a directive" (recall Ted Kennedy, Strom Thurmond, Mark Hatfield, and Ted Stevens).

One more weapon possibly wielded by the establishment was vote
fraud. This is a frequent technique of machine politics but almost impossible to prove, as a succession of rueful U.S. attorneys in Chicago
has learned. In Honolulu, the evidence was only circumstantial. In
1994, Swindle lost a part of the First District where voter turnout was
80 percent, nearly double the statewide average that year of 41 percent.
In 1996, the Swindle campaign decided to place its own poll watchers
in those precincts. Mysteriously, turnout fell to 64 percent, and the
challenger won that area this time. These numbers are curious but by
themselves prove nothing, as Swindle admits.

"This is supposition," he said, "but I have no doubt there is voter
fraud. Democrats control the voter registration and polling process [as
in Chicago]. To find the evidence, one must first get inside. Without an
insider to tell of it, who will ever know?"

Looking back, Swindle said, "My support came from middle-
income voters and small-business operators—people trying to survive
on their own skills rather than on government largesse. . . . Lucrative
government contracts were rewards for contractors and the unionized

work force. Permanent employment in government is a virtual lust and provided willingly by incumbent politicians."

Like all Republicans, Swindle was dismayed by the 1998 election returns. Even though Hawaii had endured eight straight years of economic distress and out-migration, Democrats kept control of the Islands. The GOP thought it had a good chance to elect a governor and at least a fair chance of beating Abercrombie, opposed in 1998 by a state representative—but no.

"Rushing headlong into a 'banana republic' existence of the very rich and low-income working class, the people of Hawaii . . . prefer the performance of recent years rather than change," Swindle said.

His final words were a sardonic battle cry: *"Liberate Hawaii before Cuba—please!"*

CONCLUSION

In 1968, a young African American activist named Maynard H. Jackson Jr. ran in the Georgia Democratic primary against Senator Herman E. Talmadge, then a southern institution on a par with Strom Thurmond. This was during the first cresting of the black power movement, and the state's Democratic leadership was dismayed by Talmadge's seeming indifference to his challenger. With a drawl that could be poured over pancakes, the senator explained: "I don't mind a boy runnin' ag'in' me to get ex-pos-yuh . . . but he better never run ag'in' me *again*."

Jackson, a gifted, silver-tongued politician, would joke in stump speeches later that he "had 207,000 votes *counted*" in 1968—"counted" implying that the white courthouse machines had robbed him of votes, which they probably did. Jackson went on to become a four-term mayor of Atlanta, the first African American mayor of a major southern city, but he never challenged Talmadge again. Indeed, he resisted his supporters' suggestions that he run for senator, governor, or even president as a Democratic or third-party insurgent, and now practices law in the private sector. Once again, the national electoral system had roughly shoved aside a highly talented citizen-politician.

Only the rare incumbent today would greet any challenger with the equanimity of a Herman Talmadge. More than thirty years after the

Talmadge-Jackson race, the nation's politics is profoundly different. The size and powers of Congress as an institution, of the lobbyists' class that funds its incumbents, and of the media class that sustains them, have all grown dramatically. The post-Watergate campaign "reforms" of the 1970s actually *deformed* the system. Far from showing the bemused tolerance of Talmadge, incumbents now have created institutional and financial protections that seem to drive them not just to defeat but to crush their real or potential challengers, for example, by the standing six-figure bank accounts of Deborah Pryce in Ohio and those of many other incumbents, or by the assaults of the Ted Stevens campaign against David Cuddy in Alaska.

Congress watchers Roger H. Davidson and Walter J. Oleszek have written that the political science field has produced "a veritable cottage industry" seeking to analyze why incumbents are so formidable. It is curious that academics would puzzle over such a question. The ways and means of incumbents' re-elections are far from opaque, as this book has demonstrated. Unfortunately, the operations of members of Congress and the PACs that finance their campaigns normally are examined in Washington—"inside the Beltway"—instead of at the precinct-by-precinct level in various election jurisdictions across the country.

Perhaps a tabulation of the successes of incumbents in the races considered in this book might tell much of the tale. The following chart reduces to ratios of X to one the incumbents' spending advantage and voting-return margin over their challengers in selected races. The figures count only documented hard-money expenditures, not unregulated soft money. Also, the voting returns relate only to incumbents and principal challengers, not the entire field in multi-candidate races.

Election Race	Incumbents $ Margin	Incumbents Vote Margin
Romney/Kennedy '94	1.51	1.42
DioGuardi/Kelly '94	0.72	1.15
Gerow/Goodling '98	2.82	2.09
North/Robb '94	0.27	1.06
Miller/Warner '96	1.55	1.96
Close/Thurmond '96	1.38	1.21
Coles/Gingrich '96	1.67	1.37
Coles/Coverdell '98	1.24	1.16
Arnebeck/Pryce '96	40.01	2.42

Election Race	Incumbents $ Margin	Incumbents Vote Margin
Simpson/Rostenkowski '94	4.01	3.64
Paul/Laughlin '96	1.43	0.85
Minnick/Craig '96	1.4	1.43
Lonsdale/Hatfield '90	1.84	1.16
Cuddy/Stevens '96	1.11	2.15
Swindle/Abercrombie '96	1.07	1.08

Discounting Oliver North's funds, Cliff Arnebeck's "experiment" in an unfunded campaign, and Ron Paul's defeat of an incumbent, the pattern is clear. Incumbents normally outspend their challengers by a significant margin and end up winning re-election by somewhat of a lesser margin.

What can be inferred from this table and the foregoing narratives of these campaigns? First, money usually determines election outcomes and special-interest dollars flow to incumbents, regardless of party. Second, incumbents enjoy institutional advantages. The following lists those advantages and indicates which of the incumbents featured in this book enjoyed their benefits.

Federal limits on campaign contributions. All of them.

Congressional staffing, travel, and franking perquisites. All of them.

Constituent casework. All of them.

Gerrymandered House districts. Many of them.

State election laws and election officials. Especially, Sue Kelly, John Warner, and Ted Stevens.

"Bigfoot" support by national party leaders. Especially, Ted Kennedy, Sue Kelly, Charles Robb, John Warner, Strom Thurmond, Newt Gingrich, Dan Rostenkowski in his primary races, and Mark Hatfield.

"Bigfoot" support by the opposite party's leaders. To name three overt examples, Charles Robb, Dan Rostenkowski, and Mark Hatfield; and, to a degree, Paul Coverdell.

Automatic claims on media attention. All of them.

Local media and business support. All of them, but particularly Ted Kennedy, Bill Goodling, Strom Thurmond, Deborah Pryce, Larry Craig, Mark Hatfield, Ted Stevens, and Neil Abercrombie.

Dirty tricks. Unknown, but at the least, Ted Kennedy's exploitation of the religion issue, John Warner's contrivance of a Margaret Thatcher "endorsement," Greg Laughlin's "push polling" in his unsuccessful race in Texas, Larry Craig's advertisement that falsified his challenger's

taped remarks, and the Ted Stevens campaign's elimination of his opponent's campaign consultants.

Intimidation of the challengers' supporters. At the least, Ted Kennedy,
Sue Kelly, Strom Thurmond, Ted Stevens, and Neil Abercrombie.

Vote fraud. Not documented, but perhaps a factor in Dan Rostenkowski's primaries and Neil Abercrombie's general elections.

If this system does not amount to an established political class of incumbents, PAC special interests, and the media industry, it is hard to
imagine what such a set-up would look like in America. The democratic
bedrock of free elections and the free marketplace of ideas has fissured,
if not crumbled.

In 1968, national civil-rights advocates could give however much
money they wished to Maynard Jackson. But in 1998, the challenger to
Paul Coverdell, a successor to Talmadge's Senate seat, could collect
contributions only in $1,000 dribs and drabs.

To reiterate, the current congressional electoral system is a contemporary creation of the past quarter-century. The point needs reinforce-
ment because an alternative school of thought holds that American
politics has never been cleaner. Some analysts recall that George Washington, Thomas Jefferson, Abraham Lincoln, and Franklin D. Roosevelt were victimized by the most vile slanders from a partisan press; that
the nineteenth century congressional giants Henry Clay and Daniel
Webster openly solicited bribes from business interests; that dirty tricks
and vote fraud and outright envelopes-stuffed-with-cash pay-offs have
been suppressed; that no direct connection can be proven between
PAC contributions and actual floor votes on legislation; that today's
members of Congress are the best educated and most public spirited in
history, and so forth.

In fact, many droll anecdotes could be told about the tribulations endured by members of the American political pantheon in the old days of
unregulated bite-scratch-and-kick politics. Mark Twain famously said,
"It could probably be proved with facts and figures that there is no dis-
tinctly native American criminal class except Congress," and it may well
be that fewer crooks serve in Congress now than previously.

However, the case for reform does not rest on contemporary congressional scandals, despite the allegations against Ted Kennedy, Newt
Gingrich, Dan Rostenkowski, Mark Hatfield, Bob Packwood, Ted Stevens, and the House bank check bouncers reviewed in this book or various grafters and sexual miscreants or other wrongdoers. Rather, the
congressional electoral system itself is both corrupt and corrupting.

Washington, Jefferson, Lincoln, Roosevelt, Clay, Webster, and the others did not operate under the Federal Election Campaign Act of 1971 and its later amendments or twenty-four-hour C-SPAN and other news outlets or in a capital city now dominated by thousands of lawyers, lobbyists, and political consultants. When President Lyndon Johnson took office there were thirty-one people in Washington trying to influence legislation—attorneys, lobbyists, and consultants—for each of the 535 representatives and senators. Under Bill Clinton, the ratio is 125:1.

The tardiness of the opinion-making class to fully comprehend the incumbency-protection impact of these developments is somewhat of a riddle. The evidence that the general public has recognized it is found in ever-declining voter turnout rates. Also, it is seen in the scornful rejection of the system by such credible but unsuccessful challengers as Maynard Jackson, Mitt Romney, Elliott Close, Walt Minnick, Harry Lonsdale, and David Cuddy, who say they never intend to run again.

Alarmed by the drop-off in voter participation, the elite media perennially scold the electorate for forsaking its civic duty of voting. Actually, voters might be reacting perfectly rationally to a system of effective bid rigging by staying home on election day.

If an incumbent has won the previous election, or is leading in current polls, by 55 percent or less of the voters, the district is judged to be "marginal" or "competitive." Now, if as few as seventy-five or so out of 435 House districts are seen as competitive, the public is deemed to be in a revolutionary, storm-the-Bastille mood. Again, this was not the case as recently as the 1960s, when the vulnerability of many incumbents during the Vietnam War was taken for granted. In 1966, a now-inconceivable number of forty representatives was thrown out. In 1998, just seven lost their seats.

Today, threatened incumbents in competitive districts strive to inform all voters that only they, not their challengers, can deliver favors and pork. Then, for insurance, they entice their committed marginal right-wing or left-wing supporters to the polls by striking poses on emotional issues such as abortion, which actually have little to do with the real work of Congress but are pathways to specialized PACs.

Meanwhile, incumbents pocket both general interest-group and narrow ideological PAC money, while challengers scramble to sweep up $1,000 crumbs to get their message out. Incumbents win because they are purveyors of pork and puppets of PACs. This process explains why Congress has become harder-edged in ideology and partisanship even as the electorate has become *less* partisan and more independent. To win competitive seats, incumbents appeal to their ideological voters, especially in primaries. Then, they return to business as usual. For instance, whatever the merits of the December 1998 articles of impeachment of President Clinton for perjury and obstruction of justice, House Republicans drove the process, even though polls consistently documented Clinton's national popularity with only a minority of public support for impeachment. Some GOP members of Congress who voted for the articles might have feared a contested primary in 2000 from a right-wing challenger who could brand the incumbent as a member of what one conservative publication, *Human Events*, labeled the Republican "pro-perjury caucus."

All the while, most PACs are largely indifferent to an incumbent's ideology as long as they gain access and influence through campaign cash. Which is easy to do. A mere legally limited $5,000 contribution from an interest group, or, better, a "bundled" donation of tens or hundreds of thousands of dollars from its members, will ensure that the chairperson of the committee overseeing the group's interests will return its phone calls.

Distressed by this state of affairs, "goo goos"—to use the Chicago term once more—strive always to pass still more campaign financial reforms. Their expressed aim is to restrict big-bankroll private interests from corrupting national politics, thereby promoting the public interest. To accomplish this, they propose a menu of changes, such as governmental funding of House and Senate campaigns; outlawing PACs outright; establishing voluntary spending limits, in exchange for which candidates would be guaranteed a certain amount of free media access; or increasing the contribution limits at least enough to match monetary inflation since 1974. Respected lawmakers such as Senators John McCain, Republican of Arizona, and Russell Feingold, Democrat of Wisconsin, have teamed up to push such legislation annually. For these efforts, they are lionized by the elite media, while opponents such as Mitch McConnell, Republican of Kentucky, are derided. The reformers' goal of cleaning up politics is laudable, but their reformist campaigns are wrong on three counts.

First, they overestimate the efficacy of regulations. Their philosophy is that federal campaign financing laws have not worked, so write more of them! This zeal to regulate and codify politics dates back at least to the Progressive movement at the turn of the twentieth century, which expressed the middle- and upper-class moral drive to cleanse politics of big-city machine corruption. Sure enough, big-city bosses have mostly disappeared, despite the vestiges of bossism that have installed Dan Rostenkowski and Rod Blagojevich in Chicago, Ted Stevens in Alaska, and Neil Abercrombie in Honolulu. But bossism is nearly extinct because of societal processes such as the burgeoning of suburbia more than codified statutes.

The first federal Corrupt Practices Act to regulate campaigns was enacted in 1925. Not a single prosecution ever was brought under its provisions. Reformers are driven by the middle-class intellectual belief that politics should be rational. But politics is largely irrational, animated by emotional and self-interested contingencies at least as much as by black-letter regulations. That is why the Corrupt Practices Act was ineffective and why the Federal Election Commission favors incumbents to this day.

An ordinary citizen, even a public-spirited one, spends only a small amount of time thinking about politics and government. Incumbents think about it all day, every day. Thus, reformers cannot write a regulation that some members of Congress cannot contrive to circumvent. For instance, members of Congress are legally prohibited from receiving campaign funds at their Capitol Hill offices. After this law was passed, some of them opened post office boxes at U.S. Postal Service stations near the Capitol to collect contributions, then dispatched taxpayer-paid staffers to retrieve the envelopes at the satellite stations. These couriers then delivered the checks to Capitol Hill, enabling the congressmen to claim that the money was not "received" at their offices but merely arrived there secondhand.

Currently, reformers are upset by the corrupting influence of soft money, but there was no such thing as soft money until reformers and the courts invented it. Or, if these examples are not convincing, consider that U.S. law forbids corporations and labor unions from spending a single dollar directly to influence federal elections. The reality is that, through their PACs, these groups spend immense sums that increase in every election cycle.

The reformers' second error is their conviction that money is the essence of dirty politics. Money is fundamental, and yet it is but the ground-level plank in the entire scaffold of incumbency preservation. Even if something like one of the McCain-Feingold bills—or even if public financing of campaigns—were passed and signed into law, other institutional planks of incumbency protection would barely shake in the reformist wind. No conceivable reform law that could survive a First Amendment judicial challenge could offset congressional staffing, casework, gerrymandering, partisan support, automatic access to media coverage, local establishment backing, and other built-in incumbency advantages, nor could any such law prevent interest groups from endeavoring to win federal tax and regulatory advantages.

The third mistake involves a crucial misunderstanding of the national polity. Reformers fervently hope to free the nation of corruption by private special interests. However, they overlook the fact that *government itself is a special interest*. Government institutions, including Congress, are self-protecting and self-enhancing bodies just like their counterparts in the private sector. The difference is that government institutions are ensured of eternal life through taxation. In contrast, private sector entities survive only by courting fickle consumer preferences. Thus, by downgrading the private sector and upgrading the public sector, reformers might actually be inhibiting rather than expanding the citizen autonomy that they claim to champion.

Governor Richard Lamm, in his Foreword to this book, suggested that the present two-party structure cannot bring about meaningful reform. After all, incumbents placed and protected in office under the current system hardly would be eager to overturn it. While not necessarily disagreeing with the governor, the authors have reluctantly concluded that true reform requires a radical change: a constitutional amendment imposing limited terms on members of Congress.

This conclusion is our own; we do not presume to speak for any of the challengers, who hold varied views on reform. We further state that the case for reform does not mandate acceptance of the term-limits remedy. Almost any constitutionally permitted measure to impinge on incumbency sovereignty would be welcome, and some advocacy groups present persuasive briefs for revising the campaign financial laws. However, no new regulations could effectively repair our broken electoral system.

Arguments for and against term limits have been explored at length in other works (examples are cited in the Bibliographical Essay). This debate unfortunately has focused on political arrangements rather than on its proper ground of constitutional rights. The accounts of campaigns delineated in this book demonstrate that citizen-challengers are being denied their rights: the right to a free and open electoral contest and the right to an untrammeled marketplace of ideas.

Term limits would not amount to a mere shifting of institutional practices. By insuring a regular turnout of incumbents, a term-limits amendment would restore to citizens who seek public office their basic rights. In addition, it would revive the Jeffersonian ideal of citizen-lawmakers, an ideal honored by Abraham Lincoln, who left Washington, D.C., for Springfield, Illinois, in 1848 without complaint after a single term in the House.

Commentators have objected that term limits on the tenure of congressional chairs placed by Republican rules in 1995, and on state legislators' terms in California and other states in the 1990s, have inconvenienced incumbents and altered their behavior. But that is precisely the point.

Skeptics need not take either the authors' or their featured challengers' word that the current system oppresses basic freedoms. Some incumbents are candid about how things work. Representative David Dreier of California said, "What we in Congress do is in a small way similar to how [former dictator] Danny Ortega tried to fix elections in Nicaragua." Former Representative Tony Coelho of California, who chaired the Democratic Congressional Campaign Committee but resigned from Congress in 1989 under an ethical cloud, said, "You have tremendous, tremendous tools you can use that a challenger cannot use." Term limits would sheathe at least the sharpest of these tools. Further, term limits probably would increase voter turnout when citizens realize that their votes really do matter.

Still, is a term-limits constitutional amendment really needed? The history of constitutional amendments is that of the steady expansion of individual rights. The Bill of Rights guaranteed fundamental freedoms and the Fourteenth Amendment imposed this guarantee on state governments; the Thirteenth abolished slavery, and the Fifteenth held that manumitted slaves could vote; the Seventeenth provided for the direct election of senators; the Nineteenth recognized that women have the right to vote; and the Twenty-fourth outlawed poll taxes because they were used to prevent African Americans from voting. The pattern of nourishing and sheltering individual rights is clear.

However, a Civil War was required before the Thirteenth and Fifteenth amendments could be adopted. Even after the latter amendment, the civil rights acts of the 1960s were needed before minorities had a firm franchise. The lesson is that sweeping change comes incrementally, not suddenly. As every election cycle turns off more citizens, the case for term limits gradually grows.

A constitutional amendment is necessary because the Supreme Court ruled in 1995 that congressional term limits imposed by state legislatures or voter referenda are unconstitutional. This means that an amendment either must be delivered by Congress to the states for ratification, or else thirty-four states must call a constitutional convention to pass the measure.

The first option, congressional action, is impossible. In 1995, a congressional drive to pass a mere statute (not a constitutional amendment) to allow states to enact term limits was killed by none other than Newt Gingrich. Whether such a law could survive judicial scrutiny was a question hardly even asked. Congress, plainly and simply, will not threaten its incumbents, either with a majority vote for a statute or a two-thirds vote for a constitutional amendment. (Incidentally, Gingrich wrote a book in 1998 in which he once again endorsed term limits and pledged to try to pass them.)

The second option, a convention by the states, has never happened in American history. Yet there is reason for reformers to hope. Every election cycle disgusts and alienates more voters, persuading them that some kind of structural change is needed. Citizen action by female suffragists and civil-rights champions secured the right to vote for women and minorities, despite all the exertions by defenders of the status quo who defied them and confidently predicted their defeat. The republic has continually sanctioned wider latitudes of individual rights. The time is drawing near for citizen-challengers to reclaim their rights.

Pending a term-limits amendment, there is much that both voters and challengers can do. As voters become increasingly aware of how the system is stacked, they will look beyond the rhetoric, the staged campaign events, and the manipulative commercials to insist on real and regular debates in all congressional elections.

Already, televised debates by presidential candidates have become a political fixture. The first such debates in 1960 played a critical role in John F. Kennedy's victory over Richard M. Nixon. Presidential nominees in the next three elections regarded televised debates as such an unpredictable box of fireworks that they were not resumed until 1976, when President Gerald R. Ford, a threatened incumbent, agreed to face Jimmy Carter (indeed, Ford stumbled in one debate by claiming that the Soviet Union did not occupy Poland). In any case, debates have been taken for granted in every presidential election since—not having them would be unthinkable. Races for the House and Senate deserve the same expectation.

Critics of our elections sometimes say that debating skills—the ability to think fast and talk glibly on one's feet—do not readily translate into skills in governing, which often requires slow deliberations and tedious inching toward compromise. However valid this objection, it is irrelevant. In the media age, the basic need of any challenger, more urgent even than campaign contributions, is media coverage. Institutionalized debates to insure exposure of all bona fide candidates would shorten much of the incumbents' head starts in media attention and campaign funds.

The courts no doubt would hold that states cannot regulate federal elections by passing laws to require debates, or even to subsidize candidates' campaigns in return for agreements to debate. Congress could enact such laws, but that nest of incumbents is unlikely to do so. However, other avenues for citizen action are open.

State and national political party organizations can be pressured to write into their rules that candidates must consent to debates in order to participate in party primaries or conventions. Local media outlets also should be lobbied to demand debates—activists will find willing ears, for the media favor real debates. They provide news, and the media score public relations points by promoting and sponsoring them. Further, voters might press state officials to find statutory means to encourage debates for state legislative seats, the governor's chair, and other statewide offices. These can only build momentum for debates in federal elections.

Potential challengers would be well advised to demand multiple debates from the outset and keep hammering on that theme. But they should be warned that reporters will concentrate on the process of "the debate about the debate," the often rancorous wrangling between campaigns over the times, places, and formats. Ordinary voters pay no attention to this and challengers should stay out of it as well, at least publicly. Squabbling over these details can make a candidate look like just another politician, obsessed with the insiders' game rather than public concerns. As a challenger, take the stand that you want debates, period, and let your staffers negotiate the details.

Otherwise, the best overall advice for challengers perhaps is: Go into it with your eyes open. Know what you are in for, the obstacles and potholes in a long and winding road. If, after careful consideration, you still believe you are the best person for the job and want to seek it, more power to you. Really—*more power* to you.

As Orson Swindle quipped, "Liberate Hawaii before Cuba—please!" Our slogan is, *Liberate citizen-challengers—now!*

BIBLIOGRAPHICAL ESSAY

Serious students of Congress constantly consult *Congressional Quarterly (CQ)*, in either its weekly or annual *Almanac* versions, and the biennial *Almanac of American Politics* by Michael Barone and Grant Ujifusa, published by the *National Journal* in Washington, D.C. *CQ* is a paragon of impartial, fact-laden reporting. The Barone/Ujifusa volumes are totally reliable in matters of fact and, despite what some critics see as their conservative bias, highly reliable in matters of interpretation.

Guidance on the social and political history of the states considered in this book was provided by the somewhat dated but still valuable *The Book of America: Inside Fifty States Today* by Neal R. Peirce and Jerry Hagstrom (New York: W. W. Norton, 1983).

Campaign financial figures were taken from the *Almanac of American Politics,* the Federal Election Commission's Office of Public Records, and Public Disclosure, Inc. The FEC Internet site at www.fec.gov is helpful but not, in computer jargon, "user friendly." For instance, it usually does not break down candidates' filings according to the percentage of PAC versus individual, or in-state versus out-of-state, contributions. Public Disclosure, Inc. performs this needed service at www.fecinfo.com.

A wealth of studies examines how Congress operates, but there is a dearth of inquiries into how members of Congress regularly win re-elections. Analyses of the workings of the post-Watergate Congress, the PAC system of campaign financing, and modern media politics are too numerous to list, especially in a brief review. However, two recent contributions deserve notice. *The Buying of the Congress: How Special Interests Have Stolen Your Right to Life, Liberty, and the Pursuit of Happiness* by Charles Lewis and the Center for Public Integrity (New York: Avon Books, 1998) is readable and thoroughly documented. Somewhat oddly, given its advocacy-group provenance, the book does not prescribe specific remedies but merely calls on citizens to become politically active. A fresh study of a related problem, contemporary public cynicism toward politics, is *Spiral of Cynicism: The Press and the Public Good* by social scientists Joseph Cappella and Kathleen Hall Jamieson (New York: Oxford University Press, 1997)

For an objective overview of the campaign financing controversy, see Kenneth Jost, "Campaign Finance Reform," in *CQ Researcher*, February 9, 1996, 123–138. The FEC is scrutinized in *Broken Promise: Why the Federal Election Commission Failed*, a Twentieth Century Fund Paper by Brooks Jackson (New York: Priority Press Publications, 1990).

Some features of the incumbency protection system are outlined in the highly regarded *Dirty Little Secrets: The Persistence of Corruption in American Politics*, by Larry J. Sabato, a political scientist, and Glenn R. Simpson, a journalist (New York: Times Book, 1996), especially chapter 8, "Perks," 207–243. Among the more polemical attacks on Congress is *The Political Racket: Deceit, Self-Interest and Corruption in American Politics* by Martin L. Gross (New York: Ballantine Books, 1996), especially chapter 6, "Our Unethical Congress," 157–195.

Readers who wish to keep up to date on expanding congressional salaries and perquisites are encouraged to visit *CQ*'s Internet site at Custom.Research@cq.com. The National Taxpayers Union provides detailed analyses of each congressional member's office expenses at www.ntu.org.

Opinions expressed in this book are the authors' and not necessarily those of any other persons or groups. However, "The End of Representation: How Congress Stifles Electoral Competition," by Eric O'Keefe and Aaron Steelman (Cato Institute Policy Analysis No. 279, August 20, 1997) was broadly informative.

The book mentioned in chapter 1 that prompted a Senate Ethics Committee review of allegations against Senator Ted Kennedy was *The Senator: My Ten Years with Ted Kennedy*, by Richard E. Burke with William and Marilyn Hoffer (New York: St. Martin's Press, 1992).

Oliver North tells his life story in *Under Fire: An American Story*, written with William Novak (New York: HarperCollins, 1991). A critical biography is *Guts and Glory: The Rise and Fall of Oliver North*, by Ben Bradlee Jr. (New York: Donald I. Fine, 1988).

James Miller's views of his Senate races in Virginia may be found in his book *Monopoly Politics* (Palo Alto, CA: Hoover Institution, 1999). "Jim Miller U.S. Senate," an unpublished paper by Tyrus O. Cobb, provided background for chapter 5.

For an even-handed review of Strom Thurmond's career and the white leadership's side of the civil rights story, see *Strom Thurmond and the Politics of Southern Change*, by Nadine Cohodas (New York: Simon & Schuster, 1993).

Newt Gingrich did not mention challenger Michael Coles by name in his memoir *Lessons Learned the Hard Way* (New York: HarperCollins, 1998). His only comment on the 1996 race in the book was, "I was running for re-election in Georgia against a candidate who ultimately spent $3 million of his own money in an attempt to defeat me" (114).

Much of the material in chapter 9 appeared in slightly different form in James Merriner's *Mr. Chairman: Power in Dan Rostenkowski's America* (Southern Illinois University Press, 1999). The cooperation of the press is gratefully acknowledged.

Helpful information on Harry Lonsdale's race against Senator Mark Hatfield in chapter 12 came from "Harry Lonsdale vs. Mark Hatfield, U.S. Senate, Oregon 1990," an unpublished monograph by Dan Walter, who served Lonsdale as press secretary. Lonsdale also is writing a book about his campaign experiences.

The Conclusion observes that George Washington, Abraham Lincoln, and other American political heroes were slandered frequently. A witty popular history that traces the phenomenon up to the Clinton administration is *Scorpion Tongues: Gossip, Celebrity, and American Politics*, by Gail Collins (New York: William Morrow, 1998).

The authors suggest in the Conclusion that no revision of the campaign financing statutes can produce adequate reform. Arguments to the contrary can be found in publications by various advocacy groups. See, for example, "10 Myths About Money in Politics," by the Center for Responsive Politics, 1995 (the Center lobbies for public financing of campaigns). Campaign financing issues were examined from many viewpoints in "If Campaign Finance Reform Is the Beginning, What Is the End?", a special issue of *Social Policy* (26:1, Fall 1995).

The insight that government itself is a special interest was offered by Larry P. Horist, a public affairs consultant in Chicago, during an interview. The case against term limits is argued by Victor Kamber in *Giving Up on Democracy: Why Term Limits Are Bad for America* (Washington: Regnery Publishing, Inc., 1995). The other side is presented in *Cleaning House: America's Campaign for Term Limits*, by James K. Coyne and John H. Fund (Washington: Regnery Gateway, 1992). Although the Cato Institute lobbies for term limits, it published a collection of essays on both sides of the issue, *The Politics and Law of Term Limits*, edited by Edward H. Crane and Roger Pilon (1994). The institute's publications advocating term limits include works by Doug Bandow, "The Political Revolution that Wasn't" (Policy Analysis No. 259, September 5, 1996), and "Real Term Limits: Now More Than Ever" (Policy Analysis No. 221, April 6, 1995).

INDEX

About the Authors

JAMES L. MERRINER is a former political editor and columnist for the *Chicago Sun-Times* and *Atlanta Constitution* and has covered national politics since 1975. In 1996 he was the James Thurber Journalist in Residence at Ohio State University. He is the author of *Mr. Chairman: Power in Dan Rostenkowski's America* (1999).

THOMAS P. SENTER is a practicing physician in Alaska. A free-lance writer, grounded in both precise research and public affairs, he previously collaborated on *The Black Seminoles* (1996). A former V.A. Clinical Scholar in the combined UCSF/Stanford Robert Wood Johnson Program, Senter has been active in health care reform in Alaska. He was also the state coordinator for the Ross Perot campaign of 1992 and the former finance chair for a U.S. Senate challenger in 1996.